CROSSING
THE
BORDER

Crossing

t h e

Border

AN EROTIC JOURNEY

❧   ❧   ❧

Kim Chernin

FAWCETT COLUMBINE   ◆   NEW YORK

FOR א.א.

A Fawcett Columbine Book
Published by Ballantine Books
Copyright © 1994 by Kim Chernin

Library of Congress Catalog-in-Publication Data
Chernin, Kim.
Crossing the border / Kim Chernin.
p. cm.
ISBN 0-449-90522-5
1. Chernin, Kim—Biography.
2. Authors, American—20th century—Biography.
3. Women—Sexual behavior. I. Title.
PS3553.H3558Z47 1994
813'.54—dc20
[B] 93-22131
CIP

Design by Ann Gold

Manufactured in the United States of America
First Edition: March 1994
10 9 8 7 6 5 4 3 2 1

Contents

A
Small Farm
Near the
Border

❦　❦　❦

SEPTEMBER

1971

W hat will be told took place. It happened to people I knew. Their names and faces will be changed and the name of the small collective farm on the mountain near the northern border, in Israel. My name will not be changed. What innocence have I to protect?

This story, true as I can make it after almost twenty years. Memory is a liar, a cheat, a thief, a pirate. Who doesn't know that by now?

There was a walk-in refrigerator on the farm. I know this because I worked in the kitchen for a time, I went in there regularly. Yet, when I recall the refrigerator I remember the metal cans of yogurt that came up to my knee. They were very cold to the touch, had a tight-fitting round lid with a curved handle, you reached in with a pitcher or a big cup to scoop out the thick curded yogurt. Whatever else was in the refrigerator I've forgotten.

Out of so many small daily occurrences why twenty years later this particular one? And then, once the selection has been made (by what process exactly?), who is to say if the detail has been transposed, condensed, heightened, made to stand for more or less than itself, for itself too, simply. Who would dare to say, after all that, what truth is?

When I first left Israel I remembered too well. I knew exactly how things looked on the farm, where the chicken house stood, the dining hall, the children's playground (although there were not yet children on the farm. The first was born while I was there). I remembered the soldier, and the woman who used to sit bent forward, her elbows on her knees, her long hair falling over her face, practically covering it. Was this a way of hiding? The evocation of one who wears a veil, promising future revelation?

Until recently I didn't know how long I had spent on the farm. Was it eight months or nine? I could have dug out my passport, wrung a confession from it. There is something to be said for not knowing for certain. Eight months meant it went by too fast. To remember eight instead of nine suggests a contraction in the experience, as if cautioning not to make too much of it. It went by so fast, I knew even at the time it was going too fast, later there would be trouble from that. I tried to hold on, staring at things, repeating them, clutching them as they fled, still they fled, the eight months were gone. But I had planned to stay, become an Israeli citizen, take a Hebrew name. The soldier suggested I take the name Mika because it contained three letters of my own name. The woman looked scornful. "She will never be anything but Kim." A cryptic statement. Why not? I wanted a Hebrew name, everyone else managed to find one, why not I? But, she was right in the end.

Nine months? The larger period suits the larger ambition, to stay, become a farmer, learn Hebrew, bring my
daughter from America. (Children were expected, several
women were pregnant when I arrived.) Since then, since I
left Israel, twenty years later, I've divided my time on earth
into a before and after. Everything that has happened since
has happened after Israel. Everything else, from birth until
my thirty-first year, came before.

Time hammers away at what has been remembered.
Tears at it, lets memory tear, what lasts, what survives this
abuse, that must have had meaning. The story spits out the
rest. Everything incidental has been burnt off, all stray re-
memberings, only those have been kept that carry the reason the story went that way and no other, out of all the
other possibilities, took up that one.

Then one day, not long ago, there was a visitor from
that time, someone from then, a voice on the telephone,
that particular name unspoken by that voice since that
time. What is it that holds? What is it, between two people twenty years later? Love? Desire? Passion? But surely
the words are a warding off, act of exorcism. Chalking
mystical symbols on the wall. To drive out, lay to rest, get
power over the far too powerful for naming, the still mysterious no matter how often named. What are they dreaming these two after twenty years when one of them drives
down the hill to meet the other?

How dare they! Twenty years later? They're headed
straight for disaster, that nightmare in which, catching
oneself in a mirror, one suddenly grows old visibly, skin
parches, eyes puff and pinch, wrinkles cut in around the
mouth. Won't the very sight of each other be a betrayal?

Their beginning, on a day in the late fall near the border, must already have held this particular event, although no one could recognize it then when certainly no one thought of an ending. Love? Desire? Passion? If you give up the words, humbly, because you acknowledge they have been wrung dry, how will you describe what has happened to the person who one day suddenly wants another person to touch her hand, move closer, so that now their shoulders are touching? If any other stranger suddenly touched, moved closer, it would be an affront, assault even. Is it the beginning of downfall, an undoing? What has happened? Is it a sudden grace, in which one is given to know how sweet is the flesh of a fellow mortal?

T he umbrellas are dusty. Looking up, you would have to shade your eyes. There is no breeze, nothing moves. Like it or not this is homeland.

In the resort town from which the bus will depart, there is an avenue of linden trees. The trees go down all the way to the Sea of Galilee with cafés on either side and small shops. There is (maybe) a fountain in the square. There is also a white dog lying in front of the bus depot, a cigarette store with a few pinball machines. The ticket window at the depot is closed.

She is there too, the person I was then, in leather sandals. These sandals were made by hand in Berkeley during the sixties. The skirt is even older, was bought used, a long black skirt with green and yellow flowers. Most likely she is wearing her yellow blouse. Also, the straw hat with a wide brim, recently purchased at the airport in Lod. When that person I was, that woman whose state of mind I can imagine, walks into the cigarette store for a package of Camels, the men look up. I am, back then, the sort of person who likes this attention. That is one reason I have decided to refer to the woman back then as she.

She is feeling lost. I'm sure she is, although she wouldn't admit it, doesn't speak a word of the language, can't even read a street sign. It must be something a small child might feel, perhaps from a time before language, suddenly marooned, who has lost touch with her mother's hand.

Maybe that person I was back then would have wanted to cry. She would not have cried sitting on her backpack in the shade near the depot window waiting for the tickets to be sold, the bus that will travel up to the farm. In the town there are cheap cafés where you can get pita bread, hummus, french fries, Turkish coffee, grilled lamb. It isn't the sort of food she lets herself eat. She would prefer a plate of sliced cucumbers, white cheese made from yogurt. She likes the seedy romance of cafés, could spend her life (she often says) sitting in a corner, writing in her French notebook.

She wonders if there is time to walk to the Sea. She gets up, draws the straw hat down toward her eyes, sits down again, sits on for a long time.

She, the smoker, thinks she is tough. Other people don't see her that way. Wouldn't I love to see her from outside, to poke some fun at her, deflate her pretensions, have a good laugh at her expense? A few months from now, after working six days a week in the sun, her brown hair will

turn auburn. Then, although she thinks she is hardening
herself through physical labor, she will look more a waif
than ever. Large eyes of no particular color. She is the sort
of woman men approach. Then they find out fast they
can't take advantage of her. She looks young for her age,
especially in this country where women age fast, work
hard, worry about wars. Twenty-two, twenty-three—since
she arrived that's what most people here have been taking
her for.

Is this portrait fair? Of course it's not. She's intelligent,
a thoughtful person, full of great dreams. That would have
to show, I'm sure it does, the easy carriage of her shoulders, a defiant something or other in the way she holds her
head. Children take one look, grab hold of her hand. I
know what it is about her eyes. There is nothing hidden.
They give the impression you can see through them right
down to the bottom.

I can't offer her as the ideal heroine, worthy of the
story in which she got involved. She has some good traits,
why deny it? For instance, the capacity for overwhelming
risk. She must have had that or she wouldn't be sitting in
the heat, in a foreign country, on her backpack, desperate.

Of course she's desperate. Haven't I made that clear?
A woman, about to fall in love and hard, has got to be desperate. (This is not an idea she'd go for, believe me.)

I can't be expected to approve of that woman who has
left her daughter behind. I can't be expected to endorse
her, not even to like her. She's irresponsible, the way she
falls in love, imagines her desperation sufficient justifica-
tion for almost anything. If I could like that Kim Chernin,
that woman I was twenty years ago, if it were easy, there

wouldn't be this gap that has grown between us. There would be an enduring I, a continuity. Something must have happened along the way, a wrenching more than a gradual change, splitting us off from each other. She would be outraged to think of me, her biographer. Outraged to hear how I keep her at arm's length, calling her she, calling her Kim Chernin.

That would-be mother who has left her daughter behind, has also left behind a man who would happily take care of her for the rest of her days. A tall man with light brown hair, blue eyes that look at her without flinching. If she had to explain why she is sitting here in the dust, looking at the white dog, why she is here rather than in the arms of that man, who certainly loves her, she would repeat, she is looking for a new life. When she finds it she will send for her daughter.

She probably would not tell you it was the man who gave her money for this trip. That Kim Chernin had nothing. Before she left, she was working a few hours in the late afternoon at her daughter's school, taking care of the children in the playground. Once a week she taught remedial reading to adults at night. A writer, she lives inexpensively, lives for her art, is young enough to believe in these words, old enough to know better than to say them aloud to anyone, ever.

It wouldn't do to take Kim Chernin too seriously. That's what she'd like but it just won't do. It's taken me years to get her far enough off to be able to laugh, not so far there's no point telling her story. She's not the only person wandering the world by herself. Most of the others are men. When she was traveling in California, visiting communes in the mountains, before she left for Israel, there were always spare men around, offering to share her sleeping bag. One night a ten-year-old boy crawled in and put his face to her breast. She made him get out but she felt sorry for him. To this day she doesn't know if it was right to send him away without comfort. If a woman travels around by herself she has to put up with a lot of ideas about why she's doing it. Since she left California, several men have moved in, she's had to put them off, even though she likes to be admired. Why else would she wear the kind of blouse she's wearing?

She doesn't notice the people who get on the bus with her. But I do. I distinctly recall a large, somber woman in a print dress. Her hair is caught back in a bun with a wooden spindle. She takes her knitting out of an oriental carpetbag. Up there, on the farm, she is the kitchen boss, although of course there is no such thing as a boss or a hierarchy on a collective farm. Her name is Hagit, it used to be Gertrude. Her face is lightly pocked from a childhood illness. She takes an instant dislike to the woman with the straw hat.

A few seats back, a slender man with refined, sensitive features. It is clear from his clipped mustache he believes himself attractive, even irresistible to women. In a few moments he'll sit down next to Kim Chernin and tell her his life story. When she meets the soldier she will notice the way his hands move with a life of their own through the hidden chapters of his story.

At the back of the bus there are several other men, whom she will never come to know. They live in the small villages up and down the road from the farm. Although she will, after a time, take to visiting these villages, there is no indication she meets them again.

The bus goes up to the farm every day at four o'clock, except on Saturday, the Sabbath. It goes only to the farm, although there are villages up there where it ought to stop. When someone wants to get off at one of those villages the bus driver pulls over along the road, waits impatiently while the person, usually an Arab man in a white kaffiyeh, jumps out. Then the bus pulls off again. On the Sabbath, although people from the villages might want to leave or return, the bus is forbidden and does not go up the mountain.

It might have been nice if Kim Chernin had wondered about some of these facts. As her biographer, I'd like to say she was sensitive to political arrangements. But, no, not she. It took her a long time to wake up. Or maybe Kim Chernin never woke up. By the time she got to wondering about the world, she was probably on her last legs. Then I took over. Her main characteristic those days (this is not fair) was a capacity to be swept off her feet, surrender to swift and violent emotion. These traits don't usually promote the capacity for minute social observation.

For instance, a few weeks from now a young man (let his name be Simon), who works in the orchards and broods a lot, will point out that the farm, the land on which now grow its peach and apple and pear orchards, all its banana fields, avocado trees, orange groves, had once belonged to the Arab villagers, their neighbors, who live without electricity, indoor plumbing, or any of the so-called civilized amenities enjoyed by the farm. If you walked around the farm any afternoon after work around four o'clock, you would see all the small windows of the bathrooms on the ground floor covered with steam. In the Arab villages no one could take that kind of shower. But until then, until Simon spelled it out for her, although the situation was clear as light from the beginning, she hadn't noticed.

This bus isn't going anywhere fast. It waits, door open, muscular driver slumped over the wheel. One of the passengers knits. While she knits she casts furtive glances at the woman across the aisle. This one, she suspects, in her low-cut yellow blouse, will want to stay on, after the harvest. The knitter has made up her mind to speak out against her. When the harvest is over, there will not be enough work. Until next summer the farm does not need another mouth to feed. In the kitchen there is already scarcely enough work to go around. A few days from now she will say all this publicly in a grim, tight voice at a special meeting of the work committee.

The woman with the bun is not wrong. Her suspicions are correct. Kim Chernin has come here with the intention of staying on through the winter, to make a life here year after year if possible. Devora, the woman she knows up there, her Australian friend, has already told her she won't be able to stay unless she can find work. But there is no work, hardly enough to keep the members busy until new industries are begun. There is talk of a dairy, new members would be welcome then, but for now there are only chickens, in long, wooden shacks filled with cages. There is kitchen work, some gardening, the work in the orchards, a few office jobs, which in any case Kim Chernin wouldn't be up to as she knows no Hebrew, not even the alphabet, and therefore cannot read the street signs.

Kim Chernin has made up her mind. If she likes it up there, if the mountain is beautiful, if the people match the romance she's concocted about border pioneers, she'll manage somehow.

It is a small collective, there are no more than fifty people, all of them under thirty. There are Americans, Scandinavians, a few new immigrants from eastern Europe, one guy from Egypt, some French, a few South Americans, two men from South Africa, a woman from Australia, a reserve unit from the army is stationed up there, a dozen or so kibbutzniks. They have come from older, established kibbutzim all over Israel. They are there to help the community get established. A collective, here on the border, on the same site as the farm, has failed before. Its ghost had been seen on the threshing floor, weeping.

There is a right way to join a community of this kind. You ought to be part of a *gar'in*, a group that lives, works, trains together, studies Hebrew, arrives together on a date worked out in advance. (That is also the way most people join the army.) Kim Chernin is not friendly toward covenants of this sort. She moves by impulse, quickly, not looking back, a burner of bridges.

The kibbutz movement no longer goes for romantics of her sort. It will settle new immigrants and unruly people on a small farm at the border. There they will build up a community from scratch, through egalitarian collective effort. In this way the older kibbutzim will be spared the intrusions of a generation that has trouble staying married, wears its hair long, wanders about in neckbeads and tight blouses, takes drugs, is fascinated with sex, has turned religious in ways people who have been here a while tend to find peculiar. Down the road from the kibbutz, in the neighborhood of Mount Meron, there is a collective of people who cook macrobiotically. In the brochures Kim Chernin received from the kibbutz movement it was unambiguously set forth that drugs and homosexuality would not be tolerated. Vegetarians, however, would be accommodated.

Kim Chernin has no idea she is sitting across the aisle from a woman who doesn't like her. Not even once does Kim Chernin notice this woman, her dismal bun, her knitting, her brooding face, furtive glances. But she has been remembered.

At her window Kim Chernin leans out for one last look at the resort town. There is a spin of dust as they grind out of the station. That's it for the fountain (which may or may not have been there). But who could forget the alley of linden trees kept alive by East European settlers who planted them.

Kim Chernin, the woman knitting, the man with a mustache, the three dark men at the back of the bus, the muscular driver. I can uncover them any day, the white dog, the french fries, quickly scrawled on the margins of memory, the umbrellas in the seedy cafés, the upcoming sorrow of the German optometrist whose wife will die in childbirth, less than two months from now.

T he valley is greener, more lush than the land she's passed on her way from the south, where she spent a day or two on a collective farm, weeding between the rows of spinach in the vegetable garden.

Until now, she's been disappointed. Most of what she's seen so far has been dusty. Young dusty soldiers in shorts hitching rides along the road, clapboard towns, transistor radios. Parched desert men in heavy army boots. Fig trees eating dust along the road. It's hard to imagine regeneration from this place. It doesn't fit her idea of homeland. So far she has seen nothing in this harsh, walked-over, ascetic land to justify her yearning. To tell the truth, she's already thought about moving on. Maybe to Scotland, where friends have invited her to live with them near the sea, in a small farming village, some miles outside of Saint Andrews.

She would be capable of taking to her heels before she gives the place a chance or gets to know it. When she wrote to her friends in Scotland, in a long letter with many apologies and circumlocutions, giving them a way out in case they didn't want to invite her, telling them she was in need of a place to go, they sent back a telegram. She has the telegram with her. If she unfolded it on her lap, there would be one word. COME.

Fortunately, the valley looks good. A land, as the book says, of corn and wine, bread and vineyards, a land of olive oil and honey. Otherwise she might never have stopped even one night, driven right back down with the muscular driver without even stepping off at the farm.

At the farm, you can stand in the dining hall, reach out and practically touch the border with your hand. On the border, up there in the mountains, there are crossings by terrorists who come over from Syria and Lebanon to hide in the caves. There is shelling on that border, other farms up there have been attacked at night. When the alarm goes off, women, children, the men too go down into the shelters. The farm is patrolled at night. There are guard towers up there. The Australian woman who lives on the farm, whose name is Devora, has written to Kim Chernin about these dangers.

There is an archaic tilt to this valley, in spite of many details that place it squarely in the twentieth century. She sees a donkey piled up with firewood. It reminds her of a donkey painted on the wooden cover of a notebook that belonged to her sister before she died. This donkey has the same broken look, usually called virtue or patience.

In the valley most things are headed for home. There is a languor you wouldn't find at midday, not even in a country hot as this. A cart filled with oranges is about to roll out into the road. Dark women in black dresses, long-sleeved in spite of the heat, watch from across the road. They are carrying sickles; one of them carries a basket of figs on her head.

The bus rumbles by tilled land, orchards. A few months from now Kim Chernin will view them critically, with an expert's eye. For now she recognizes orange trees, each growing up out of its own shadow. The light in the valley comes from the Sea of Galilee. It rolls through fast, by late afternoon already making its way toward the border. By nightfall there will be no trace left of the Mediterranean, of which this country likes to pretend it is a part. Bone desert, troubled mountains, too many troubled borders.

The man with the mustache, who has been sitting a

few seats behind the woman knitting, moves up next to Kim Chernin. The knitter, noticing this, probably misses a stitch, picks it up again. Kim Chernin is still looking out her window. For a time, the handsome man leans over to point out the sights, although she would rather see what she is seeing. They pass men on tractors, they sit straight up on their metal seats. There are army trucks, some of them covered. The men in them, in khaki uniforms, are armed, one or two wave to the bus. The small man with a mustache, who has just invited Kim Chernin to go with him to Greece, leans out her window, shouts a name. The soldier answers.

The handsome man has been living on the farm for eight months, since the beginning. Now he's sick of it. He wants to go home, back to England, but first he's going to take a vacation in Greece. He's been down in Safad making travel arrangements. He's going to pack up his stuff; by tomorrow morning, when the bus comes up again, he'll be on his way. He says he wasn't cut out to be a farmer. He says this with a clipped, sharp accent with great contempt.

They are passing a small village with mud-wattle houses. In ten days, on Yom Kippur, Kim Chernin will go to the village to hear the ram's horn. She will walk all night with the village girls in the dirt streets. I think these girls will remind her of her daughter. They have eyes that know too much for any age.

Three dark-skinned men walk shoulder to shoulder through a field of millet. Kim Chernin makes a characteristic observation. When a whole field of grain has that much light, it seems to be praying.

Her neighbor points out a moshav, where everything

is owned privately although the people work cooperatively. This settlement is more prosperous than the mud-wattle villages, where Jews from Algeria live. In the moshav one might have seen luxuriant vegetable gardens, a large swimming pool, two-story houses painted in pastel colors. In this valley, no one knows another war is coming in two years. No one imagines it will nearly be lost.

The bus turns sharply to the left, begins to climb. Kim Chernin has told her companion she does not want to go to Greece.

"You'll see," he says. "There are only two kinds of animals in Israel. Peasants and warriors."

"No women?"

"The women are animals too."

At this he laughs quietly into his mustache, as if to say, I can get away with this joke. We both know I am a great lover of women.

Kim Chernin is not paying attention to him. So far as she is concerned, she is going up to a place where redemption can happen. This redemption will come upon her through hard work, through the land above all, her kinship with comrades, the kibbutz movement, in this case the Mapam, the left-wing movement, to which her farm belongs. Because she thinks of redemption, she does not worry about the dangers of the border, the gossip of the man next to her.

The road is steep, it twists back on itself, throwing out beneath them a sudden view of the intensely still Sea beneath silent winds. Here and there, through the raked violet surface of the water, small white foam patches rise up wistfully. Within minutes the bus has climbed high, along sharp crags, open rocks. The earth up here is a deep, rust red orange, uncompromising in its seduction. Against this fecund red, white stones are scattered everywhere in the fields, the fields falling away below them, back toward the valley, suddenly visible now and again as they rise. At times, the stones make an impression of a long-toiling, upward-struggling, jagged wisdom. Higher up she sees black goats, picking their way among the rocks. She is pleased by the barbaric face of this mountain. If the man from England were not sitting beside her she might have had bold thoughts about the meaning of life.

Across the aisle the knitter knits on. She does not once pick up her head to observe this wild landscape that makes Kim Chernin feel the presence of large possibilities, otherwise known as destiny. The rocks, the goats, the rust red earth, offer her a sense of vindication, as if she were right all along, as if the whole time she knew what was waiting for her and would, if nowhere else in the world, feel at last truly at home here. Next to Kim Chernin the man speaks about Oxford, where he went to university. Once in a while she looks at the man. Probably he is having the experience that makes people trust her, as if it were possible to see down to the bottom of her eyes.

Behind them, near the back of the bus, an Arab man lowers the window. He calls out to another man in a white head covering. He speaks a musical language with many *l*s and vowels. The other man has been coming down the mountain along a steep dirt path. He is walking with a wide-flung gait, rolling forward on his toes as if he could stride down the mountain blindfolded.

"Animals," says the man next to her. "Don't trust yourself alone with them."

"Animals," she repeats, "and what shall we call you? A
racist?"

Her tone has no humor, very little animosity. She
seems to be stating a fact, or perhaps she is only sincerely
wondering. Because of this tone without inflection he
blushes. Probably that was the moment he figured out, in
spite of her yellow blouse, the promise of intimacy, her peculiar eyes, she was not a woman to be approached lightly.

K im Chernin's father died on a Sunday in June, some
four years before she left for Israel.

On that same day, June 7, 1967, Jewish soldiers occupied the Old (Arab) City of Jerusalem.

Exactly 858 years earlier, on June 7, 1109, Crusaders
showed up before the walls of Jerusalem to reclaim the
Holy City from the Turks.

To Kim Chernin the most important of these events
was the death of her father, although most people would
probably think the arrival of the Crusaders more significant, when Godfrey of Bouillon along with his fellow no-
bles and all their knights and foot soldiers threw
themselves on their knees and wept shamelessly.

Probably it was a coincidence her father's death fell
on the second day of the war in which Israel was acquiring
the territories that would from then on cause it the greatest possible uneasiness, would lead to further wars and
demonstrations, ambushes, terrorism, the hatred of neigh-

bor for neighbor, the deaths of children. All of which her father exactly predicted. He (who called himself, in that order, a Marxist and a Jew) would have regarded the fall of Jerusalem as more significant than his own.

On June 7, when her father had been dead three or four hours (he was killed in an automobile accident, her mother had been in the seat next to him, nothing had happened to her mother), Kim Chernin made a claim, on behalf of the Jews, to the land of Israel. She based her claim on certain archaic matters, not on broken agreements, international resolutions, not even on battles fought in 1948, when as a girl of eight in Jewish day camp she first heard about the founding of the state of Israel.

When everyone in the living room talked vehemently about Israeli imperialism, Kim Chernin described, very passionately, the battles recorded by Josephus, when the Romans conquered Jerusalem in the year 70. That was how far back her sense of homelessness ran, I guess.

Kim Chernin's father was a storyteller. Every day, usually at dinner, but also sometimes when he was driving her to school, he told a story. His stories were not the brooding, inspirational, often somber tales her mother told about madness, revolution, the struggle to survive, the death of Kim Chernin's sister who died young. Her father's stories were the kind that made you shake your head about people in small towns far away in countries almost forgotten. Because of these homespun tales she had come to respect the power of a story to make you care about matters far from you and otherwise, apart from the story, irrelevant.

Therefore, when she told the group of friends assembled in the living room (she was the only person who stood up for Israel as a homeland, probably because she was already thinking about redemption, always a selfish business) how the Jewish tendency to repeat stories was solely responsible for the Jewish return to Eretz Israel, she was indirectly speaking a tribute to her father.

He would not have appreciated it. Certainly, no one else did. Sensing this, she talked faster, said more than she'd intended. She wanted to know why the possession of land twenty or fifty or eighty years ago was a more valid claim than a story about having possessed it two thousand years before. So long as Jews were identified as a people through this story they would sooner or later be impelled to enact the story, to prove that it had been true. For if it were only a story, and not indeed a true story, Jewish life over the past two thousand years would have had no meaning. Yes, she went on, talking fast, that is how we must understand Israel, as testimony to the sheer narrative bravado of bending history to the story's will.

Did she travel all the way to Israel because of her father, because of the unresolved disagreement? She has lost him, the only person who will ever be what he was. This is so large, she does not believe in it, while at the same time it has brought her low. Is she going about the world looking for him? But then why would she have chosen a place of which he didn't approve? When people tear up their lives and start going restlessly about in the world, you can be sure there's more than one thing driving them.

No matter how stubbornly I place Kim Chernin in the year 1971, insist she is moving about in the world four years after her father died (the very year Meir Kahane, founder of the Jewish Defense League, fled to Israel from the United States, where he had been indicted for manufacturing weapons, to begin his relatively short, violent rise into the Israeli Knesset). No matter how persistently I remind her, two years from now there will be another war. Even if I assure her in 1982 there will be the invasion of Lebanon, will it do any good? I doubt it.

Kim Chernin believes all Jewish men are like her father. They like to play chess, recite Pushkin, sing along with Lensky in *Eugene Onegin.* If you screamed into her ear the most recent news about Israeli intelligence agencies, she would never have heard of the Mossad, the Shin Bet, the Aman, would simply not believe a Jewish man could murder an Arab during questioning, kill an innocent Moroccan waiter working in Norway. She probably imagines an Israeli intelligence agency gathers information from libraries.

T he year before Kim Chernin traveled to Israel, in September 1970, Palestinian guerrillas hijacked three passenger airplanes and brought them to Jordan. In retaliation King Hussein attacked the Palestinian refugee camps in Amman. The PLO fought back, but Arafat was defeated and forced to flee to Lebanon (disguised as a woman).

This event, known to the entire world as Bloody Sunday, had escaped Kim Chernin.

Her eight-year-old daughter, who kept her ears open, probably knew more about these things than the mother, whose internal map of Israel included the significant location of the biblical tribes. She could have placed the

Edomites, the Amalekites without difficulty, but probably did not know where the Syrian border ran.

I do not apologize.

The bus has pulled into the farm. The young man next to Kim Chernin has taken down her knapsack, the knitting woman has put away yarn and needles and lumbered off the bus, the Arab man is waiting for the rest of them to get off, even the muscular bus driver has climbed down. Now it is her turn, in her straw hat.

Some kind of party seems to be going on. There are people jostling and milling about all over the farm. Whenever they get within a few feet of one another, they shout, *"Ha Shonoh Tovoh."* That is the New Year's greeting, as even Kim Chernin knows. She gets the impression these words have been spoken so often in the last few hours, the words have entirely lost their meaning. Therefore, they make everyone laugh, which makes her laugh too, which makes people notice her.

Her beautiful laughter has nothing at all to do with innocence. It has been built up drop by drop out of slow death, unappeasable sorrow, the terror of a small child awake all night in the same room as a sister who is dying, the silence of a father who had been trusted, who in his silence about death has betrayed her.

If someone had listened carefully he might have heard in the way she laughed, with her head back, feet planted firmly, the note of early death. Then my task would be easier, that listener would understand how this woman would fall in love, what desperate hope love would contain, as if it had the power to call back the dead, as love should. What else is it for?

Probably the man with the mustache is simply a fool. He will go home, lead an existence far more ordinary than any he might have found here at the border. He would like her to be the woman he remembers, with tragic overtones. She will be the woman for whom, for the rest of his life, he is yearning. All he has to do is persuade her to go to bed with him.

For now, he watches her. Her wrists tucked back on her hips, her head turned slightly to the side, her eyes narrowed to small slits, she is laughing at the dozen men and women, and a few men in army fatigues, with their legs tied to one another, trying to make it down the narrow course, marked off with cans and bottles a few feet from the bus all the way to the end of the driveway, where a beefy tall man is waiting with two circlets of woven banana leaves, waving them high up over his head, to pronounce the victor.

Kim Chernin's family did not celebrate Rosh Hashanah. Neither did the Jewish people before the Babylonian Exile. Relatively speaking it is a new holiday, not much more than 2,500 years old. Here, on the collective farm, a few men are walking around with toy trumpets, blasting them hard. They have to make a lot of noise because they are trying to get God to remember them. This is hard work, the trumpeters are sweating.

From here, where the winding road from the valley is not visible, the settlement, with its dozen or so buildings, seems to have been lowered, piece by piece, from above. When Kim Chernin manages to look away from the three-legged races, the trumpeting, the exchange of sweets, the excited, sweating faces, the settlement lurches toward her.

If things turn out right, this is the place where she will spend the rest of her days.

Most of the buildings are two stories high, maybe ten or fifteen years old, painted a dull yellowish beige. They are placed at slight angles to one another at the far edge of the narrow plateau that forms the living space of the farm. Beyond, there is a grass strip of several yards, then a drop straight down into the valley.

To the left, on the eastern boundary of the farm, there are smaller, more ramshackle buildings, which later will turn out to be the chicken house, the laundry, some tool rooms, the engine house. On the far right, across a rectangular lawn, a ranch-style building encloses the farm on the western side. It contains the *mo'adon*, the club, where (as she has been told by the man on the bus) most people gather after dinner to play chess and cards, knit, listen to music, socialize, gossip. Dances and celebrations are held there.

From where she stands, near the bus, she can take in the entire farm, could walk it in a couple dozen strides in any direction. Over there on the west, empty at the moment, is the house for children. They will be raised collectively, going to visit their parents in the late afternoon, between four and six o'clock. Kim Chernin scrutinizes everything. She is trying to read the signs. The modern buildings are a bad sign. She would rather the kibbutz were old, had some history to it, a few worn patches here and there. Instead, it has the look of a tasteful country motel on a back road in America.

The view, on the other hand, is a good sign. Right then, without the least embarrassment, Kim Chernin swallows up the chain of purple mountains that rise up to the north along the horizon. Bound by mist and cloud, made up of withdrawals, invitations, refusals, enticements, the mountains suggest massed billowing waves perpetually swelling out of one another, as if just then giving birth to themselves. It was hard to imagine that this elusive humped-back primeval hoard would be there daily, whenever she lifted her head.

She glanced back at her knapsack, saw the man from the bus leaning against the low, flat building (the dining hall) on the farm's northern edge, beyond which the road, the orchards, the hills of Lebanon, the highlands of Syria. She set off fast across the farm, in a couple of dozen long strides, to the settlement's farthest southern edge, where the yellow buildings stood, separated from one another by a few yards, each turned at a discreet angle, to offer privacy, take advantage of the view, or contribute a slight rakish touch to the complacent architecture of the farm.

Below her, right at her feet, the river valley with its dry beds. The lure of this valley, so different from that of the mountains. There was something forbidden here, to which you needed the password, you might otherwise wander forever, yet wasn't that precisely what you wanted when you longed to go down among dry grass, abandoned riverbeds, blossoming thistles, black goats? She could make out, at the farthest edge of vision, what later she would easily recognize as Arab boys, going after their flock.

This was the place for her. High up, unashamedly overlooking. It had been made for her, finally sufficiently wild. She was at home here, wasn't she? As never before on earth?

She ran back, across the grass lawn where the New
Year's festivities were coming to an end. She gathered her
hands in two fists, pressed them hard against her shoulders. She would make them take her on. They had no idea
how she could work. Twelve, thirteen hours a day if
needed. She, the daughter and granddaughter of working
people, the great-granddaughter even.

On Rosh Hashanah you are supposed to eat sweets.
Everyone knows this, even she. According to the laws of
sympathetic magic, in which people always believe, if you
eat sweets on the New Year, the whole year will be sweet.
Not that anyone needs much encouragement to stuff
themselves on a festival day. One of the men in fatigues,
who has been playing a sort of ball with twisted rags, ap-
proaches Kim Chernin as she walks back toward the dining hall. He offers her a handful of raisins mixed with
almonds.

S he looks him over quickly. Is this he? A meaningless
question. She has no idea she's going to fall for a soldier. Both are excited. Her eyes are wide, she's slightly
holding her breath, she's taken her bottom lip between her
teeth, he has cupped both hands to offer her the raisins
and almonds. That gives him a chivalrous air. He's talking
too much about himself; he has to catch her attention before she wanders off into her new life and forgets him.

If this man comes to her room, proposes a hot romp,
I bet she'll accept him. That's why the story rears up,
thinks about changing direction. I think there was some-

thing brief and hot between this soldier and Kim Chernin. A single encounter. Up in the guard tower out behind the evening room, that's what I think.

She's leaned toward him, to take him in, her left hand suspended near her shoulder. Maybe a great love throws its shadow from where it is soon to happen backward to where the beloved waits? Maybe she has been informed through the singing of a small bird? Coded messages may have been arriving (she thinks the wind can bring messages of that kind).

Some people say for every one of us the exact place, the exact hour, of death is written down, precisely. If an earthquake doesn't come to get us, a tile falling from a neighbor's roof will take us down. It is lovers who are worked into the universe like this, Kim Chernin thinks. For every one the exact place, the exact hour of love is written. She means the kind of lovers who are prepared to put everything else aside. (But there have to be two of them who love like that. One loving another that way won't do.)

She watches his lips. She likes the way they press firmly against each other when he finishes a sentence. She notices his hands, hooked into his belt loop. His shoulders are broad, he lifts his left arm when he talks. She watches him for a moment, eyes blazing, when he is called back into the game. Her hand has dropped to her side. By the time he throws the rag ball, she's already looking away.

The code for this little encounter is not obscure. The man she's looking for would not have heard when someone called him. This one, who is showing off, to please her, undoubtedly because he thinks she's cute and sexy, has no idea he has just lost her, forever.

So, what about the guard tower?

I could censor out these shadier doings of my earlier self, that Kim Chernin who loves to break rules, if it shouldn't be done she's likely to do it. But memory, as we all know, is a law unto itself, a complete pagan. Memory probably made one patchwork soldier out of many encounters. The sound of fast climbing, the cold metal of the ladder, hands groping, the thrusting and receiving of what is certainly sublime pleasure; seriously, says memory, with all that, does it really matter who the soldier was?

There is another reason for not censoring these minor transgressions. When it comes time to fall in love (to play her part in the great wet universal drama), we need to know Kim Chernin will run right out and climb the ladder, without fear of the slippery rungs. Love of the kind she imagines does not wait. One knock at the door, a branch scratching along the windowpane, love passes you by, on the way to someone who reacts faster.

A blast of trumpets, simultaneously, all over the farm. There are no children taking part, playing games, eating sweets, blowing horns, running in and out of the dining room. A brace of clouds has passed by. Shadow is laid down with egalitarian discipline, as appropriate. Fortunately for her, everyone up here speaks English. She probably won't have to use her carefully memorized sentence. "*Ani mechapesit et ha Devora.* I'm looking for Devora," my Australian friend, who may or may not be thrilled to see me.

The dining hall is a long, narrow building. The kitchen is on the far side, close to the road. Swinging doors open from the farm into a foyer on this side, where

Kim Chernin is standing. She is looking for the name of her friend among the six rows of boxes. They are wooden boxes, none of them have locks. They play a significant role in the life of the farm, especially in winter. Within weeks the farm will close in on itself, the mailboxes will grow larger, crowding the foyer, growing over into the dining room.

More than once Kim Chernin will see people (usually they are women) crying secretly over dinner because of those square wooden boxes inside the foyer, separated from the main hall by another pair of swinging doors. Then her time will come too, when the wooden boxes will assume an importance out of all relation to their true significance.

Inside the dining hall there is a haphazard arrangement of wooden tables, some round, some long and narrow. There is a battered piano in one corner, kept well tuned by the musician who lives on the farm. Although sixty people eat here regularly, there is always room for guests, extra workers, advisers from other farms. No doubt the room could hold a hundred people, all seated comfortably, without crowding. But in that case extra tables would have to be brought in.

Usually, the room is bare. Today it is decorated with balloons, folded-paper hangings. It is scrupulously clean, a consecrated nutritional temple, free of graven images, as has been commanded.

Kim Chernin goes back to the grass lawn. She is scanning the farm for her friend, hoping she won't have to use her ridiculous Hebrew. Up here, night comes down fast. One minute it seems to be late afternoon, filled up with a sense of slow return. The next minute you are shut out, dogs barking. For some people it is simply unbearable not to know where they are going to sleep that night. The light and the dark have nothing to do with it. The wind carries it, some people are more sensitive to it than others. The minute the soldier ran back to the game, before she went into the dining room to look at the mailboxes, she had begun to feel homeless.

There is always a sober side to the New Year's celebration. The toy trumpets may sound, but God may not listen. He might remain deaf to us, forgetting us altogether. What should we feel if that happened? Wouldn't that be a sort of homelessness? Or, even worse, suppose he remembers and judges us, as he promises to do on Rosh Hashanah? By Yom Kippur, the day of Repentance, which falls some ten days later, our fate will be sealed. And so really, with our little trumpets and our sackcloth balls we are playing at life and death in the night wind that is already looking down on us.

Three books are regularly opened on Yom Kippur. In one book the names of the righteous are enscribed. In another the names of the wicked. The third, the largest book, is for those not altogether good or entirely bad, the ones in between. In which book would her name be written? Probably, she thinks, it would go into the book of fallen women, sinners, and witches. The book of death.

Hopefully the farm, the hard work, the comradeship, will cure Kim Chernin of these thoughts. That's why she must persuade them to let her stay. Probably she is tired, she's hardly slept since she left home. Why otherwise would she suddenly be unable to keep up with the laughter, the trumpets, the reassuring sight of her friend Devora, who has just found out about the woman in a straw hat and come to see if it is Kim Chernin.

D evora is wearing blue shorts. They are the kind of shorts you cannot wear (they have a tight elastic high up on the thigh) unless you have beautiful legs. She jumps up twice, waves tentatively at first, then with her arms up over her head. When she is sure the woman in the long skirt is Kim Chernin, Devora runs to her the way girls used to before they became athletic. Then she grabs the straw hat, puts it smartly on her own head. Usually she is a shy person. But that business with the hat, pulling it down over her eyes, taking Kim Chernin by the shoulder, right away telling Kim Chernin about her room for the night, Kim Chernin likes that, although she thinks Devora is behaving more like Kim Chernin than like Devora.

Devora grabs Kim Chernin by the hand. She says, "Have a shower in my room. I'll make tea."

Kim Chernin extends a dusty foot. "Still work in the laundry? You'd better put me through a good wash. Look at me. A talking dust ball."

"So who will make tea?"

This banter cannot be kept up for long. Devora is already wondering what to say next.

She stops walking. She does not look at Kim Chernin or give back her hat. All that is exactly right. Having nothing to say, precisely when she most wanted to say it, because she too was deeply moved, was Devora. If you knew her at all, you knew this stopping still was as good as words and maybe better.

The storeroom was next to the laundry, you didn't need a key, Kim Chernin could take whatever she needed. They gathered up sheets, blankets, pillows, towels. There were also work clothes, dark blue shorts with elastic, women's work pants with five buttons on the side, faded work shirts, a few pair of battered boots. As a three-day guest Kim Chernin did not have to work. Still, she selected a pair of green knickers. It was possible they had never been worn before, although they didn't seem new. Devora thought they belonged to the other collective, the one that had been up there before and failed.

Devora, balancing on a stack of sheets near the window, wondered why Kim Chernin needed work clothes.

"Maybe I'm not cut out for this life," she said. "I didn't like Dani's kibbutz either. Don't ask me how many pots I scrubbed, numbers don't go that high. It was better after I met Dani. But his mother was always after us. So we thought, Dani and I, it would be better to move somewhere else and then we heard about Araht. He's already come three times to visit. He was here until yesterday. You would have met him if you came yesterday. If you stay, the day Dani's discharged you'll see him, you can believe me, climbing off the bus that very same day."

Devora was the soulful type, frequently heartbroken. Her eyes had an I-would-endure-anything-for-your-sake look to them. This look had always been dangerous, attracting the kind of man willing to let her prove it. Usually, Devora wore her hair parted in the middle, falling below her shoulders on both sides of her face. She certainly was a beauty. She had large, almond-shaped dark eyes. A finely turned, delicate nose. She even had a wide mouth with some shy secret turning up the corners. But frequently, in a crowd or gathering, Devora was overlooked. Maybe she was just too good, a bit meek, not sufficiently a bad woman, selfish, taking her own pleasure.

In the room on the ground floor which would be Kim Chernin's for three days, she and Devora made up the bed. Kim Chernin put a few books on the shelf. She had been carrying an enlarged photograph of her daughter, a dreamy eight-year-old girl with wispy blond hair, a space between her front teeth, eyes with a searching expression. But there were no tacks to hang the poster. The room, small and narrow, with a stone floor, bare yellow walls, a single bed, a plain wooden desk and chair near the window, was scrupulously clean, monkish, a perfect cell. Devora found a large pickle jar behind the building, picked a few flowers, put them in it.

"I never knew home could be so easy," Kim Chernin said.

She lay down on the bed. The minute her head hit the pillow she was in one of her euphoric moods. Of course they would let her stay. She'd make them, they'd have to. The green knickers, from the collective that had failed, were another good sign. She had always liked knickers, they reminded her of German students she used to see on the S-Bahn in Berlin, before the Berlin Wall went up, when she was seventeen years old, the first time she was traveling about in the world by herself. A pair of knickers meant serious study, hard work, Old World charm, an eccentric sense of style. The more she talked about the knickers to Devora, who sat down next to her on the bed with a sad smile, shaking her head at her friend whom she especially liked, would always help just because of this foolishness, the more Kim Chernin was convinced the green knickers with brown buttons at the cuff were the very charm she needed.

"If you stay you can get a bedspread from the laundry," Devora said.

On their way to the dining room, Devora talked for ten minutes.

Sometimes Kim Chernin was a good listener. She held her head slightly to the side, said an occasional *um-hm* just at the right moment. Her eyes, although usually giving the impression that you could see straight through them, on these occasions suddenly let you know she had brought you into focus, that you had been seen. This can be very helpful to a shy person.

"There's something strange up here," Devora said. "You wouldn't see it at first, none of us do. And you especially wouldn't because you get so excited. You make up your mind someplace is the answer for you, then you see everything as if it were a sign you've found what you're looking for. You're in ecstasy even about a pickle jar. You have pickle jars in America. You could put a few flowers in them and make a vase. That's not special. Okay, it's special if I do it for you, to make you welcome, because we're friends. But the pickle jar itself is not special.

"Sometimes I think I should just get out. I could stay

with my parents until Dani's discharged. I told you, remember? If you want to go to Jerusalem, you can stay with them. I'll call them tonight. They'll be in Jerusalem for the whole year. I might really leave, it is just possible I might leave. Araht is one weird place. Some people say it's the winds coming over from Lebanon. Nobody even knows why the other kibbutz failed. You think you're coming to be part of this great experiment in social living. That's what we all thought. I think the other kibbutz failed because it's so lonely up here. You'll see. Nothing but goats. It's better now, it's still almost summer. In the winter, people get so mean. You should see how they gossip. Up here gossip has been raised to the level of high art. It's the only form of culture on this kibbutz. Especially the women in the kitchen. There are three of them in there. They all knit. The minute they get into the *mo'adon*, they drag out their needles. There are four knitters, one doesn't work in the kitchen and she's not fat. She's in the laundry, with me. I don't think she knows how to talk. Maybe she only knows how to gossip. I swear, she's never said one single word to me. You know what they say about me? They say Dani isn't coming here when he gets out of the army. They say he could come every weekend. One of those women, the kitchen boss, she's the one in charge of the room assignments, she's trying to move me out of my rooms because she says Dani isn't coming to live here so why should I have two rooms, I'm just single like anyone else. I won't move out. Even if Dani weren't coming, which he is, I would not move out. If I have to move, that's it. I'm out of here. Who needs my rooms? All the couples already have two rooms. She's always calling on kibbutz principles. There's other principles, why doesn't she call on those? Like compassion? Like fellow feeling? It's not the easiest place in the world to be, Kibbutz Araht, if you get used to rooms, maybe you just don't want to be moved around and have to start over again decorating and everything somewhere else? If I went to Jerusalem I could study Hebrew. In a city Ulpan. Only I don't know what Dani would do, because I do know he's coming back when he gets out. We could go live on his parents' kibbutz. You could go there if you want, if you can't stay here. Then I could see you when we come to visit. If we move there you'd be there. It's hard to make friends on a kibbutz. If you were there I'd have one friend ready-made. There's an orchestra on Dani's kibbutz, his father plays in it, you could choose any work you liked, there's plenty. I'll mention it to Dani. Araht is a place for desperadoes. The Israelis are learning English, no one is learning any Hebrew. When you come in for dinner they'll all speak Hebrew. That's to show off. In three minutes they'll be stuck. I'm in the same fix. They've sent advisers, every week we get more advisers. I think it's the mountain. We're completely isolated up here. No one visits the Arab villages. It isn't done. Now that you're here, maybe I'll go with you. People say the winds are weird, maybe they are, coming over from Syria. They say the winds drove the other kibbutz away. It failed, completely. There's all sorts of gossip. It just degenerated, I think there were love affairs, fights and stuff, they say a man broke down the door of a woman's room, one woman almost got killed, but it's all hush-hush."

I n her backpack Kim Chernin has a small book printed on heavy paper. Dog-leafed, arrows in the margins directing the reader to obscure passages on front and back leaf, here Kim Chernin carried on an embattled discourse with Sigmund Freud.

Fortunately, her dog-eared theories have never been subjected to serious scrutiny. If I wanted to make a complete hash out of this transcript, I'd unleash them wherever they pop up. They are as pesky, persistent as memory, as they must have been when she lived them. Why was she thinking about Sigmund Freud on her way to the dining hall with Devora? She would probably say the coming of night drew her thoughts back to the archaic, primitive world of the body. Freud, the dream interpreter, namer of the unconscious, was a shade too tepid for her taste.

Kim Chernin was attached to her books. If a few hours had gone by when she had not clapped eyes on them, she would grab for her backpack, unzip hastily, rummage around. Kim Chernin thought Freud had been wrong that the infantile sexual capacity for taking hot pleasure indiscriminately all over the body was destined to be replaced by the dominance of genital experience. Kim Chernin disliked the idea of anything being given up, left behind. Where Freud imagined organic processes Kim Chernin detected cultural coercions. It amused her that Freud thought children, the "average uncultured woman," prostitutes, and other females giving way to "primitive human tendencies" had not been sufficiently impressed by shame, loathing, and morality, to which men were imagined more devoted. Kim Chernin saw no reason for the polymorphous tendencies Freud had detected in infancy to be outgrown. Why not allow them to flow unimpeded, majestically, along with all subsequent organizations of pleasure, through every adult sexual encounter?

Should Kim Chernin discuss these ideas with Devora? Probably not. Over the years Freud had shown a tendency not to understand her either.

Perhaps Freud's sexual experience had been different from hers because he was a thinker not a doer. Kim Chernin did not think higher cultural activity depended on the sublimation of primitive sexual desire. She thought gothic cathedrals entirely compatible with sex because inspired by forces as ecstatically primordial. If it were true (she devoutly hoped it was true) that women had retained their infantile capacity for engaging in primitive sexual delights, that would fate them to be the world's great artists.

These errors of Freud's irritated Kim Chernin. Looking, gazing, touching, fondling, these partial impulses later on supposedly made subordinate, through which the mature Freudian sexual being then passed hurriedly, without undue lingering, on the way to the supreme genital goal, Kim Chernin thought deserved the same high cultivation as any other art, as she let Freud know with exclamation points and comments in at least ten different places. His text never showed the least receptivity to these recommendations.

This may be the reason she left him behind when she left Israel, next to the ashtray in some taxi to the airport on her way by that time to somewhere else. She thought all of culture a conspiracy to take women's preordained, capacious, multiorgasmic sexuality away from her.

She would not let it go!

That refusal, renewed on this occasion once again, walking along in apparent serenity next to Devora, caused her to frown darkly, narrow her eyes, come to some familiar, violent resolution as they crossed the security road that enclosed the kibbutz in an undulating perfect ring, along which even now the guard towers stood in solitary, metallic early-evening splendor.

When the world is equally divided between light and dark, it is a good idea to make a wish or have a vision. No one guarantees this wish will come true. But how can it hurt to make it?

Animals start for home, where hopefully a good meal of hay or mash will be waiting. A bird is likely to snatch up the last worm, donkeys start braying with their rusted sound, a soulful cry on a register to which human beings are not for the most part very sensitive. Up here, on the farm, people head for the dining hall.

Usually, they are dressed in clean shirts, jeans and skirts, freshly ironed by Devora. They arrive in couples, threes and fours, on their own, overtaking others. They all walk with the same languid stride. To walk this way, you keep your shoulders back, take long, slow steps, assume an air of slightly scornful affability. If you go to live on a collective farm, if you have dinner regularly with the others, that's how you'll walk. Kim Chernin thinks there is something beautiful about this movement out of one's individual life back into the collective. She hears people say, "*Lila tov*, Good evening." They look older than they had during the

New Year's celebration. No doubt they have settled back into the grave business of running a farm.

A man with a blue headband has just said good evening to Kim Chernin. She whirls around to look at him, her eyes filling with pleasure. She is the excitable sort, for whom all casual, small gestures can suddenly seem significant. This is the first time anyone has greeted her in Hebrew since she arrived on the farm.

He has a massive head of unruly black curls, a wide mouth, small brown eyes, a flat nose. These incongruous features, which should have made him homely or worse, have been egged on to a condition remarkably like good looks. He is a passionate man, brooding, darkly thoughtful. The sort of man who takes one look at Kim Chernin and finds a sister. His small, worried eyes seem to be full of high drama. Or maybe it is just the evening light that makes him seem fired up when he is in this moment very sad. Just before he left his room Simon ben Zvi, who works in the orchard, had stopped being a Zionist.

She takes a few steps toward him. His dark eyes cover the farm with a fierce, brief scrutiny. He crosses his arms, leans back on his heels, presses his chin against his chest. This posture suggests a man digging in against an assault he has called up on himself.

He says, with not quite an American accent, in a husky voice, "Give no sign. Don't let them know you want to stay. You're here for a few days. That's all, to visit Devora. Talk to me later. I have an idea."

She wants to ask him who "they" are, how he knows she wants to stay, why he has decided to help her. He searches her eyes. His inner world must be peopled with men who go out barefoot into the desert. The speed of the conspiracy astonishes her, she who is not easily taken by surprise.

Then, all at once, his face withdraws, as if the cover of a heavy book, an Oxford dictionary or an Old Testament, had been closed just when you wanted to go on reading. She returns to Devora, puzzled.

"That's Simon, he works in the orchard."

Devora smiles her sad, endearing smile. This particular moment, when she has to leave her room and enter again into the collective, has always filled Devora with dread.

There are five or six dogs on the farm, some of them wear brightly colored neck scarfs. They are sleek, pampered creatures, who have arrived for dinner on their own, ahead of the other members. They have gathered at the swinging doors that open into the foyer where the mailboxes are. A few of them, who don't know any better, keep trying to get into the dining room. There is a large black dog with a grave, intelligent head. He is beyond this nonsense with the doors. Devora shies away from him with an anxious hop; the dog ignores her. He is close pals with a short-haired yellow dog, not much larger than a puppy. The yellow dog batters the other with delicate paws.

Devora and her friend, the enthusiastic new arrival, make another loop around the farm, across the grass lawn down to the *mo'adon* on the west, then down a few paces to the children's house, where they walk out behind the building. It is still hot. The air is crowded with a dense humming and buzzing. You have to be careful, or you could breathe in a mouthful of mosquitoes or get one into your eye. The mountains are fading out. Let them go. They've done enough for today. She's soundly in love with their remote pale glimmer. She will never stop yearning for them. Long after other loves have come and gone, this love for the mountains will hang on.

Kim Chernin looks down at the lights on the Citadel. Or maybe they are the lights from the English mission in Tiberias. A city stands solitary at the sharp curve in the road. That may be Safad, city of mystics. That was the moment, Kim Chernin always said, when she first fell in love with the soldier.

On that same evening, the eve of Rosh Hashanah, the soldier had been in his parents' house, in the room he shared with his grandmother. His sister had her own room. She did not get along with Abuela, her mother's mother, who spoke Ladino, the Spanish spoken by Sephardic Jews, who at some point in their history came from Spain, although Abuela who was then ninety-two years old, had come to Israel from Syria, where her family had lived for so many generations no one could count them anymore. The soldier already knew he would be going up to Araht, as the senior officer of his reserve unit. He knew how many weeks were left before he went up and got changed so much, only Abuela would know him when he came back down.

Later on, when he worked it out with Kim Chernin, sifting through the fine details, in her room on the second floor where he was completely at one with himself for the first time in his life, it became clear that on the eve of Rosh Hashanah he had gone up to the Citadel as it got dark, was looking further up the mountain toward Araht, while Devora pointed out Safad, city of solitudes, where he was standing.

Maybe that was why, when the wind Devora had mentioned came over from Syria, passed between the children's house and the evening room and found Kim Chernin, her arm linked through Devora's, Kim Chernin inexplicably wanted to leap off into his arms.

Why did Kim Chernin take off for Israel, why did she leave her daughter at home, why did she wish to fall madly in love? Don't ask too much of me. I'm here to throw putty (where possible) into the gaps of this narrative of inner states. It has been imagined that I, because I came after, would be better placed than someone else to divine what might have been. No one has suggested my opinion is worth beans when it comes to why. I am only an outcropping, as passionate or not as the next person, certainly not neutral, not even particularly given to introverted speculations. Human behavior, if you ask me, should remain a mystery.

Not mystery as Kim Chernin used the word! I accept the limits of knowing. For Kim Chernin, who accepted no limits, mystery could be known. It only could not (easily) be spoken. If she was addicted to falling in love the way others go for a good pipe, I suppose this hankering grew out of her certainty she would find in love the unthinkable, which nevertheless one late afternoon when most or least expected seizes you by the hair. Being seized by the hair was, for Kim Chernin during those years, the only legitimate way of acquiring knowledge.

For the last year Kim Chernin had been kept awake by banging doors. At home, in Berkeley, she sat at the edge of her bed, ready to bolt. Where would she go? From what was she fleeing? Sometimes, when she went out of her apartment to fetch her daughter from school, the street was suddenly no longer the street that had always been there. The lopsided hydrangea bush in her neighbor's garden, the aging redwood fence across the street, the deck with twenty-six stairs, were no longer familiar. If she walked down the street, turned a corner, she might fall off the edge of the world. The neighborhood had an ominous brightness, as if it were just then being thought up. This was not a pleasant sensation.

She sat down on the red steps in front of her door to wait it out. (What would happen if she got up, tried to go back inside to call the daughter's school, found the door locked by a key not her key?)

Kim Chernin had been frightened. Maybe that is why she was thinking of falling in love. She had the gift of forgetting. She never once remembered she had loved before. Each time was the only time, the first time. I don't know what plucked the feathers off the meanings she'd been running around with. Does anyone ever know why people come to this pass? Back home, things had been growing away from Kim Chernin. They looked at her with sad miscomprehension, confused about why she was abandoning them. This happened also in the rose garden down the hill from her house, every single rose in the garden followed her with an expression of despair and grief.

That was when Kim Chernin set off looking. She went south, to the Zen monastery in the Santa Cruz mountains. Her job there was polishing kerosene lanterns in a small room behind the temple. She traveled north, up the coast almost to Oregon, to visit rural communes. She carried a sleeping bag, a small tin for cooking on an outdoor fire. After one or two attempts she knew it was impossible to tell anyone what had happened to her. The minute she spoke, her fears were tamed into what was possible for language. (Language has no way to explain how you could die of a feeling.)

The man who loved her would do anything in the world for her, take her anywhere, give her anything, give her his undivided attention, take weeks off from work to walk up and down Stinson Beach if that would matter. She couldn't figure out how to tell him, how something you feel could be so terrible you'd be broken in pieces if it went on one second more, and then it does.

Her daughter, who was eight years old, had been looking into her eyes at bedtime. This, she thought, is bad for the little girl. She is seeing too early what should not be seen in a mother's eyes, ever.

Sometimes she said to herself, *All this is happening because something in me has to be shattered into life, called back from out of the deep slumber of its exile.* This is the way she talked. Kim Chernin thought falling in love was the surrender (finally, after long resistance) to what was struggling into new life from the deep dark of oneself.

I guess, for the man to be relevant, he too must have been hatching up something, surrendering, giving way finally after long struggle to the birth of himself. That cast him in a very feminine role where love was concerned. Made each midwife to the other, brought them together pregnant with themselves.

I laugh. I sit in Kim Chernin's blue swivel chair, I hold my elbows hard against my sides, laughing. I used to believe these things. I believed them passionately. When I was Kim Chernin, I too tried to live them.

B y now it is dark enough for people to imagine other people creeping across borders, hiding in caves. The night air (warm, heavy, scented) is filling up with whispers and rustling, plots and conspiracies. Was it a bat or a nightingale winging out with a mute, uncomprehended cry for help?

For Kim Chernin and her friend Devora, strolling shoulder to shoulder at the far edge of the farm, there is no reason to hurry. Devora would just as soon avoid dinner. She would rather head for her rooms to offer Kim Chernin another slice of crumb cake. Kim Chernin likes it at the edge of the farm, head tipped back, eyes half closed, chin lifted slightly as if she were listening to music.

Sometimes, Kim Chernin hears something calling. It has no sound (not yet), or maybe it has the muffled whoosh a mallard makes landing on a small pond in the woods behind her flat on Euclid Avenue, where she went in the late afternoon with her daughter. If it had that sound it would be sad and far away, the sound of loneliness in a mother who has abandoned a child. When Kim Chernin wants to throw herself into the arms of the soldier, he means for her the vaguest hope that such a man might be possible. In someone as passionate as Kim Chernin this small hope carries an enormous sustaining power. When that particular hope called falling in love finally died, Kim Chernin was snuffed out practically overnight.

Devora says, "I've been in love three times. I'm twenty-three years old. If Dani doesn't come back, if we don't get married, I'm never going to fall in love again. Not ever. You'll see. I'll go back to Melbourne, take Bubbe out of the home, live with her the rest of my life."

Kim Chernin thinks Devora has been trying to convince herself no man could possibly be as good as her father. That's why she always picks scoundrels. Should she say this to Devora? Probably not.

Devora listens, then she laughs. She leans up against Kim Chernin as if she were laughing so hard she couldn't stand straight. It is hard for her to catch her breath. The laughter of a woman who does not yet know she is without hope probably sounds like this.

Kim Chernin is in that susceptible state akin to desperation, out of which there may arise the abrupt suspension of the critical faculty common to all forms of falling in love. Gone the usual dread of getting too close to the imperfections of the other. One needs them so much one is prepared to lay down one's arms, see them in the best possible light.

Devora drags her heels, she watches the white shoestring of her newly washed sneakers work its way loose. She has lived up here for eight months now, would rather give up dinner altogether to be looking at old photographs in her room with Kim Chernin.

Devora has told Kim Chernin there is a small refrigerator in the dining room, built into the wall near the kitchen. Anyone who gets hungry after dinner can go there for yogurt, bread and butter, cookies or cake and jam, fruit and cheese, you never have to worry about enough to eat. But, says Devora, eating by yourself in your room isn't looked on in a friendly way, it slights the collective. Almost everyone shows up for meals unless they're sick. Then someone is sent to take them lunch or dinner.

When Kim Chernin met Devora one summer several years ago, Devora taught her how to bake crumb cake. It was from a recipe by Devora's grandmother. Devora knew how to put just enough butter into the sugar and flour so the crumbs came out light, not greasy. That summer Kim Chernin had just moved from San Francisco to Sausalito. The following year when Devora came to visit, Kim Chernin had moved from Sausalito to Berkeley. That time too they baked crumb cake. Devora was on her way to Israel to make a new life. Kim Chernin had been longing for a new life. The two women walked by the marina, sat on the sand, ate cake, cast their visionary yearnings out on the dark waters. Devora spoke about regeneration through hard work on the land, Kim Chernin mentioned the dissolving of one's individual loneliness in collective life; they wanted to help create, as had the early pioneers, an enduring form of social life, the kibbutz, the finest flower of socialism here on earth. Devora found the equality of the sexes very appealing. Kim Chernin (anachronistically) mentioned free love.

Eighteen months later Devora no longer believes in collective life with the same fervor. On every kibbutz she's visited, the women are cooking, ironing, taking care of the children, cleaning toilets, working in the dairy. The men are driving tractors, pruning trees. In a grim, determined voice she tells this to Kim Chernin, who drags her by the arm toward the dining room. Devora would just as soon do another loop. If Kim Chernin left it up to her they'd stand looking down at Safad, have visions, cry silently because Dani hasn't called since he left yesterday.

Devora reasons, "If Dani were really in love he would have had to call, wouldn't have been able to stand even four hours without calling, would he?" Kim Chernin thinks a soldier would probably look a fool if he called his girl every four hours. She thinks he'd probably fall under suspicion, be court-martialed for passing secrets to the enemy. Devora, bravely, attempts a laugh.

Devora has already looked through her mail earlier in the day. She glances at the empty box three from the left in the bottom row. When they are about to enter the dining room, one behind the other through the second set of swinging doors, Devora has to keep Shimshon, the long-haired spotted dog with bad breath, from sneaking in.

K im Chernin had always known her father loved her mother so much there was no room left to love anyone else the way his daughter wanted to be loved. This state of affairs could certainly make a daughter yearn for the unattainable. It might also make her fall in love with a man before she's met him.

Of course, Kim Chernin objects on principle to anything that makes the mystical pragmatic. She hates science, especially the science of inner states, which belonged to mantic women, lyric poetry and Dostoyevski until a Viennese Jewish doctor came along. Kim Chernin does not like the Viennese doctor although she can't stop reading him. In her backpack, she carries a small volume of *Totem and Taboo*.

As it turns out, the soldier from Safad will be in every respect a dead ringer for Kim Chernin's father, who played chess, recited poems, held his palms pressed together in front of his chest when he was thoughtful. Kim Chernin's father had graduated from MIT, the soldier will turn out to be a senior student in engineering at the Israeli equivalent. So really, there was nothing mysterious about Kim Chernin's falling in love with a man before she met him, nothing mysterious about the eventual arrival of the soldier on the kibbutz, nothing calling Kim Chernin to Israel to precisely this farm, where the soldier had been assigned to reserve duty.

All premonitions, forebodings, panted yearnings, erotic imaginings were father-bound, father-determined. There would be no need to invoke, as Kim Chernin persistently did, fate, doom, mystical destiny of love. Anyway, Kim Chernin said to her analyst before she left for Israel, it is not the paterfamilias for whom the daughter is longing, it is the dreamy young man not yet snuffed out by life, the boy with destiny in his face, autumn in his heart, the youth-father, wiped out long before his daughter was born, the father before he had become a father, before the mother got to him, crushed him. That is why there is always so much nostalgia in love. Love is always for the beloved who vanished by the time one knew him. Isn't it?

There are times in her life when Kim Chernin is very shy. This isn't one of them. She walks into the dining room alone. The rules require her to leave in three days. Several summer volunteers, hard workers, whom everyone knew and liked, who had lived through the apple harvest, working sometimes twelve hours a day, have tried to get around the rules. None was permitted to stay. With the harvest over, a good third of the members will work off the farm, on farms in the valley, even farther away. Some are going to school, learning mechanical skills or dairy farming.

No one needs or wants another stranger. That is clear from the flint in their eyes. Especially the sort of woman who one way or another is always trouble, has already antagonized the kitchen boss, would have broken a mustached heart if it could be broken.

Kim Chernin intends to win hearts, every one of them. Although I myself am glad she went under, has never been heard from so far since, most people like Kim Chernin. Still, it won't be easy. People are scared up here, close to dangerous borders, they stick to rules. She has just crossed over from everything she's been until that moment into whatever is now possible for her. She intends to work hard (she will work hard, it won't do a bit of good, she's going to cause trouble).

Everyone stops talking. Most stop eating, lift their heads, turn to look at her. It is almost winter, the volun-

teers have gone down off the mountain, the grim cold time
is coming. The rains will come, Kim Chernin has reddish
hair in waves and tangles, my hair has gone straight, disil-
lusioning snow has come down on it. I believe almost
nothing I once believed, not in belief itself, certainly not in
that high, austere religion called falling in love, with a
place, a tree, a destiny, a group of people.

She stops at the entrance to the dining room, waiting
for Devora. Take a good look at her. Here is a woman who
has found what she is looking for. If she looks powerful,
that is not surprising. Here, in this border kibbutz where
people work sometimes twelve hours a day, rising before
dawn, in every kind of weather (later on it will even snow),
she has found her setting. Whatever it is she is running
from, whatever drives her, whatever is calling her, this is
the place to set up camp, gather her forces.

K im Chernin is wearing a skirt with small black-and-
brown checks. It has been shortened to leave her
ankles visible. She got this skirt from the mother of one of
the kids she took care of after school in the schoolyard. In
exchange, Kim Chernin gave the mother an oval copper
saucepan. It's not much of a skirt by most standards, long,
slightly flared, it makes her look taller and more slender
than she really is. She's wearing another one of her low-cut
tops, wrinkled because it ended up at the bottom of her
knapsack. She's changed her sandals. This pair too was
handmade in Berkeley, at the leather shop that used to be

on Telegraph Avenue, then moved to Shattuck, then disappeared.

Her method of styling her hair could be recommended to anyone about to spend their life on a collective farm. She washes it, shakes it off with a violent shake, rubs it hard with a towel, combs through it with her fingers. If a clump of curls or waves isn't hanging in the right place she snips it off with scissors. Sooner or later she gets around to all the waves and curls.

I admit to some fondness for her. This waif, thirty-one years old, who to all appearances might be scarcely out of her teens, making the very best of being tosseled, tired, out on a limb and rumpled.

Kim Chernin looks over the room fast. If she is to give herself to them she'd better size them up.

The room is noisy, filled with diverse tongues, a regular Babel. There is a diffuse roar, in its own way very pleasant, an orchestrated pandemonium of tapping and cutting and placing, knocking against, brushing away, sweeping under, chomping, sneezing, coughing with a sudden outbreak of sociability. There is not one person in the room over thirty-one. The advisers have gone back to their home kibbutzim for the holiday. Where will she sit?

Kim Chernin does not glance back at the door for Devora, who has taken Shimshon, the spotted dog, back out onto the lawn. To her right, near the kitchen, the man from the bus is standing next to his table. There are two empty chairs. On the other side, across the room to her left, the man with the headband is trying hard not to catch her eye.

At a table across the room, next to the windows with eight panes, everyone is leaning forward. They seem to be staring at the tureen of soup. Some are pointing, others shake their heads. Even from here their voices seem hushed, violent. A woman, who has not yet said anything, raps the table next to her plate with her forefinger. She does this three times. It is an expression of disagreement. The table reminds Kim Chernin of the dinner tables of her childhood. Probably here too the soup has nothing to do with it; a political discussion is taking place. The man with the headband, who said *"Lila tov,"* who works in the orchard, who is no longer a Zionist, is sitting at the end of this table. His eyes are fixed mournfully on the speakers, three men who constantly interrupt one another. Maybe one of them is saying Ariel Sharon blew the campaign in the Sinai.

The table next to the table where people are arguing is not full. There are two empty chairs facing each other at the end of the table. One person at least is expected. Several times, a jumpy man with corkscrew curls glances at the door, stares at Kim Chernin, looks past her. Others look at the door too. After that they pick up a conversation full of jokes that are probably funny because they've been told so often, it takes an insane courage to tell one of them again.

At the table closest to Kim Chernin some kind of desperate struggle is going on. Kim Chernin definitely doesn't want to sit here. There is a perceptible rattle of knife and fork. Whenever anyone moves a plate everyone looks over eagerly, as if here finally might be a topic for conversation. There is a dedicated woman with narrow eyes, a jaw squared by too much concentration. She has just made yet another attempt to rouse the conversation. A word, then another pulls itself free, takes off bravely, is shot down squarely by the embarrassed silence.

Maybe shyness has overcome Devora; she may have gone back to her room to get a photo of Dani. Devora is the last person to leave a stranger alone choosing a table.

(I think someone from the kibbutz office, who was on her way to the dining hall, gave Devora a telephone message from Dani. Dani wouldn't be able to make it on the weekend, his unit was being posted for special duty, he couldn't say more than that. Devora, although of course she believed him, started crying. Devora would have died rather than give the gossips, the kitchen boss especially, the satisfaction of tears.)

There is a large table on this side of the room, toward the center. Here, clearly, no stranger will be welcome. Conversation is proceeding at a dignified, slow trot. People might just as well be wearing fine clothes cut by an exclusive tailor, although they have on the same well-ironed wash pants, open-collar print shirts, sandals and socks. From their ease, their arrogance, their suntanned pleasure in their own company, anyone would know these are the native born, the Sabras, the prickly ones whose inner world is said to be sweet and juicy if you can get to it. Kim Chernin wants to take her place at that table, penetrate the aloofness, the formidable reserve, the insolence. When she falls in love maybe after all it will be with one like this, who must be courted, breached, made to surrender. For her, such falling in love would be in the sign of the mother, love far more dangerous than any other kind.

It is said that the Romans attacked Masada by building

up an iron-clad tower. From this tower they made use of a battering ram to assault the walls of Masada, a fortified stronghold in the wilderness of Judah, beside the Dead Sea. Inside the walls a thousand Jews, including women and children, resisted the Tenth Roman Legion. The Tenth Roman Legion was composed of fifteen thousand men.

A few days after the tower was erected, the soldiers of the Tenth Legion opened a breach in the walls. The Jews, ever resourceful, quickly made another wall. The Romans failed to breach this one, they were not able to set it on fire, the flames they launched were driven back against their own troops by the south wind. The Romans retreated, prepared to return the next day to lay siege. During the night the Jews committed suicide. Two women and five children remained to tell the tale.

All this took place in the year 71. Some people would say Masada is a symbolic tale, its meaning valid to this day. Maybe this is the way Israelis will fight and die, heroically without compromise, maybe tomorrow. Maybe it is a cautionary tale, warning about the tendency to suicide in a headstrong, reckless people who believe they have a right to a land lost more than two thousand years ago. It might be also a tale about what it takes to love a Sabra of a certain type, for whom the breach of that splendid insolence spells death.

K im Chernin can see the outline of Devora's teeth. Her cheeks have sunken, a terrible pallor has worked over her features. Eyes puffed up; fine, deep lines have broken out around her mouth. That is grief, a terrible cosmetic.

Kim Chernin whispers, "Let's get out of here."

Devora grabs her hand. She is moving fast, headed straight for the table where Kim Chernin does not want to sit, where the man from the bus had jumped to his feet. He's making one of his absurd gestures, a low Russian bow, arm outstretched, sweeping the floor.

Devora says, "Why should I hide? I am not afraid of her and her gossip. If Dani says something's true, I don't care what she makes of it."

Devora leads them to the empty seats directly opposite the knitter, whom Kim Chernin has not yet noticed. Devora glares so hard her face regains possession of itself. It blazes with indignation. Devora throws back her head, laughs a loud, false laugh. The man from the bus has just grabbed Kim Chernin's hand, lifted it to his lips. The man next to him, a big guy with hairy hands says, "Oh, shit. Oh, shit, man."

Once, when Kim Chernin was small, she heard a child cry when her father walked out of the room for a few minutes. There was something in that desperate, unreasoning wildness that makes Kim Chernin wish Devora would not laugh. What if the others heard the cry Devora pretends is a woman laughing?

Across the table, next to the knitter, is a man whose hair is still wet from his shower. It has been combed back absolutely flat, the way no one then would ever wear their hair. Kim Chernin thinks he probably adored a father who died young, leaving behind a framed photo of his wedding day during the thirties.

Next to him, the knitter from the bus has been looking down at her plate. From Devora's hectic stare it is not
hard to figure out who she is. Her hair and bun are so
smooth Kim Chernin imagines a can of shellac has been
used on them. Next to her sits a thin, fastidious woman
with brown braids crossed in two drab bands over her
head. Devora nudges Kim Chernin significantly. This is
the woman from the laundry, the confidante.

Everyone at the table knows Dani will not be coming
this weekend. Even people from other tables know. It is
clear from the way no one looks at Devora, while at the
same time they are observing her minutely. As soon as dinner is over, her name will be on everyone's lips.

The man from the bus has pounced on Devora's hand.
This gives her a chance to glitter hectically as he raises her
hand to his lips. Kim Chernin just manages to cover
Devora's far-away sobbing with her own beautiful laugh.

Kim Chernin has made up her mind to defend
Devora, who is frail. Even if it costs her the chance to stay,
even if she finds herself desperate, back on the road, she
will take arms against the contempt they show Devora. As
if none of them could break because of love. She will tell
them love is a game for gods, the very sport from which
Yahweh, the Patriarch, was always in flight. If they manage
to escape love's sweet pagan ravages, they will go down
drab into the grave.

Devora, who is twenty-three, has already three times
never kept herself from falling in love.

The man from the bus immediately begins to show
off. He has been a student in Paris. He knows the original
location of the first Paris coffeehouse, the Procop, which

opened its doors in 1648. The big man with hairy hands thought Kim Chernin was from Melbourne, like Devora. He is surprised to find out she comes from Bezerkly.

The man who adored his father passes a bowl of chopped cucumbers. Next to Devora there is another bowl of onions and tomatoes, thick sour cream. The evening meal is cold, except for soup, usually made from broth of chicken or meat served hot for lunch. Kim Chernin accepts a bowl of yogurt from a plump woman with horn-rimmed glasses whose eyes have such an intelligent, kindly expression, she is suddenly no longer homely.

Devora tells Kim Chernin the woman with kind eyes is an Israeli, a Sabra, who has come up to Araht after her discharge from the army. Unlike some others who have kept to themselves at their exclusive table, she has taken seriously her job as emissary, changes tables at every meal, answers questions, encourages people to speak Hebrew.

There are two kinds of bread. They are brought up from a village in the valley, from a small bakery next to the ruined mosque. Only the white kind has been passed to Kim Chernin and Devora. It's a pale loaf with a thin crust. The dark bread is standing between the kitchen boss and the small woman from the laundry. Kim Chernin is no fool. These two have not looked at her once since she sat down. Kim Chernin does not like ceremonial failures. She could certainly on occasion fly into a rage, let off steam, lose control of herself. She would not deliberately slight even an enemy.

Kim Chernin is reckless. If they kick her out of here, she's in bad trouble. A woman about to fall off the edge of the world has no time for nonsense. Moving slowly, in gestures that call attention to themselves, she unfolds her napkin. She smooths it against the table, lifts it by a corner to regard her achievement. Everyone else looks too as Kim Chernin squeezes the napkin into a dense paper ball, tosses it lightly across the table. It lands on the plate of dark bread. Two sets of hidden, startled eyes look up fast. Kim Chernin has an ambiguous expression. No doubt the kitchen boss has read it correctly. It will be better, even for three days, not to make an enemy of this woman.

Devora watches Kim Chernin from the corner of her eye, fighting back waves of impossible laughter. Kim Chernin does not lift her eyebrows, point to the bread, say one word in English. The woman with braids draws in three sharp breaths.

It is not natural for seven people to sit in silence staring at a plate of bread. The man from the bus darts forward, reaches out convulsively. He is stopped by the Israeli woman in horn-rimmed glasses. Just in time. Otherwise, the kitchen boss would not have had a chance to get the plate of dark bread across the table. More of a shove than a friendly offering, but still.

Kim Chernin helps herself to hard-boiled eggs, chopped vegetables, half an avocado, a bowl of yogurt. She puts butter on the dark bread, a thick-crusted, moist, heavy loaf of the same kind she ate as a child in the Bronx. The man with hairy hands says the evening meal is usually more substantial. The night before, they had hummus and pita. The kitchen boss scrapes back her chair. Maybe she doesn't care for criticism of the food. Probably she is not happy with the attention given to this stranger. No doubt she would like to know how she was forced to pass the bread. How, exactly?

After dinner you gather up your plates, cups, the utensils, and take them into the kitchen. First, you scrape off the food into a rubber pail, then put the dishes into the metal sink of hot, soapy water.

Who makes the rules? Who breaks them? Is there a committee? A single person, in charge of the place, elected official, appointed by the kibbutz movement, a court of appeals, where do you turn, whom would you petition if you wanted to stay?

Kim Chernin is scraping the last tomatoes off her plate when the woman washing dishes cuts her hand. Someone has left a sharp knife in the sink. When the dishwasher reaches down to pick up a dish, the knife gets her.

The dishes are all plastic, the cups too. But the kitchen knives are sharp. There's a lot of blood, the woman has grasped her wrist with her right hand, she keeps sucking in her breath with a sharp wheezing sound, there's a great bustle in the kitchen, someone bangs the wooden door that opens onto the road, the orchard, Lebanon. The farm truck draws up fast, stands panting. The small yellow dog squeezes into the kitchen as the bleeding woman is taken out.

The kitchen boss, smoothing her dark hair into the bun, asks for a volunteer. She wears a faded blue immaculate apron. She looks over the people gathered in the doorway. In the dining room behind them most people are still at the tables, eating compote, drinking light brown coffee.

Kim Chernin has stepped up to the sink. Maybe there are more knives? Put there on purpose? She grabs a long-handled fork, scrapes around on the bottom, finds the plug, drains the water. It is not a pleasant sight. There is blood on the dishes at the bottom of the sink. (There is also another sharp knife.) Kim Chernin is very excited. She's been living on pure nerves. Already, three times this evening she's fallen in love. First with the mountains, then with the unknown soldier. Then, briefly, with the comrades in the dining room, the man with corkscrew curls, the woman with bent glasses, the man with hairy hands, the seven insolent Sabras, Devora in her grief, the man who lost his father at an early age, with the whole room full of them, those who laughed at bad jokes, those who told them, the three men who kept interrupting one another, the woman rapping the table with her index finger, the man with the headband. Kim Chernin's love was so large there was enough even for the kitchen boss, for the fastidious woman in braids who only knew how to gossip. But the brown plastic dishes in the metal sink with something on them that must have been blood made her think of carnage, slaughter of the innocents, trench warfare.

Someone has opened the door behind her back. In comes the wind from Lebanon, from the wild hills across the border. It is like no other wind anywhere in the world. There's something smooth about it, with a lingering entice-ment, no matter what weather blows it at you. It makes you long violently for what is right there to grasp, only you don't know it. Whether or not she has a right to this land (she thinks she does, I think she does not), something of Kim Chernin will never get away from this place. Inwardly violent, contradictory just the way she is, this land is the same sort of bloodthirsty visionary.

K im Chernin had always liked to wash dishes. When she was a child she and her father, both wearing butcher's aprons, took care of the dishes after dinner while her mother, a political organizer, organized meetings on the telephone in the hall outside the kitchen. Kim Chernin's father had a sense of fun. Once, he brought over the metronome from the upright piano in the family library, where there were shelves filled with books mostly about Marxism. While the metronome ticked from the small table in the corner of the kitchen, Kim Chernin and her father washed and dried to a steady rhythm, as if they were playing a Bach fugue. On other occasions they raced each other, Kim Chernin's father insisting he could dry dishes so fast he'd be done drying the last dish before Kim Chernin finished washing.

Here, the sinks were much larger. There were three of them, two sinks for the first rinse and wash, a third sink for the final rinse. Next to that sink was a large draining board with wooden racks.

Kim Chernin did not bother with an apron. Although she washed vigorously, in a quick, steady rhythm, rinsing the plates with a quick, efficient dip, gliding them over into the soapy water, scrubbing them twice with a circular motion of the large sponge, tossing them into the rinse water, she didn't spill a drop. When the sink filled up or the rinse water got soapy, she leaned way over without taking a step, pulled the plug, changed the water, without missing a beat. The next time someone came from the dining room to hand over a plate, she was there to receive it.

No one had ever seen dishes washed with such effortless grace, serene goodwill, enthusiasm for work. That is why a lot of them hung around talking: the knives in the sink, the woman with a cut wrist, wild speculation about where the knives had come from. A few people insisted some Arabs from the village up the road must have got through the patrol, hidden out in one of the guard towers before dark, made their way into the storage room behind the kitchen, to wait for a moment when the kitchen was empty. Most people thought this nonsense.

Several times the kitchen boss found it necessary to point out how they were blocking the doorway. Some people drifted away, but on the whole the group grew larger. Before Kim Chernin had finished washing dishes, there were even some people coming back from the *mo'adon*, where the chessboards had already been set up. Eventually most people stopped trying to speak in Hebrew; there were even two men who came forward to help dry the flatware and utensils. (Had this happened even once before that night? Definitely not, according to Devora.) They had to be shaken out on a huge cloth, rubbed vigorously, organized into gender, stacked in the drawers in the cabinet next to the kitchen door.

Kim Chernin changed the dishwater frequently; there was something pleasing about the immaculate white suds that foamed up magically when you ran the jet of water into the tub.

The man with springy curls carried the dried dishes across the room, to the storage cupboards. This unexpected sight (a man carrying dishes) made a couple of women wonder whether the Messiah had come. The man with springy curls smiled sheepishly, came back fast to get another rack.

Because of this dishwashing Kim Chernin had arrived at one of her exalted moods. This made her feel she had known everyone for a long time, a lifetime perhaps, on terms of greatest intimacy. Tonight perhaps was a homecoming after long absence. But the old familiarity was still there, as it might have been between cousins, close when growing up, meeting for lunch after a ten-year separation. Each time she looked up from her sudsy work, every time people came into the kitchen to hand her a plate, she received them as if they were shining as brightly as the plastic dishes she stacked in the wooden draining racks. This openness, of the woman who has just fallen in love, made her shine too with a contagious warmth and sympathy.

According to Kim Chernin's memory, this dishwashing became a veritable orgy before it came to an end, touching everyone still hanging around the sink with royal spasms of awe and desire, marked by the melting down of barriers, the sublime coming together such as probably overcame worshipers of Bacchus or Pan.

It even happened that Kim Chernin saw how the man with the headband looked quite a bit like Pan. The sly, slanting eyes, pushed almost closed by high cheekbones, the wide, curled mouth with its dangerous invitation to entirely innocent pleasure, he was standing with his hands pressed against his thighs, one ankle crossed over the other, near the doorway, next to Devora, sizing up the scene with meticulous calculation.

Devora stood with her hands behind her back, smiling secretly. She knew Kim Chernin would be up at Araht as long as she liked. The unwelcome stranger had already found herself a job, met just about everyone on the farm, captured the general imagination. Things like that didn't happen much on a collective farm, where ceremony was kept to a minimum. For a time as Kim Chernin rinsed and washed and rinsed you could hear a regular splash of names introducing themselves. Yehudit, Amos, Tali, Boaz, Dan, Elana, Arik, Simon.

Several people, two men and one woman, who had never spoken to Devora before, gave her regards for Dani. A tall woman whom everyone took for an American, who had not spoken a word since she arrived eight months ago, broke out in three sentences of perfect Hebrew. People seemed reluctant to leave the kitchen. A couple who had been waiting to get extra compote, straightened out the salt and pepper shakers. They had fallen into serious disorder, pepper mixed in with salt, salt with pepper.

Simon ben Zvi talked to Devora from the side of his mouth (he had never exchanged three words with Devora), never taking his eyes off Kim Chernin. Devora said Kim Chernin could charm the brown socks off a white dog's paws. Simon ben Zvi said, in his gruff voice, in an accent that was not quite American, "Wherever you get sixty humans together, six will be thugs or fascists. The fascists will try to keep her out. They won't like her free spirit. It's not clear what the thugs will do. They might fall in love with her, they might try to kill her."

Devora decided he was not serious. Her father had told her she always mistook humor for insult, irony for bitterness. Since then she had been on guard. She said, "Kim Chernin is the sort of person who wants to experience everything once."

Simon said, "But the fascists won't succeed, I'll stop them."

"You won't," said Devora, "because I'll save her."

Kim Chernin thought love always involved the breaking of rules, men helping with the dishes, too many people crowded in the doorway, conversation breaking out between people who had been until then silent, this sudden, unpredictable willingness to welcome an unwanted stranger. During all that time washing, rinsing, drying, Kim Chernin had not said one word more than her name.

Yes, I know, it has taken sixty-nine pages to get Kim Chernin on a bus, up a mountain, into dinner. Later on, months will be wiped away with a single sentence. Is that my fault? A story has to conform to the shape of memory. Literary considerations (pace, narrative continuity, etc.) must be suspended. Memory will throw off these strictures at every turn. *"Eyn mukdam u-meuhar ba-tora,"* as the old saying goes. "There is no 'earlier' or 'later' in the Bible." Memory is even worse. Everything happens at the same time, is invested with equivalent status. You might as well read it from right to left, upside down, in retrograde motion.

I sift every detail, knead it, core it, cut away skins. I

am looking for evidence that will establish time, place, sequence. No one said I had to put down everything. Unless hidden in every detail there are clues to what comes later? Is memory out to get me? Is it on my side, hoping I'll figure out what is hidden in its fragments? I doubt it.

The memory of a single individual has as many codes, laws, legends, stories, as the whole Jewish liturgical tradition, with its layers of archaic Hebrew, Aramaic, Septuagint Greek, to say nothing of its Yiddish translations and instructions. If I go on like this I will no doubt have to develop a commentary on my commentary on Kim Chernin's memories, which will surely flow back to some common racial source, from there into the fertile bed of humanity from which restless Abraham set out merely a few generations ago. If it has to stop somewhere, it also has to have a beginning.

Kim Chernin was making her way through the slowest patch of memory in the whole terrain, saying to herself, I am walking to the *mo'adon*. I am high up on a mountain near the border. I am part of a collective, I have brothers and sisters, we will observe the holidays together, when Pesach comes it will be I who find the afikoman.

The Israeli woman with horn-rimmed glasses walked a few feet behind Kim Chernin, arm in arm with two women friends, also Israelis. Kim Chernin thought they should be singing a Hebrew folk song, an invocation to the night. The man still mourning his father, the man with hairy hands, and Simon ben Zvi made a group. The hairy man knew who had put the knives in the sink. It was the man from their neighbor village, who had slaughtered the goat and left it for terrorists, skinned and cut up in pieces, in the border cave.

Simon ben Zvi said furiously, "Give up driving that tractor. It's shaking your brains into your boots. No? You think that's a compliment? You never had brains to begin with."

The man with slicked-back hair, who came back two hours early from work every day to practice on the old upright in the dining hall, put his arms around their shoulders. That calmed them down. There even was some pushing and shoving of a contrived sort in an effort to get closer to Kim Chernin, who was facing them, walking in front of them, backward. Devora rarely went to the *mo'adon* anymore. Alone in her room she wrote letters, pasted photos in her album, read scholarly articles about Yemenite Jews. The man from the bus walked beside Kim Chernin. He was telling her the Arabic names for the constellations.

They were joined by a pregnant woman with a loud voice. She was speaking to a man who walked protectively with his arm around her waist, both shifting rapidly from Hebrew to English. Kim Chernin thought they were practicing the bilingual capacity they would soon bestow upon their child.

Everyone thought the stars looked like holes punched out. Kim Chernin said the sky up here reminded her of the exploratorium in Griffith Park, where her high school class had been taken every semester, where you could see every star and constellation with perfect illumination, where James Dean had mooed like a cow. That is how Kim

Chernin, too, felt, she said. The night sky made her want to moo or bleat.

This declaration was followed by sporadic outbursts of mooing and bleeting, which sounded different in Hebrew than in English. Kim Chernin was walking forward now, slowly with her head back, then Simon ben Zvi put his hands on her shoulders. He had a smell Kim Chernin liked, of plants recently watered, dark earth mixed in with sweat and contagion. Here was the pure sexual surge Kim Chernin thought the ancient Hebrews in their fall away from Yahweh had been celebrating, here in the way Simon ran hot through her was the archaic pleasure Freud imagined had abandoned the body and gone to live in patriarchal obedience to the genitals.

I linger over the detail. It establishes this memory as unmistakably the record of a first night, when Simon is still able to call up sensations that will grow tepid, then cold, when she comes to admire his brooding, perspicacity, fidelity, the traits that make him as intimately individual as the mother and father from whom sexuality, all through childhood, had to be beaten away, thus destroying forever all future commerce, Kim Chernin thought, between love, intimacy, family life, and hot sex. Kim Chernin believed, after a history like that, sexual pleasure of the kind she sought, the archaic, Canaanite, pre-Hebrew kind, was possible only between strangers. She had not decided whether this was or was not a tragic part of the human condition. Unless you cared for marriage and the family, what was so bad about strangers?

Most people went to the *mo'adon* every night, to read and gossip, play cards and chess, drink tea, eat cookies, discuss politics. There were people up there who saw the *mo'adon* as the supreme accomplishment of collective life. Work over for the day, (future) children at rest in their collective house, here was the in-gathering of the community to affirm its existence, exchange small stories. People who like that sort of thing would have been at home there.

The *mo'adon* was a large, rectangular room, with comfortable chairs, short, narrow tables arranged along the walls near the windows, shelves of books, and games stacked up almost to the low ceiling. There were two large metal urns for tea and coffee; every night it was someone's scheduled job to make sure they were prepared. The men did not seem to be written down for this rotation, although later, when the children were born, the men took their turn sitting up in the children's house, to keep watch at night. Even very young babies did not sleep in their parents' room.

Kim Chernin's group was standing near the bookshelves. The Israeli woman with horn-rimmed glasses brought Kim Chernin a cup of tea. Then Kim Chernin got a cup of tea for her. It turned out she liked hot water with lemon and honey. The tea was accepted by one of her friends, a pretty woman in a blue-print dress, who told Kim Chernin how to say *tea* in Hebrew, she pointed to the glass, name it, she pointed to herself, said her name. This went over very well, other people joined in, Kim Chernin repeated everything (*cup, tea, Zipora, man, woman, me*) but with the most peculiar accent.

The man with the mustache would be leaving when the bus came up the following morning, before dawn. He said, in Hebrew, choosing his words carefully, "I'll never see any of you again, not ever, after tonight."

He seemed sad and contrite as if he'd ruined his best chance at a good life. The pretty Israeli woman in the print dress patted him on the arm. He gave Kim Chernin a hungry look. Maybe she could still save him?

Kim Chernin hardly saw him, she was adrift in their love for her, a hand brushing hers on the way to the coffee urn, the many times she found herself shoulder to shoulder with a perfect stranger. Then, all at once, she was swept up by an acute mystical awe. It made her want to burst out in tears, fling herself down, worship something. She had come home. She would tell them that. She had, after much wandering, found them at last.

Unfortunately, ecstasy is not a close observer. Kim Chernin did not notice the pinched faces, wary eyes, watchful frowns. Her mood flew up over all obstacles; she did not once see the four women who had set up camp, knitting together on the far side of the coffee urn, the man in overalls who looked down at his feet, spoke to no one, leaned against the wall on the far side of the room, near the back door, biting his nails. Hating Kim Chernin?

I f you want to know Simon watch him walk. Hands behind his back, stopping in the middle of nowhere to gaze at nothing. He takes two steps, shoves his hands into his pockets, takes two more steps, kicks a pebble out of the way. Maybe he is composing a roster of people likely to vote for Kim Chernin if a community meeting is called?

On the other hand, how did Kim Chernin's memory get hold of Simon on the way to her room when Kim Chernin is nowhere in sight? Never mind. Memory is permitted these small filchings. Like anyone else it wants to make a good story.

Simon believes he is the man for whom Kim Chernin has come to Araht. To prove this, he will bring her his journals, copy out pages, slip them under her door. If you ask me, there are quite a few memories here plagiarized from Simon.

Kim Chernin became aware of his inner world only after it had been assembled, analyzed, written down, brought to her room. I, cutting back through memory, know what Simon is feeling the moment he feels it, when Kim Chernin could not possibly know. I have the advantage over Kim Chernin. In this limited sense I have become omniscient.

Simon has noticed the light in Kim Chernin's window. Although it is hours past midnight Kim Chernin has been moving about, dragging a chair after her. She knocked in a tack with the heel of her sandal, stood back to see the poster, took it down again. It was clear she would never find the right place, would keep moving and adjusting for months into the late night until she managed to bring the girl to the farm.

Simon thought that would be even harder than arranging things for Kim Chernin.

He went around to the door, knocked louder. He was answered, "Come in, Simon," by an amused, tired voice.

She was sitting on the desk facing the poster, her knees pulled up close to her chin.

"How did you know it was me?"

"The man from the bus has already been here."

"You'd never go to bed with that creep."

Simon did not find this statement dignified. The next day, he scratched it out, went over it with a thick black line, wrote it in again.

Kim Chernin looked at him with wide-open eyes, her head to one side (definitely one of her gestures). She said, "Do I know you from someplace? Another lifetime? In that one you probably knew me so well, you had developed an unerring judgment about my taste in men?"

Simon did not know if Kim Chernin was joking.

He said, "When I saw you with Devora, you recognized me right away because you were waiting for me to show up, because that's the sort of person you are and I am too."

Kim Chernin said, "I don't want help, Simon ben Zvi. Go away, park your white horse somewhere else. I can work things out on my own. That guy you call a creep, he had a good reason to visit. What do you want?"

"You can't work things out on your own. No, you can't. Not up here. Impossible."

He sat down next to her on the desk opposite the poster of the little girl.

"She doesn't look like you. Not one bit. Even the eyes. You can't stay here without someone's help. Devora's okay, she's sweet, but you can't count on her. And don't make fun of me, don't try. I see right through you. In the *mo'adon* you would have started crying, or worse. I saw it in your face the whole time you were there."

Kim Chernin would have been pleased if Simon ben

Zvi had lifted her up from the desk, carried her to the bed. He was strong enough. And kissed her, hard as he could, as he lay on top of her. Simon sat still, still swinging his legs, looking at the palm of his left hand, which was blistered.

He said, "I play the guitar. I don't like blisters. Araht isn't everything you think it is now; you'll find out if you stay here. If I help you."

Kim Chernin put her head on his shoulder. She did things like that, she was consistently in that way irresponsible. She said, "Why is it I always get stuck with someone like you? No matter where I go in the world, one of you shows up. I always end up trusting a type like you."

"And then?"

"No 'then'—your type is infinitely trustable. Never betrays the woman he loves, never lets her down."

"You're making fun of someone. Maybe it's not me."

"How old are you, Simon? Twenty-three? Twenty-four? Almost old enough to marry my daughter. But what happens when I want to get rid of you?"

"Supposing you don't?"

"Then, sooner or later I'm still in the same kind of trouble, if it is trouble, whatever it is."

"Sure is, trouble. Anyone can see that. I saw it the first minute, even if you are pretty and you look young."

Early in life (at the age of eleven or twelve), Kim Chernin had discovered sex was the answer to everything. Sleeplessness, fear of the dark, the rage a child accumulates sometimes for grown-ups who don't listen. All later desperations could be put to rest the same way, might still be that night too if Simon were not there so chastely, on a nobler mission, to save her.

Simon ben Zvi jumped down from the desk, turned to face her. She moved to make room for him up close.

"Don't worry," he said, having come to the conclusion that she was acting tough but was really fragile, "I'm not planning—"

"I'm not exactly worried, Simon."

"I see you're not. But I still won't. Word of honor. No matter what happens, I want you to know that's not why I came here."

"No matter what happens? What could happen that you or I did not want to happen? You give me your word of honor, no matter what happens? But if something did happen, your word of honor would be meaningless, wouldn't it? If your word of honor really counts for any-thing, you have no reason to add 'no matter what happens.' Very intriguing, this 'no matter what happens.' "

"You have a nice laugh, when you're not laughing at me. I have something to tell you. I don't want to shout. If you think I'd try to get you to go to bed with me in spite of my word of honor, that's not true."

"You might have meant, 'I would try to get you to go to bed with me.' What good would your word of honor do then? As a matter of fact, it wouldn't do you much good."

Simon had never seen anyone laugh so hard. That laugh was as misleading as the face she wore behind the face everyone saw, which didn't fool him.

Kim Chernin liked desire. It put an end to banging doors, grief-stricken roses, the shriek of a child who knows she is soon to be abandoned by her mother. Simon shook his head, "I want to help you. I don't want to be another man taking advantage of the situation."

Although it was very late, and walls were thin, she laughed again. "Wrong story, Simon."

Simon ben Zvi would have married Kim Chernin the next day, although there was no need to marry someone on a kibbutz, you just moved in with them. But he wouldn't go to bed with her, not even if she wanted him, not even out of male pride to be the first man to have her. He had to be a very young man, Kim Chernin thought, to look like that, there to serve, but not to take advantage.

T he night Simon left Kim Chernin's room, when he could have made love to her and didn't, he was already planning to tell her about his vision. It would happen one day at the Roman ruins, above the wadi, toward sunset, when the Arab boys were calling the goats back from the dry riverbed.

In Simon's vision, there were old men walking at a fast pace one behind another. There were children, buses, army trucks, women carrying bedding, sacks, and bundles on their heads. The road was cluttered with kerosene stoves, lanterns, chairs, beddings. Children were left along the road because the soldiers would not let anyone stop to save the children. It was hot, there wasn't enough water, the children were dropping down into the dust.

The column drew closer. It came from a distance along a dirt road winding down from a mountain. There were thousands, tens of thousands, old men, young men, women and children.

Simon was absolutely certain Kim Chernin would understand this vision, but Kim Chernin knew some things Simon did not yet know.

She had known them since 1947, when her parents told at the dinner table how Zionists had recruited, from displaced-person camps in Europe, people who did not want to go to Palestine. They wanted to go to America. Her parents said President Roosevelt had been willing to take in the Jewish refugees after the war but had been talked out of it by Zionists.

The first time Simon saw his vision, he imagined the soldiers were German. When the forced march came again, when he was repairing his workboots the next day in the toolshed, he understood the soldiers could belong to any army, all those armies simultaneously that had persecuted the Jews. The Jews were the universal image of human suffering, driven on, beaten down, left to die of exhaustion along the way, at the hands of Romans, Assyrians, Cossacks, Nazis, the Czarist army, Chmielnicki's hordes, the Babylonians.

Kim Chernin would have known who the soldiers were. She knew things Simon did not yet know because her parents had told her. That was why Simon's vision couldn't impress her the way Simon hoped. It is to this failure I attribute much of that will soon go wrong for Simon, Kim Chernin, even for Devora.

Kim Chernin had made her peace with Zionism by the age of eight. (She was a lonely child, she read a lot.) She accomplished this feat by tracking the impulse that draws a people out of the land in which they have been dwelling. Kim Chernin had her own views about what drove history forward. When the old way has collapsed, when people leave their homes to go elsewhere, because the reforms of the early years of Czar Alexander II have failed, the charges of ritual murder are renewed, the police stand by while people are beaten to death, synagogues desecrated, homes looted and burned, when boys of twelve are rounded up to serve in the army, beaten to death or into conversion, the Jewish bootmaker is displaced by manufactured boots, the innkeeper loses his livelihood, the masses of people are cornered in a Pale shrunken to nine-tenths of its size by administrative restrictions, the May Laws are pronounced, Jews may not leave their towns and hamlets, cannot hold leases or merchandise outside, the Pale grows more congested, the sanitary conditions become worse, people live from hand to mouth, the school system breaks down, there is mass flight into the cities from which those who have fled there are now expelled, then people get going, they flee from Minsk to Vilna, from Vilna to Vitebsk, from there to Chernigov, Poltava, Kiev, Moscow, Saint Petersburg, Berlin, Warsaw, Jaffa, New York. Two generations before Kim Chernin hundreds of thousands of Jews from the same part of Russia where her grandparents lived set out for the United States, the parents of Kim Chernin's parents among them. Others traveled by sea to Palestine. Kim Chernin, eight years old, who knew all this by heart, did not think this was a question of ideology or the class struggle. She thought these people were desperate, their sisters had died, they were falling apart, they stood at the window staring into the street, they could not go on in the old way, they grew silent, they invented their own land, which had to be far away, impossible, some had invented Eretz Israel. Kim

Chernin on the way to California from New York had imagined mission cities filled with orange trees, a place substantially better than the place a sister had died, the innkeeper's wife been raped, the bootmaker's son conscripted. California would be better too than the highlands of Ethiopia, where a million Ethiopian Jews had been cut down to twenty-eight thousand by rebel armies, by bandit gangs roaming the countryside, the violent Jew-hating Cossacks of the Great Rift mountains. When California let Kim Chernin down, a desert land with dead seas and date trees grew up in its place, that was in 1948, when Kim Chernin was eight years old, when she saw for the first time in Jewish day camp the blue-and-white-striped flag of the new Jewish homeland with the star of David at the center.

At the dinner table Kim Chernin's parents said the Zionists collaborated with the Nazis during the war, cynically paying them to rescue the elite of the Jewish community to take to Palestine. Kim Chernin's mother had said, "So, what's an elite? Someone who knows how to dip a spoon in caviar?" Kim Chernin did not need Zion to be all good. In desperation, people behave in ways they will regret later. Should she say that to her mother? Probably not. I think she might have tried to say some of it to Simon.

Maybe Simon had heard just enough in the Arab village up the hill from the ruins, something he read might have set off an intolerable thought that might erase him if it ever got loose. Maybe what made him Simon and not his father was planning to be a high priest of an inner world where Zionism waited patiently for the coming of the Messiah. Perhaps he had choked back his childhood despair, because his father hated him, because his mother protected him too much from his father's hate, by telling himself that one day in the land of Israel he would make sense there. Of the ten pieces that made up Simon, which might have come apart, patchwork, maybe his love for Israel was the single binding thread? Therefore, the vision had to come again. The procession started moving, kicking up its insinuating dust, soldiers, army trucks, dying children, kerosene lamps thrown along the road, soldiers in the uniforms he was unable to recognize, each time he was about to understand the meaning of it hot, the land so parched, only small shrubs and bushes growing on the low hills, the image fragmented. Close up, he observed minutely the crushed silver ring on a child's hand. Close up, strands of a woman's black hair tangled into the ropes of her bundle. Simon called the bundle pathetic. He found it sad, even worse than the crushed silver ring, so desolate Simon, who did not allow himself to cry, suddenly knew who the soldiers were and the name of the conquered towns (yes, they were conquered, the [Arab] people in them were forcibly expelled. According to contemporary Israeli historians, who had not yet written a word when Simon saw his vision, the marching column could have been the one that marched from Lydda and Ramla in the neighborhood of Tel Aviv, in 1948, under order from Yitzhak Rabin, lieutenant colonel of the Israeli Defense Forces, to pitch its tents near Ramallah.)

Thoughts ahead of their time are disturbing. Anyone in Simon's position could be forgiven for not at first naming correctly the army or the oppressed. Most people would have given up the whole business long before. A few years before when Simon was living in Alexandria, he had smoked a lot of hash. He could have said he was having a flashback, a breakdown, insisted on sick leave, taken days off to wander the shores of the Sea of Galilee or through the holy streets of Safad. (Eventually he added Safad, a city of winding streets, twisting alleys, eggshell roofs, brocaded windows, medieval stone bridges, to the list of cities from which people had been forcibly expelled by the Israeli Defense Forces. Simon, along with a number of men from the kibbutz, was due to go into the army the following year.)

Simon did not have one friend on the kibbutz. Alone with his unthinkable thoughts, he faced them out until they delivered their message. He never planned to tell a soul until he met Kim Chernin in a straw hat, wandering about on the farm with Devora late one New Year's Eve.

If Kim Chernin had not come to Araht to come between them, Devora and Simon might have met outside the laundry one late afternoon when Devora was humming a Yemenite song. Simon would have understood the yearning for a god in exile. She in turn would have loved Simon for his heroic silence.

Simon believed in magical images, Devora in baking, Kim Chernin in washing dishes. She had washed so many dishes during the last three days the dishes could now literally wash themselves. Kim Chernin did not intentionally lie. When she said she had not slept since she left home, five days earlier, she meant her nights had been sleepless. Why bother to count the half hour of sleep snatched here and there (on the sacks of grain in the storage closet outside the kitchen)? No one could possibly keep on at that pitch without dropping. Sooner or later Simon had better decide to take her to bed or she will fall right off her feet and never get up again.

Kim Chernin loved exaggeration, it enlarged the world, gave it depths and dimensions it otherwise lacked as it turned its dreary daily round. Where I live, people don't get swept off their feet when they mop the kitchen floor after lunch. As memory Kim Chernin is seen, as she always claimed, standing five or six inches above the floor, while she chased the water with a suppressed whoop from under the sinks, around the stoves, out the door.

People do not rise up five inches off the floor unless they are desperate. If Kim Chernin kept moving, eating mostly yogurt and hard-boiled eggs, she would get to a state where moving fast had become an exaltation. The dishes rinsing and stacking themselves, the chromatic levitations with the mop, were sure signs of impending trouble. Kim Chernin's thoughts moved fast too, flitting from this to that in a continuous whirl. When she closed her eyes she saw batches of colors mix and dissolve from a primal template. Or her feeling of rapture would mount up so high she knew she had knocked through to the meaning of all things. There, for a moment or two, she would be hammered by a soundless weeping for pure joy or the pain of knowing the moment was already passing, leaving perhaps not even a memory or any trace of itself behind. It was a dangerous state, it had been known to suddenly puncture, then she could hardly manage to get off the bed. All the fatigue she had not felt before came in; the lethargy could go on longer than moving fast had lasted, high up and fast as she had gone before, she was now cast down, meaning shredded. From the high place she never once remembered it was going high that would bring her low. If she had remembered she would not have renounced the fling upward. Down below was bleak and desolate beyond what can be told. Anyone there is, in her own way, close to death. Kim Chernin had been in that somber place.

When someone offered Kim Chernin a toke of this, a snort of anything else, Kim Chernin flung back her head, put her hands on her hips, laughed recklessly. *Would I need them?*

Back then, people found it easier to believe some things we scoff at. Devora's grandmother had told her to put one lemon pit in every cake she baked for her husband. Along with the pit Devora was to say, loosely translated from the Yiddish, the charm for keeping a husband faithful. ("One, two, one two, he loves me, he don't love you.")

Devora also baked a cake for Kim Chernin. Her grandmother had taught her no particular charm for persuading people to cast a vote in favor of a stranger at a community meeting on a kibbutz. (The meeting had been Simon's idea. No one had suggested it to the volunteers. In order to work, more than half the members would have to agree to break the rules. Why should anyone want to break rules for a stranger?)

Devora thought the charm for falling in love would

do for the community meeting. When she had finished the crumb cake, wrapped it in a foil-lined shoebox to send Dani, she started in on *lekach*, an extravagant honey cake with six eggs for a finer texture. There was a good quality cooking brandy in the kitchen, Devora planned to make use of it.

While adding the six eggs one by one to the sugar, with a circular scooping motion of the whisk, Devora beat so hard the batter underwent a remarkable transformation. Kim Chernin was there, she saw it. As Devora whipped and folded, the batter rose up out of the bowl. A creamy, yellow ribbon of egg and sugar arched into the air, then spiraled down again into the container. Kim Chernin had to run for another bowl, then another, as Devora, a look of profound "I told you so" on her face, quickly poured the frothing foam.

Kim Chernin was watching the batter with a wary eye. People who exaggerate are nonplussed when the world behaves in a way that needs no exaggeration. She said, "Simon's working on fertility charms. Did he tell you? He's conjured up this guy making it day and night with his girl against the chicken house. This cake could usher in single-handed the postnuclear age. The two of you show great confidence in my ability to arrange things for myself. Not that I want to insult Bubbe's cake. I'm grateful to it. And to you, of course."

Devora, working up a sweat, had tied back her hair with a kitchen towel. In the last few minutes the towel had tucked itself into shape as a turban. She was wearing long jade earrings, her eyes blazing, patches of color had come up on her cheeks. Kim Chernin thought if Dani could see Devora now, he wouldn't need the lemon pit to stay in love with her.

Devora stopped sifting and measuring. She wiped her hands in two swift strokes just where the apron curved over her belly. Devora blinked her eyes several times. She looked up sharply at Kim Chernin, then down again.

"Come on," said Kim Chernin, "out with it."

Devora put both hands around the cake box. She had small hands with long fingers and silver rings. She wondered who would call her if anything happened to Dani. The army would call his parents first. If she and Dani were married, that would be different, but the army would otherwise not first call a girlfriend. So, if not the army, someone else would have to call her. Dani's father didn't talk much. Devora had never seen him talk on the telephone. Dani's mother talked on the telephone the minute she got home from work. What would happen if the army was not able to call through if something happened to Dani? Suppose they got through and Dani's mother got the news, what if Dani's mother deliberately didn't call Devora?

Kim Chernin was keeping an eye on the batter. The dough was threatening another transformation as Devora, having diluted the honey with hot coffee, stirred it into the uneasy mass.

Kim Chernin was leaning on her elbows against the counter. There was an enormous baking oven on the wall to their right, two other good-size ovens in the black iron stoves that stood at the center of the kitchen. Kim Chernin jiggled the dial on the wall oven, opened the door, removed a blackened baking sheet. "There are only two possibilities with Dani and his silence. Either the army won't let him call you, or he doesn't want to. In the first case, you'll hear from him sooner or later. In the second, if you don't ever hear from him again, we'll give that guy a shake he'll never forget, we'll stuff him with *lekach* and lemon pits, wrap you up in the bed with him, with your turban and your wild eyes and you'll have this guy right in your pocket where you want him."

Kim Chernin leaned all the way across the counter to pull Devora's earlobe. Exaggeration was very soothing to a broken heart. Devora laughed, sifted the flour and baking powder, the soda and allspice into the cake. She muttered Bubbe's charm over the bowls, her face rapt and peaceful, as her wide forehead had always intended.

They were practically out of bowls, Kim Chernin had to gather in the big pots just to hold the batter so Devora could add raisins and nuts and then practically the whole bottle of brandy, two tablespoons would not have been enough for all that cake.

"You've got to speak at the meeting tonight, Simon's right," Devora insisted. She tasted the batter, pursed her lips. "Something's missing. You try it."

Kim Chernin said, "I won't speak because I can't. Look at me, I'm six feet off the floor already. If I go in there and start talking I'll be buzzing around the ceiling before I've said ten words. Let Simon do it for me. As soon as we've tamed this primordial ooze I'll type out my life story. You read it for me. They all know me already. You think anyone who doesn't want me will want me because I tell them a sob story about myself?"

Devora shook her head. "Some people are waiting to

make up their mind till tonight. There's always people on the fence. Simon made a list, if all the so-so's turned out to vote against you, you'd be in trouble. Simon's sure of it. And I am too. And anyway, it's not the words, it's your personality. Simon and I can't read that. People believe you when you say things, I don't know why because you're a born liar. But even I who know you, when I hear you talk, I believe anything you say because you believe in yourself, you say everything with conviction. If you were in my situation and you wanted Dani to go on loving you you wouldn't need lemon pits, you'd just tell him he does love you and he would. Damn this cake. What's wrong with this cake?"

Kim Chernin tasted it from the spoon. "It needs tons more brandy, more cloves. Did you use citron?"

"Citron? How do you know?"

"Taste it."

Devora looked worried. "We'll be baking all afternoon at this rate. You'd better go write your speech. I never put citron in before. Should I use all the brandy?"

"All and then some. Where's the store around here?"

"It's only open on Tuesday nights. It's just our kibbutz store. You-know-who distributes the supplies. She writes everything down in a ledger. I don't know who's keeping the ledger on her. I bet you anything the kibbutz would be a lot richer if that one went on a diet."

Devora laughed so hard she started choking. Kim Chernin had to pound her on the back. The sudden uproar was upsetting to the cake, which rose up again and performed one of its spectacular gyrations.

Devora shouted, "Look at the cake! Maybe this is

what happens to *lekach* in Eretz Israel? But Bubbe was a socialist. She never once believed in God!"

Usually Kim Chernin loved dogs. She understood their confinement and their suffering. Whenever she passed them on the street, she would look into their eyes. The dogs always returned the look. Once, she healed her own dog, a brown and white springer who suffered from burrs. The dog had been whining and scratching until Kim Chernin pressed her hands against its ears. Her hands grew hot, the dog grew quiet, it lay still, staring up at her. Kim Chernin knew it was this look she would have directed at God if he had managed to save her sister.

There was one dog at Araht Kim Chernin did not like. He was a sullen bully. He belonged to the man in overalls, who had hated Kim Chernin since the first night in the *mo'adon* when everyone else loved her, although Kim Chernin did not yet know he hated her or that the dog named Zigefuss belonged to him.

Kim Chernin stood at the kitchen door, a bowl of cake in her arm. "Zigefuss, you like cake batter?" The small yellow dog came running instead. Kim Chernin took the little dog in her arms. Right away, Zigefuss came lumbering over.

"Don't growl at me, you fiend," Kim Chernin snarled back. Zigefuss was drooling a long strand of green spittle. He had stiff grayish hair, it stood out in sharp spines all over his body. Sometimes, when he was scratching himself with his big foot, Zigefuss gave the impression of several heads, each more flea-infested than the next. Kim Chernin, who used to weep on the rare occasions her father hit her black cocker with a rolled-up newspaper, was sometimes visited by a wish to strangle Zigefuss.

The dog lapped up a spoonful of batter. Then another. Finally the whole (small) bowl.

Devora watched from the doorway. "I wish he would have convulsions and flop down dead. There's something about that dog. If this cake is supposed to make people fall in love, somehow I just can't see Zigefuss as a lover."

Kim Chernin had been examining Zigefuss through a microscope made from her thumb and first finger. "He didn't turn into the Ba'al Shem Tov. But he's not shaking and foaming either. We may not get any votes out of this cake tonight, but I think it is safe enough for the dogs. Eh, Zigefuss, you sublime ugliness? You gonna let me pet you between the ears?"

"Kim, he'll bite you. He bit the kitchen boss when she was giving him a piece of meat. I'm not kidding. Don't touch him. She had to go down for tetanus. Even Hiram can almost never touch him. Wroooogh, Zigefuss. Go away, get out of here."

Devora ran faster than you'd imagine, heels turned out, knees in, flapping her apron at Zigefuss, who was not impressed. "Kim, please, just leave him alone. He's vicious. Wrooogh, Zigefuss. Scram."

It took a while for Zigefuss to heave himself up, shake once or twice, lumber away. Even then, he looked back menacingly at Devora. "Someone beat that creature when he was a puppy, I'll bet you anything," Kim Chernin said. Devora took a few steps after him, still flapping the apron.

"We can't afford to pity him," she said. "Even if he let you pet him once, the second time . . . disaster!"

After that, Kim Chernin let all the other dogs into the kitchen.

Devora's victory over Zigefuss was due to the cake batter Zigefuss had consumed. If it hadn't wrought love, Kim Chernin said, it had made him a shade more sensitive to fear and danger, the beginning of love.

"Don't ask me about love," Devora insisted as she ladled a spoonful of batter into a bowl for the small yellow dog. "You're the expert. You've already got Simon in love with you. What happened to you-know-who, the guy from the bus? Did Simon spend the night in your room?"

"Not the way you mean, not exactly."

Devora rubbed her hands together hard. "I like that. I like that 'not exactly.' I bet. I can just imagine. Listen, tell me the truth."

"Not likely."

"I don't mean that. I mean, most people in the world would say I was beautiful, wouldn't they? I mean, when I meet a man, I say to myself, 'He's bound to think I'm beautiful. Everyone else does,' but it carries no conviction. I don't believe in it, except as something people have always said. You're not beautiful that way, then suddenly you are; I don't know if it's beautiful exactly. It's some way you're alive, suddenly you turn yourself up and then you're even better than beautiful. You remember that time Barry and I were in Berkeley, and Michael was visiting from England? We called you and you came over and Michael was more or less your date? You know what he told Barry? He said at first when he met you he didn't even think you were attractive. Then, by the time two hours passed, he thought you were the most attractive woman he'd ever met. That's why Barry wanted us to come back with them. All four of us. I said yes. Yes, I did. I yes, you no. Come on, you have to remember. Why didn't you?

Kim Chernin looked thoughtful. "You should have been a mystical rabbi's wife. You should be married to a man who would dance for god from sundown to sunrise, a lover of peach jam and gentle women, for whom you would be the only woman in his life. You shouldn't experiment with sex; you're a completely faithful woman. Look how faithful you've been to the same wrong guy. But at least you feel, you suffer. Sex is only interesting when it's driven by an unholy desire. . . ."

Kim Chernin had started to talk fast. She had grabbed a wooden spoon, twisted it this way and that for emphasis, swinging it out with a vigorous gesture that made Devora duck.

Devora put her hands on Kim Chernin's shoulders. "It's I who have eaten too much cake? Maybe you'd better not speak in the *mo'adon*, maybe you're right. Everyone likes you well enough now, but if you go on like that . . ."

Kim Chernin said, "If I speak too fast, if I get carried away, make a sign. I'll keep an eye on you, I'll slow down. Scratch your nose. Try it. Better yet, just open both hands like this, and press down. 'Quiet, Kim. Take it easy.' Try it."

Kim Chernin talked in order to practice. "Devora, did you hear what I said? The only really blasphemous thing a Western thinker can do is regard sex as divine. Okay, I'll slow down. This is slow, what's not slow about this? But the origin of all sexuality is the divine. Even in the

Old Testament. The Canaanite goddesses are always worshiped through sexual acts. Yes, they are. I assure you. I
already slowed down. I can't think these things when I'm
going slowly."

Devora moved up close to Kim Chernin. "You didn't
slow down. You didn't even try. If you get into the *mo'adon*
and talk like that you'll be out of here before midnight.
Poor Simon, if that's what he's in for."

"I didn't know you had a sense of humor."

"It's the cake batter."

Kim Chernin put her hands on her hips. "Why
shouldn't I talk at that meeting? I'll tell the truth, if they
don't want me I'll find someplace else that docs."

"Kim, no truth, anything but that. I don't think I
could stand it here if you left. There's not another kibbutz
like this in all of Israel. Just believe me. You're too wild for
the others. You won't find a Simon there or even anyone
like me, to bake a cake for you."

N o memory could preserve for twenty years every
word of a speech spoken thousands of miles away
in a room full of tension and exhaustion. If I were to write
it down three days in a row, the same seductive, cunning,
desperate speech would emerge, in which not one word
would be the same. Does that (or does that not) make
memory a liar?

The whole room was packed, the tables had been removed, the chairs set up in a large half circle. Kim Chernin
was wearing a long dress, Chaya (another knitter who

worked in the kitchen) in brown rayon pants sat massively in her folding chair next to her, translating. Compared with her, Kim Chernin felt slight and irrelevant, as if she were about to blow away.

Kim Chernin probably slipped in a word about the founding meeting of a student Zionist organization in Russia. Her head was filled with stuff like that, highly flattering to her listeners, who must have sensed she was comparing them to people who had shouted nonstop for five hours before they agreed to take Eretz Israel, not America, as the goal of Jewish migration. That would have been toward the end of 1881, in a smoke-filled room in Moscow. Kim Chernin had another story. This one was about the time Martin Buber addressed a gathering of Russian-Jewish students at a meeting that went on for two days and three nights in a beerhall in Zurich. I doubt if she mentioned one single argument for breaking the rules. She wouldn't have bothered. The minute she started talking it would have occurred to her, she was her own best argument.

There was silence when Kim Chernin stopped speaking. Kim Chernin concentrated on Devora, who was sitting in the front row next to Simon. Devora made a victory sign. Kim Chernin had talked well. The words had arranged themselves in great arcs of sound, unexpected cadences, weighty caesuras. She hadn't waved her hands, she had spoken calmly, Devora hadn't made the slow-down sign even once. Simon's face was stony with anguish. He had made up his mind, if Kim Chernin couldn't stay, he would leave with her, accompany her all over the world until she was safe.

Kim Chernin had kept herself together long enough.
She could do nothing further, more could not be asked,
what she and Devora could do had been done. If she
was not invited to stay, she would resort to any extreme
measure, move in with Simon, go to Scotland. She was
unraveling.

She had a clear idea how the unraveling would happen. First a foot, then a finger, a whole arm with the shoulder, until soon the plausibly articulated skeleton of herself
stitch by stitch would have been unglued. She felt a quick
jab of icy panic in the same class with doors banging.

Simon jumped to his feet. He was wearing a black
headband, a pair of tight, wrinkled white pants folded
across his muscular stomach on a diagonal line to the
waist. His white T-shirt, pulled tight over his chest,
brought thoughts Kim Chernin considered inappropriate.

Devora watched him too. She'd had no idea anyone
like Simon lived on the kibbutz. Everyone was hidden. Simon, in his room playing his guitar. She, sorting through
old photographs, writing letters by hand on good paper.
She never crossed out a word. If she made a mistake she
tore the whole thing up and started again. Simon must
have been the sort of homely little boy everyone calls
adorable. It went well with how he took everything so intensely, his quick ability to size things up. Devora was
swept with a profound longing to take him in hand and
iron him.

Simon clenched both fists up close to his chest.
"Okay, here's what I think. If we want Kim to stay we'll
make it possible. We didn't come up here to be just another kibbutz. We make the rules, we break them. Let's

break them for her. Everyone's seen how she can work, she knows practically everyone. When it's time for her daughter to come, and I don't think we should make her wait a year either, that's not fair to the mother, it's not fair to the child, we'll figure out what to do then. For instance, her daughter could go down with the farm truck every morning to Kefar Blum and come back in the afternoon when our workers return. Her daughter could go to school on the kibbutz, but live here at Araht with her mother. If Kim were in America, her daughter would be taking the bus to school, wouldn't she?"

Simon grimaced. That was a slip. He pulled his headband halfway around, twisted it nervously.

"If Kim is going to live the way she lives in America, why did she bother to come here?"

This comment (in mediocre Hebrew) from the kitchen boss was not popular. She was answered in Hebrew and English. "That's low-down. That's not the same thing. That's mean. Why shouldn't we bend a rule if we want to? Araht isn't just any old kibbutz."

Young, Jewish people have been known to jump up, wave their arms, interrupt other speakers, who have certainly interrupted someone else. Chaya called the meeting to order. She lifted one pudgy hand, extended her forefinger. "I will call on anyone who wants to talk. Wait for me to call on you."

A man in faded blue jeans stood up in the third row. "If we have questions for Kim Chernin let's ask the questions. Otherwise, let's move on to the discussion and the vote. She's asking to join our community. That doesn't mean we have to put her through this shit. . . ."

The man was not bad looking, although definitely not Kim Chernin's type. He had a silky, reddish blond beard worn quaker style without a mustache. His hair bristled in short blond spikes, reminding Kim Chernin of cut grass. Or maybe the haircut was needed to make him look tough? He wore the sleeves of his T-shirt rolled up high on his shoulders, a package of Camels tucked into his left sleeve. He had a cigarette behind one ear. His whole manner seemed to suggest that you could trust him in a fight; that he'd beat anyone's head in, but the fight would be fair.

The kitchen boss, the woman with braids, had taken out their knitting. Their needles clicked out a worried, embittered commentary. Occasionally one of them tugged firmly at a dark hank of yarn. It rose up obediently out of the carpetbag, as if it had just been brought sharply to order. Devora noticed a few crumbs on the kitchen boss's lap.

Boaz, the man in faded jeans, hitched up his trousers. "I've been back three hours," he said. "It doesn't take long to see how things are. She wants to stay, why shouldn't she? Everyone told us we wouldn't make it for six months up here. We made it. Why did we? Not by having to throw a stranger off the kibbutz."

Kim Chernin watched Simon enviously watch the man in faded jeans. Simon's face had become completely transparent, one of those frogs with translucent skin whose heart you could watch beating in biology class. During his second year in the army Boaz had led his unit in a fifty mile march up to Jerusalem in 100 degree heat. People who saw him when he arrived said he wasn't even sweating.

Chaya leaned over to whisper, "Boaz is the head of the security branch. He's just back from his honeymoon a few hours ago. If we move on to the discussion, you'll have to leave the room. We'll call you back after the vote. Are you exhausted?"

The room was hot. Everyone, at the same moment, began to suffer. Several people opened windows, others went to get a second piece of cake. No one dared open a door because of the dogs, who had been howling steadily ever since Devora let them lap up the overflowing cake batter. Devora has always said they did not howl once when Kim Chernin was talking.

Kim Chernin looked at the man in faded jeans. He was leaning way back in his chair, his arms crossed over his chest. Another young man had come forward to whisper, he was kneeling on the floor behind Boaz, who reminded Kim Chernin of the boys in her junior high school, who never did their homework, slid books back and forth down the aisle, on one occasion threw a book through a closed window. When the lights were put out for movies Kim Chernin and a couple of other girls would run over to sit on the laps of these boys, who were always the most fun to be with. It scandalized the teacher and that was the point. At that age, going on twelve, Kim Chernin already knew the whole point of sex (sometimes) was to create a scandal. This kind of boy could make a comrade of a girl, if she were tough enough.

Boaz jumped to his feet. "I don't buy this shit about no work at Araht. In the orchard, there's plenty of work. The whole afternoon crew puts in extra hours to keep

up, their work day never ends on time. Simha always has
to ask for volunteers to stay longer. How old is the
daughter? Eight years old? Simha has a job for her in the
orchard."

Boaz put his hands in his back pockets, squared his
shoulders, let his grin flash around the room, one of those
men with naughty pale green eyes who will still look boyish when he is eighty. He was slight, muscular, not nearly
tall enough to carry it off. It didn't bother him. He wasn't
worried about women, it was men he was out to impress
and had and did. He'd gone straight into the army from
street gangs in Chicago, a tattoo on his right arm, just below the place where the sleeve rolled up to hold his
cigarettes.

"You, Boaz. Thanks for speech. To my mind, people
work much extra on kibbutz. That what mean to building
up collective. Not mean two more mouth to feed."

Boaz jumped up on his chair. "Bullshit, who the hell is
that?" Two of the young men Simon called Boaz's slaves,
both of them skinny, moved fast toward the back. There
must have been a dozen or more people, some standing
around the honey cake, others sitting. The obscure guy
from the Eastern European country was sitting next to the
coffee urn, but what did that prove? It could have been
anyone. He had a right to his opinion, didn't he?

Kim Chernin noticed the man in overalls. He had
turned back toward the room, his face (the same transparent skin), full of yearning. He had grabbed hold of his
overall straps with both hands, his eyes rested softly on
Boaz, his comrade. He too must have worked in the secu-

rity branch? Must have been waiting, counting the days perhaps, for Boaz to get back?

Not likely.

Kim Chernin felt tired. Fine filaments of fatigue ran down into her chair, gluing her to it. Even if they didn't vote for her she would not be able to leave. They'd have to carry her stuck to the chair to the hospital in Safad, where the soldier would come to find her, to save her.

Chaya leaned toward her. "Are you all right, you look exhausted. I've never seen them like this. They're out of control, even Boaz. Is something the matter? The discussion should take place when you're out of the room."

"Rules aren't what they promise," Kim Chernin whispered. "One hopes for so much from them. Form, harmony, the celestial order they imitate. They always let you down. Invariably, they degenerate into rigidity, punitiveness, authoritarian terror. Or they invite you to break through them, to discover what they have been trying to keep you from knowing. I have the strangest feeling I'd like to put my head in your huge lap and go to sleep practically forever."

Had she said that? Of course not. Chaya stood up, waving her hands back and forth over her head. The man in overalls had started talking.

"Let's admit, we are discussing not only the mundane rules that regulate life here on the kibbutz. Why did the collective before us fail? Wasn't it something to do with anarchy, license, the absence of some form of reliable authority?"

Chaya managed to break in. Her hands were clasped tight in front of her. "You speak of rules, but you violate them, yes you do, here, this moment. This discussion should not take place until Kim Chernin is out of the room."

He answered fast, a smooth, South African accent. "Kim Chernin is certainly charming."

The man could have been handsome, in a grim, hard, woodcutter way but his narrow, reddish brown eyes, with their fixed gaze, reminded Kim Chernin of eyes in flash-bulb photographs, demonic, mistaken.

"Certainly any community would be pleased to welcome her. But at what cost? That's all I have to ask, Chaya, then I'll stop. That's my question, I direct it to Kim Chernin. What will it cost us to welcome her as a member?"

Simon was on his feet. "Sit down, Hiram. You're out of order. That's not the kind of question Chaya means. You speak of rules, you subvert them, I see through you, you're the type to use rules in order . . . in order to . . . I don't know, take advantage of them . . . to . . . satisfy yourself."

Boaz had grown transparent too. Beneath the surface of his face ran a keen, boisterous, cunning, boyish calculation. Boaz stretched his legs into the aisle, laced his fingers behind his head. "Hiram doesn't mean us to take him seriously. He's exaggerating so we'll get the point, aren't you, Hiram?"

Chaya made four sharp staccato claps with her hands. "You, too, Boaz are not in order. We are all speaking in English, no one knows what anyone else is talking about, it was not my impression Hiram was sarcastic. I thought him sincere. But out of order."

Simon ignored her. "Whether he was serious or not, does it matter? I myself, I think he was serious, what difference does it make? Someone in this room, probably a lot more than one or two, certainly think like that idiot. What will it cost us to invite Kim Chernin? Let's work it out. The rules were made when we were not yet sure we could get through the summer. We were worried about everything then. We kept trying to get the volunteers not to eat apples or we wouldn't have enough to sell! It's not a laughing matter. Here we are, supported by the Ha-Shomer ha-Za'ir, and we couldn't even let the volunteers eat apples. Now we can't trust ourselves to offer a home to a woman and child who need one. If that's what we are, in our first year, we've already failed as a kibbutz, that's what I say. We might as well all pack up and go down on the bus tomorrow with Kim Chernin. Does anyone care where she's going? Isn't that what we're doing? Sending her out alone into the world?"

Boys at school had never liked Simon. The girls had. When he was fourteen, still living in Alexandria, an older girl had taken him in hand, shown him where and how, found him a gifted learner. The guilt of that pleasure was still with him. He would leave Araht with Kim Chernin (a man follows the woman he loves), he would never jump up on his chair, ready to knock someone's head in.

Boaz took the cigarette from behind his ear. He twisted it lovingly between his fingers. He had learned about sex in a gang rape, in Dublin. Five boys, the girl fought every one of them, Boaz told Kim Chernin one day when it rained, when they went back to the tool shed in the orchard. Boaz said the way she twisted, kicked, threw her hips, turned him on. But he never did it again. Never, didn't Kim Chernin believe him?

"Do I believe you? Do I even believe this whole story?"

Although the rape took place years before, this story gave Kim Chernin the impression Boaz had come to Israel, marched fifty miles to Jerusalem without sweating, to escape some consequence.

But he never said so.

The three Israeli friends stood up together. The pretty one said, "We'll send Hiram to the Knesset. There he can discuss the great philosophic questions." The one in horn-rimmed glasses spoke next. "Let's move to the vote. I cast my vote for Kim Chernin." The pretty one clapped her hands. "My kibbutz has more exceptions than rules. We're sick of rules. We like exceptions better." The third looked around the room. "You want to hear my solution to the problem of one more mouth to feed? I will share half my dinners with Kim Chernin. Is there anyone who wants to share breakfast? You won't suffer. She eats nothing but yogurt and hard-boiled eggs."

In the din and babble, laughter and clapping, that followed, Kim Chernin tried to get to her feet. The chair clung to her. If Kim Chernin couldn't get to her feet, she could at least add her voice to the uproar. "I believe a question has been addressed to me? Hiram, you asked me a question? I shall answer."

The man in overalls leaned forward, put his arms over

the back of a chair. Although he looked like Zigefuss, Kim Chernin did not flinch. There was no malignancy now in his eyes. They were empty. Kim Chernin, incongruously seated while practically everyone else was on their feet, opened her hands in a gesture that seemed to say, *So? What's the fuss?*

"You wonder about the cost of inviting me to remain on the farm? The cost I admit would be great. You'd have to endure breaking a rule in order to find out that a rule is just as good when it's broken. Nothing happens to it. It's still a rule, it's still there. Only now it has achieved the exception that defines it."

An uproar of applause, loud whoops of pleasure. Everyone felt Kim Chernin had somehow got the best of the exchange. Then, people shouted out suggestions, engaged in fragmented philosophic banter, laughed exuberantly, pushed each other on the shoulder, clapped, spoke in languages of origin, Hebrew, Spanish, Norwegian, Portuguese, ate honey cake, shut the windows, opened them again, went to sit farther back in the room, moved up closer. Simon and Devora had their heads together, whispering intently. Chaya clapped her hands, clapped her hands, finally gave up, sat down next to Kim Chernin. But Kim Chernin was swaying very, very slightly with a mysterious, faraway smile. Chaya pulled her by the hand. "Pardon me if I say so," she whispered, "but I think you should walk out of the room. I'll call for the vote."

Kim Chernin directed her mysterious smile at Chaya. The woman's sense of justice, although she herself would not vote for Kim Chernin, made the impression of a fine down featherbed.

Something was happening to Kim Chernin, probably because she was tired. The room had receded, it stood far off at the end of a long tunnel, a sparkling point of beckoning light beyond darkness. She made an effort to put things back the way they were supposed to be. When she tried hard, concentrating her will, the room returned to normal. The walls stood upright, resting on a floor, supporting a flat ceiling, under which were chairs with people sitting in them. Then, the organizing principle snapped, a lawless disorder returned, things seemed bathed in an ice-cold light, smells wafted by, the smell of honey cake, the smell of Zigefuss's breath, the smell of snow for a person seeing snow for the first time, the image of the soldier who was coming, he was coming to save her. She saw his face, framed by his long brown hair, his expression, a gentle intelligence.

Something had happened. Because of it Kim Chernin struggled back, gathered in the dispersed sensual pieces, forced them to make up a plausible whole. The whole group, receiving the change in one of those simultaneous tremors of awareness, relaxed perceptibly. What had happened?

A woman stood up. She walked impatiently down the rows, across the front of the room, was standing next to Chaya, who was on her feet, who immediately stepped aside.

The woman acknowledged her with a quick nod. She waited until Chaya had gone to sit in the second row, near the beardless guys who hung on Boaz's every word. Because this woman was standing simply, hands at her sides, without saying a word, everyone looked at her. That was all it took. The room fell silent. That is what authority meant. Kim Chernin had imagined, when it was discovered she could not be pried loose from her chair, when efforts were made to lift the chair, they would find out the chair had grown into the floor, just as the floor itself was attached, through a deep, subterranean structure of roots and branchings, to the core of her homeland.

The woman had long, straight black hair tied back in a single braid. Amber eyes with an exotic, upward turn at the corners, high cheekbones. An impenetrable beauty, menacing in its refusal to reveal the source of the inspiring pallor in the stern, oval face. Her glance fell on Kim Chernin resolutely, striking her with its coldness. She was tall, wearing a pair of new blue jeans, a blue cotton sweater with short sleeves, she had a cool, aloof tone to her, was one of the superior ones, the native born, the Sabras. She had come back a few hours before with Boaz, she was The Bride.

When she spoke (in Hebrew, quietly), people listened.

"Please, would someone tell me where I am? Am I at Kibbutz Araht? This is our new experiment in social living? Is it true, what I see here tonight is happening at Kibbutz Araht? I look around, I ask myself, are these the people I was missing so much I wanted to come home a week early? Come home a week early to a kibbutz that has not noticed Kim Chernin is practically falling off her chair? Has anyone offered her a cup of tea? A piece of cake? I have been sitting here for an hour but I too only noticed how tired she is."

One of the men sitting near the refreshment table

brought Kim Chernin a cup and plate. Kim Chernin put them on the floor next to her chair.

"This woman is our guest. She has done us the honor, the honor, not the insult, of asking to live with us. She has been here three days, she likes us already so much she wants to stay with us. I myself, seeing us tonight, I ask myself, what's there to like? But she likes us. I suggest, we invite her for the next six months. During that time she can take time to look around, figure out how it's possible to bring a daughter. If it's possible, the question of the daughter will be answered, there will be nothing to discuss. Meanwhile, we will get to know this Kim Chernin, who will get to know us. I suggest we invite our guest to leave for a few moments. The discussion has taken place. Perhaps someone, Simon? will show her where to wait in the office? We will now immediately take the vote."

Kim Chernin waited in the office. By this cold fish in blue jeans, by her precisely, by no one else, Kim Chernin felt slapped in the face. As if Kim Chernin did not matter. (Why should Kim matter?) Kim Chernin felt this call to abstract justice a terrible blow. She wanted to be loved, chosen, have rules broken for her. She longed for comrades in arms. She would be invited to stay, not because of Bubbe's honey cake, Simon's fertility rites, the solidarity of the dogs, the fiery championship of Boaz, her overcoming of the (necessary) opposition of Hiram in overalls, the friendship of the three Israeli women. She would be invited to stay because inviting her was the only appropriate expression of kibbutz generosity to a stranger.

A cold generosity, a heartless compassion.

Kim Chernin leaned back against the desk, a door banged shut down the hall, feet clattered toward her.

Yes, they've invited me. If they hadn't invited me no one would be running.

The
Soldier

❦ ❦ ❦

LATE FALL

1971

If you had run across Kim Chernin on her way to Devora's room she would not have told you her philosophy of life, sex, and the body. Nevertheless, she was ruminating about Theirs, a character she knew herself in part to be, whom she hated. I have not mentioned Theirs before. I thought it awkward enough, a Kim Chernin now, writing about a Kim Chernin then. Theirs, however, can no longer be avoided.

Kim Chernin will shortly go to sleep for a long time. During that absence we might as well occupy ourselves with the detested Theirs, whom Kim Chernin sometimes called Theirs the Compliant, in which "their" was collectively mother and father, first teacher, the policeman on the corner, the man in the park, the neighborhood boys who sang in harmonies roaming the neighborhood late at night. Taken together, they had made a creature who was significantly not Kim Chernin. Collectively, they had removed Theirs, a creature they had made in their own image, from the pleasure-body Kim Chernin felt she should rightfully possess, and from its sensations. That is why Kim Chernin aimed to destroy Theirs.

Destroy is a strong word. Perhaps I should say Kim Chernin wished to redeem Theirs from the disembodied, compliant state in which Theirs existed. Where I say Kim Chernin ate only yogurt and hard-boiled eggs, Kim Chernin would say it was Theirs who believed in starvation.

Kim Chernin wanted to destroy Theirs. She wanted to root out Theirs's enthusiasm for first-thing-in-the-morning ice-cold showers, she despised Theirs's ascetic leanings, Theirs's enthusiasm for transcending the flesh. If Kim Chernin was a rebel, that was because of Theirs, Kim Chernin was in rebellion against Theirs.

How rebel? Theirs was, after all, also a part of Kim Chernin. In all this the constant warfare between Kim Chernin and Theirs, the only conceivable authentic impulse, Kim Chernin said, was erotic. Kim Chernin liked to say no one had put that in her, that at least was one thing the mother, the policeman, the father, did not want her to have. None of them wanted her to be fond of guard towers. To the extent Kim Chernin felt desire, she was not Theirs, she was her own.

Theirs dwelled in a hollow behind the eyes, in a head that knew itself by virtue of its detachment from a body. It was not easy for Kim Chernin to describe Theirs's relationship to the body. Could one say Theirs had forgotten the body? Reduced it to a phantom limb? Brought it along for convenience sake or in an emergency? (It seemed that if you were gone from the body entirely, you might be said to be dead. Theirs feared death.)

The animosity between Kim Chernin and Theirs unfolded almost daily along the line of sensation called skin. Kim Chernin was eager to heat up every pinprick of sensation, Theirs hot to smother it. Theirs might win in the battle against food. Against sex and its vagaries, desire and its appetites, Theirs was powerless.

Kim Chernin's strategy was: little by little, through yielding to every occasion of temptation, in the shack down in the banana groves (maybe), sooner or later one late night with Simon, another blow would be struck against Theirs. If Kim Chernin was fragmenting, that precisely was how she wished it to be. It was Theirs who would go down. Soon the original Kim Chernin of pure sensation would be born, at the site precisely of Theirs's dismemberment.

Theirs had gone into psychoanalysis to complain about Kim Chernin. She disliked the way Kim Chernin talked about Dionysian ecstasy to a stranger in a Berkeley café. She was shocked when Kim Chernin went up into the Tilden hills to smoke banana skins, swam from the forbidden forested side of Lake Anza where there were no lifeguards, lay under eucalyptus trees naked and wet practicing strategies against Theirs.

The analyst told Theirs men were using Kim Chernin. He said they were exploiting her narcissism to take advantage of her body. Theirs admired this formulation, which set Kim Chernin down a rung, offering herself to every man who found her beautiful. (Theirs knew Kim Chernin was not beautiful, her breasts were too large, she did not have long fingers, she appealed to men because she was a slut.)

Kim Chernin did not expect the analyst to understand her radical program to liberate desire. He probably had no idea women had a desire all their own, a unique pleasure all over their body in no way comparable to a man's body, not even remotely like it. How could he know when most women also did not know?

During four and a half years of psychoanalysis Theirs constructed the sexual history of Kim Chernin, who silently read that history differently. Theirs was impressed by the discovery that the child they had both once been had gone for a walk in a Bronx park, where she had run into a naked man who gave her a dime for touching his penis. Kim Chernin regarded this story, along with the one about the boys in the cellar of her apartment building, where she and her family lived on the fifth floor, mere further instances of the conspiracy that had been exercised against her body since birth.

Every time she touched a place that gave pleasure, was frowned at for it, a piece of her body was taken from her. The sensitivity of her fingertips were the first to go, her fingers (which liked to explore nooks and crannies) went soon after. Her eyes were taken from her when the door was slammed in her face when she was curious about what her father had in his pants that made a bulge there. After that, the bulge acquired a mystery that became all later mystery. The bulge was coy, sometimes appearing, other times flatly hidden away, divided, it seemed, into three distinct parts, as was god himself who invites to knowledge but does not allow the object of all yearning to be beheld. She lost her hands at a young age, when they wanted to grab hold of her mother's breast (true ground of being, there even before the gods) By now grabbing hold had become forbidden; no one said why, but the hands were slapped.

That time in the basement, when she had been lured down by three or four older neighborhood boys who pretended they wanted to play with her, they had pushed her down on a mattress. She was not yet five years old. What happened then, what happened then could only be constructed. The memory trailed off after a memory of a boy saying, "Watch out, she's got strong legs." Maybe she fainted. Her body remembered kicking, at night when she went to bed, every night from that time phantom legs kicked and struggled. Inside, at an infinitely sensitive point high up between the legs, thrusting and burning. Although neither Theirs nor Kim Chernin could remember what went on in the cellar, the body said, "Rape."

Theirs was only too happy to be done with this body that had suffered the humiliations of growing up a girl. According to Theirs, starvation was the appropriate destiny for this body, which must take over its own mortifications and hopefully in time brand, discipline, and eliminate its wishful sensations. According to Kim Chernin, the true meaning of existence was the body, boy or girl it grew up slapped and humiliated, alienated from the meaning it found in the jagged edge of a green leaf, the pleasure the mouth took putting things into it, the body's languor. For Kim Chernin the body was peopled with hidden nature spirits all hungry to be turned on. To go that way, back to the body, stealing it back from those who had frowned, slapped, slammed, thrusted, was the way Kim Chernin wanted to go.

Theirs had gone into psychoanalysis to get rid of Kim Chernin. Instead, the boisterous Kim Chernin grew stronger as Theirs began to fall apart. The division between them, which the psychoanalyst would have regarded as unwelcome, made it possible for Kim Chernin to survive the gradual piece by piece destruction of Theirs. When Kim Chernin got glued to the chair in the *mo'adon*, that was a moment when Theirs lost hold of the phantom body.

But if the phantom body was the only body Kim Chernin had, if the new body was just now being brought up through repeated episodes of sex and sensation, where would Kim Chernin locate herself as Theirs and the phantom body went down? Where would Kim Chernin locate herself? A question that cannot be asked, cannot be answered. Worse yet, Kim Chernin was not content to elaborate this scheme philosophically. She wanted to hold on (how? where? a person without a body?) until the pleasure-body, original birthright, was mature enough to give her a home.

Clearly, a person in this condition might have to curl up in the collective body of a small farm, in the arms of a man only too keen to take her. She might have to sleep for a long time, for sleep has its own body. I think it was Theirs who kept her awake at night, knowing that in sleep the body returns to itself, takes original delight, grows innocent.

According to one memory Kim Chernin slept for seven days and nights. Maybe the sense of humor

Kim Chernin did not yet have was already at work in the way her memories were inscribed. I sometimes think she stacked them maliciously, hoping I'd have trouble sorting things out. Does that mean Kim Chernin knew she was doing away with herself? Does it mean she foresaw the eventual triumph of Theirs? Not so. She knew she would trample Theirs into the dust. Or maybe memory prefers a person like Kim Chernin? I'm sure her memories do not mean well by me. There's a trap here somewhere, some trick lying in wait, someone who lives at the edge is likely to have arresting, impossible memories. I? What will I leave to memory? Does memory even tolerate the sort of sorting out to which I'm pledged?

While Kim Chernin slept, several people left trays with yogurt and hard-boiled eggs outside her room. The hallway had a stone floor, a good-sized sink with a storage cabinet. The hall led into two bedrooms and their common bathroom with its excellent shower steamed up windows at four o'clock when work was done for the day. Kim Chernin shared these simple utilities with a talkative woman, who just now, is impatient with Kim Chernin's long sleep, makes as much noise as possible in the room next door, plays dance music, hums and whistles, treads heavily with sharp heels. Nothing works. Kim Chernin sleeps on, the sleep of those nearly at the end of their rope, a healing sleep after long and epic exhaustion.

She was safe, she had reached shore after long passage through uneasy waters, she would be taken care of, the kibbutz would pay taxes for her, arrange for her laundry to be done, take care of her food and meals, provide a room, repair a roof, settle her down among comrades, make sure she was productively employed, help her become an Israeli citizen, an honor to which she was entitled because she had been born to a Jewish mother.

All those things Kim Chernin had worried about (balancing her checkbook, paying rent on time, finding a way to write and still earn a living) would be taken care of by someone else. A doctor showed up every other week to hold office hours in the small infirmary next to the chicken house. If Kim Chernin fell ill, could not work, the kibbutz would provide for her, if necessary for the rest of her life. As it grew, the kibbutz would let Kim Chernin write four hours a day if she could prove her talent for writing. Kim Chernin had no doubt she could prove her talent for writing. She only wondered if anyone there would recognize her talent when she had proved it. She wrote mystical poems, obscure in imagery, impassioned in voice perhaps not quite the thing to do on a hardworking farm on the border that had not yet acquired its dairy?

Otherwise, the collective would help train her for work suiting her tendency to read too much. I think she would have made a good teacher, even a psychoanalyst. A teacher was perhaps the best idea. Then, she would have to work off the kibbutz, maybe on the same kibbutz where her daughter might go to school.

The daughter roams through her sleep with restless, seagull shrieks. She slips letters under the door. The letters seem to have been written on stipled paper imprinted with a yarn flower in the left-hand corner. They arrive in bright yellow envelopes on which the name Israel is mispelled, crossed out, written over. The dream daughter cups her hands to her eyes to peer through the window. She is hungry, her mother is sleeping. She tiptoes away.

The soldier comes and goes through her sleep. In one dream he walks softly into her room late one night when it is almost morning, sets down his lamp on her desk, removes his rifle, checks the clip, hangs it over the arm of her chair. She watches him get undressed. In her sleep she is curious to find out what sort of man he is. She isn't disappointed. Without his boots, socks, khaki shirt and trousers the soldier is naked, he wants her. It is possible to see the rise and fall of long muscles in his arms when he adjusts the rifle. He must be breathing fast. For the dreamer, breathing fast brings about Asahel, King David's sister's youngest son. Asahel was killed by a spear thrust below the fifth rib when he ran after Avner in the skirmishes between the armies of David and Saul. Asahel was said to be light of foot, swift as a wild roe, but he ran so far he was finally out of breath, vulnerable, easy to cut down. The dreamer falls for the fallen warrior. She cries seagull shrieks over him. She discovers the meaning of lamentation. Her long hair can be rent like a garment of grief. The skin of her soldier may have been made for him by a highly recommended tailor. Without a stitch, one single flaw or wrinkle, it spreads evenly over the entire long, taut, lean sweep of him. He is more than an arm's reach away, or she would reach out and make him come.

Wherever you are in the world the days from Rosh Hashanah to Yom Kippur are days of awe. Somber and exalted in character, to them belongs the serious examination of the inner life. These are the days of contrition, one weighs up one's responsibilities to the human community, counts out the tallys of debts, thefts, expenditures. Whether Kim Chernin, in her yoke of sleep, practised holiness through the holidays is not apparent. Myself, I think she dreamed the holidays away pagan style with frivolous thoughts and wishes. Later on, she always maintained she had been waltzing with the Patriarchs, teaching (especially) Abraham how to dance, while Theirs was stretched out beneath the altar. Theirs hoped god would take back his ban against human sacrifice and substitute Kim Chernin for a lamb.

While Kim Chernin slept, Simon and Devora came by frequently. Devora brought a stack of neatly ironed work clothes, most of them in Kim Chernin's size. Simon had found a good pair of work boots for when the winter came. They would be okay with several pairs of thick socks. Everyone, even Kim Chernin's enemies (they would have been ashamed to say otherwise) agreed she should sleep undisturbed.

Mostly, Simon and Devora sat in silence. Simon was sure Devora would not understand why he had stopped being a Zionist. He was waiting for Kim Chernin to wake up so he could tell her. Devora listened to Kim Chernin's breathing. She liked the shadows growing across the room; once in a while she caught a distant cry from the poster of the little girl on the wall above Kim Chernin's bed. On the last day of Kim Chernin's long sleep Simon brought in his guitar and sang in Arabic. "I watch over your sleep, my love, I watch over your sleep, I am waiting, my little one, I watch over your sleep, I watch over you."

Here was the love Kim Chernin had always wished for, the halfway house needed until her own born-again body was ready to carry on. Not just the love of Simon or Devora, or the shy Israeli woman with horn-rimmed spectacles who tiptoed in and out of the entryway with tea and cookies, blushing. Without knowing it, Kim Chernin needed the love of a tribe, a collective of kindred-enough spirits, she needed to be stitched into them, woven into the dark web of their common identity, nothing else would have worked. Let's forget the business of five days and nights. For the first time since the rape, the man in the park, since her sister died, when Kim Chernin was four and a half years old, Kim Chernin (she dreamed that a blade of grass was growing through her earlobe) managed to sleep through a whole night.

H ave I mentioned this yet? In 1968, the year after her father died, Kim Chernin had a fight with her mother. The fight started because Kim Chernin had read an article about Rabbi Moshe Levinger, who had moved into the Park Hotel in Hebron, in defiance of government policy that prohibited Jewish settlement on the West Bank. Later on, the Israeli cabinet voted to let him and his followers stay in the occupied territory. Before long the government established a settlement for them. It was (and is) called Kiryat Arba.

Kim Chernin's mother thought the Israeli cabinet (at that time the Labor party was in power), had once again betrayed the ideals of the Jewish people, making them collectively into imperialists. She showed Kim Chernin a poster of a Palestinian who had been shot by an Israeli soldier. The Palestinian was a young man with a serene face; he wore his death in a dignified manner. His blood spilled over the edge of the poster. Kim Chernin noticed several drops on the kitchen floor.

Kim Chernin said to her mother, "Perhaps there is always sacrifice when a great archetypal pattern is enacted? We see small, we know nothing about the larger reason for things. Couldn't it be, in the end, there will be justice for both sides precisely through the suffering of an innocent like this?"

Her mother said, "Where did you unlearn what I taught you? If you saw a picture of a Jew hanging, and this Jew was hanging because a Nazi hung him there, would you talk about, what do you call it, what kind of pattern?"

Kim Chernin did not like to be misunderstood. She longed for perfect comprehension, especially from her mother. She raised her voice, "What kind of pattern? I'll tell you what kind of pattern. When people spontaneously return to a land they have not seen for two thousand years that is the fulfillment of an archetypal longing. No one makes them do it, they probably don't even call it Zionism, it has nothing to do with ideology, it rises up out of desperation, total despair with their conditions, in the hundreds of thousands they can't go on, only one thing keeps them going, a single idea, and it makes life possible, if it were not for this they would little by little cease to care to light a fire, pull up the bed cover on a freezing night, bring hay to the cow. . . ."

Kim Chernin's mother put her hands on her hips, looked dramatically over her shoulder, calling on presences living and dead to witness her daughter. She said, "Who is talking about cows? Where did cows come in? And hay? What kind of hay is this? Is this archetypal hay?"

At that time neither Kim Chernin nor her mother had a sense of humor. Kim Chernin said, "You see? You know perfectly well what *archetypal* means. You just don't want to understand me. I've given up caring if you do or not. The fact remains, the Jewish people made their way back to Palestine because they felt the shadow of their own destruction in Europe, already before the turn of the century they felt it, I tell you, and tried to save themselves. Isn't Israel, for all its moral ambiguity, better than Hitler's ovens? Isn't the murder of millions of innocent children worse than the hanging of an innocent Arab man?"

Kim Chernin's mother tapped against her chest with a pointed finger. This meant she was angry, would soon become eloquent. She raised her voice, "Don't give me 'better or worse.' Both are worse. And also worse is the Jewish people becoming murderers. What two thousand years of persecution didn't do, what Hitler's ovens didn't do, Zionism has done in one generation. Destroyed the Jewish people. Destroyed, I tell you. I don't recognize as my own a people who takes land from another people, chases innocent people out of their villages and towns, who gobbles up fields and orchards and then shoots down the ones who protest!"

Kim Chernin said, "Maybe it is time for the Jewish people to give up their moral superiority and enter the world of nations, where one kills for a border, takes land from one's neighbor, who hasn't? what nation doesn't?

Why should only the Jews be forbidden this always morally ambiguous effort to make a land their own? You want to define the Jewish people by our homelessness, our capacity for cultural transmission, our ethical woolgathering in obscure crumbling temples of the Pale? No thank you. I love the idea of the Jewish warrior. I don't care if he grows illiterate for seven generations, just so he learns how to stand up and fight."

I am sure Kim Chernin did not mean what she had just said. She would not have liked an illiterate warrior. Her mother probably also did not mean that Zionism had destroyed the Jewish people. Neither mentioned Miriam Levinger, the rabbi's wife, the day she gathered forty women and children and marched down from Kiryat Arba into Hebron to occupy an abandoned Jewish hospital, Beit Haddash. But the day Kim Chernin had been waiting in the kibbutz office to hear how the vote turned out, when she tried to imagine how Miriam Levinger looked on her march into the Casbah, the face of The Bride came to mind. Resolute, inspired, the unearthly calm of the fanatic, the sinister power of one capable of putting principle before everything.

Keep this face in mind! During Kim Chernin's long sleep that face put in an appearance, confused at times with her mother's face, at times with the soldier, it came with her through the thinning waters of sleep to leave behind an impression of the dry, cold wind up there whose presence was responsible for much coming grief and passion. It brought also a glimpse of fleeting happiness from her childhood, when her sister took her up the hill in the Bronx park with a sled. Sister first, Kim Chernin on top, holding her around the neck but not too tight, not to choke her.

The avocado trees were not flourishing. Drippings from the banana plants were probably too potent (the avocados had been planted beneath the bananas to give them shade). Kim Chernin had to dig them out, loosen the earth from their spidery root structures, set them down carefully in a small hole she had made a few feet away. Yosif, the man with the corkscrew curls, worked along with her, helping to build shade shelters from a few branches of dried-out banana fronds.

Although Kim Chernin did not mention this to Yosif, her body had changed during her sleep. The moment she had awakened, at 3:33 in the morning, the body slipped out of bed, jumped up several times to make sure it really could suspend itself in the air the way Nijinsky is said to have done. Then down, light as rain. Then up again and so on for about ten jumps, after which the effect began to wear off.

First the dishes washing themselves. Then levitation with the kitchen mop. Next Devora's lovecake. Finally the sleep of five days and nights. Now there's a new body! Do these unlikely doings mark the path of miracles that transformed Kim Chernin when she set foot in the homeland?

These things crop up because Kim Chernin's great-grandfather on her father's side was a mystical man, a Hasid, descendant of the wonder-working Ba'al Shem Tov. I have recently learned this from Kim Chernin's uncle, her father's younger brother. But Kim Chernin's father's mother was a descendant of the esteemed Enlightenment scholar, a dedicated opponent of Hasidical yearnings, the eighteenth-century Gaon of Vilna. With this lineage it shouldn't be easy to believe in miracles even when they happen. The question is, did Kim Chernin believe them? Did she actually experience herself floating six inches off the floor? Did she really believe she had a new body?

Kim Chernin caught sight of herself in the mirror. What she saw pleased her, although the body was smaller than it had been. At a guess, she was now maybe two and a half feet tall. The small body was immature, no doubt about it. Its breasts had not yet sprouted. It looked at itself frankly. Its feet were not beautiful. They were broad, without grace, the toes were stubby. On the other hand, they were the sort of feet to get you where you are going. Kim Chernin liked them.

She lifted up her arms. There was no shadow in the pale hollow of underskin. She stroked it with pleasure. Down there, where the thatch had not yet come in, smooth, eager lips drew her attention. There was a belly with a slight curve; if you ran your hands over it they would be led down there. These were the ways of her body, chastely innocent in its serene knowledge of its own pleasures. The legs would never grow into the long legs Theirs had desired. Kim Chernin admired their sturdiness, they would get her through what she would have to go through to get back to them as they had been before they had been hated. They sprang up again in a series of kicks and twists to celebrate themselves. This body held itself in a ready state of animal joy, not yet encumbered by the shame, loathing, and morality Freud thought civilization should bring down on it.

Yosif did not seem to notice Kim Chernin's body had changed. For Yosif, she would probably always be the woman with big breasts who had walked into the dining room with wet curls and a checked skirt. She rode in the cab with him every morning (the rest of the crew sat in the open truck). It was Kim Chernin who jumped out to get bread at the Arab bakery next to the ruined mosque in the village on the way down to the banana groves. Her jump was still very light and high. The Arab boy who worked in the bakery watched her glide down as if she were a twist of spiraling paper. If so, he was the only one who ever noticed.

Kim Chernin loved the bakery, now especially that Theirs was gone, maybe forever. (Theirs gone, forever?) She had always loved bakeries, had once imagined offering herself as a baker's apprentice at the Danish bakery in Berkeley on Telegraph Avenue, across from her favorite café. Since she was up most of the night anyway, was overly fond of bread and rolls, often thinking about those she had eaten recently, or planning others she might soon eat, the night hours would leave her free to write during the day. (In addition to mystical poems, she wrote tales set in the Middle Ages. There was no hope of publication, of course.) She could imagine herself wrapped up in a white apron, smeared with fingerprints of dough and yeast. The daughter would sleep in a bed next to the ovens, raisins and cloves contributing what they could to the peacefulness of her dreams, which must not be like her mother's.

In the Arab bakery the breads were set out on a thick

wooden pallet, the small boy with a squint helped Kim Chernin gather several loaves. A grayish flour dust covered her work clothes, it was hard to get off. It gave her the smell of newly baked bread, Simon liked that. The smell of dough was still there when the soldier arrived, he said it made her edible. She said it was all right with her ("Go ahead, eat me"), but his English wasn't good enough, he missed the point.

Kim Chernin's small body was very sensitive to taste (it was also sensitive to touch. For instance, she could feel Yosif's gaze as it went over her cheeks as if it were already a kiss). The bread was part wheat, part barley, part white. As she chewed, Kim Chernin could sort out the grains, distinguishing those that were covered with salt from those that were barren. Eaten like that, half a chunk of bread made more than a sufficient meal. (Kim Chernin thought this was the secret of pleasure Theirs had never been able to crack.)

It was still hot, the long late harvest days of the farm on the border. Before her long sleep, time had been tripping over its own heels, racing ahead of itself, massing, crouching, crowding, colliding. Now time turned long and sleek, there was fat growing over its ribs. The slow time of Kim Chernin had set in, the slow growing into the place, as if she had long slow years to make memory of it.

There was time now to dawdle and stretch, watch the bananas ripen, stand for hours in the late afternoon meditating with Devora the crisp folds of the trouser pleat, while Simon perched haphazardly on the pile of laundry, drowsing over his guitar.

The suspense of the last year had been broken; she,

whose whole life had been crisis and struggle, had triumphed at last in her battle with Theirs. For the born-again body, time was a ladle of thick syrup. Kim Chernin could sip it up, watch it descend in slow amber droplets, catch the world in it, paddle through it disputing with Simon about the right way for a nation to be born. And all that would be only a single drop from an infinite cluster of sweetness. Here, for those weeks before the soldier showed up, the slow singular chapter of Kim Chernin's life, her time of languor, her pastoral.

Unfortunately, Kim Chernin did not like the work. The crew in the banana groves was mostly silent, separated from one another, wandering up and down the long, inhospitable rows, covering the trees with blue plastic bags to make the fruit ripen faster. They were the farm's introverts, perhaps they spent their days reflecting on the true nature of the soul especially now that Yom Kippur had arrived.

Simon told Kim Chernin she did not have to do work she did not like. The kibbutz had accepted her on a trial basis, but she was entitled to all the privileges of the other members. Everyone had switched around at the beginning, looking for the right work. Simon had worked in the bananas, in the chicken house, he'd done some gardening, he even drove the tractor for a week or two.

Simon loved Yom Kippur, the somber meditative self-reckoning. Because of Yom Kippur he had tried since he was a small boy to hold himself accountable. If an angel of God should come down and demand to know whether he was qualified to enter the innermost arc of the temple because he had suddenly been chosen to take the place of the High Priest, Simon wanted to be ready.

If Simon were chosen as High Priest (this his mother had told him, along with the sound advice not to mention it to his father) he would not sleep the whole night before Yom Kippur. He would eat lightly, so as not to grow sleepy. He would study with members of the Sanhedrin, the highest order of the priestly cast. That way he would know by heart the order of the service. He would learn about the final examination of the animals brought in to the temple for sacrifice.

Simon (he did not have to be told about not telling his father) liked best of all when the other priests took the High Priest into the room where the incense makers worked, so that the High Priest could practice taking incense in his hands. The High Priest's hands must not be overflowing with incense, they should be full. Simon's hands on Kim Chernin's breasts would have been overflowing.

Simon sat morosely at the Yom Kippur meal next to Kim Chernin. More than once he had renounced the pleasures of women. He had not once caught sight of the angel of God, although one day a feather had fallen out of a still, perfectly blue sky. Would Simon be willing to give up the life of a High Priest to lay his hands on Kim Chernin? Why should they go empty if Yosif's hands had been filled! Was Kim Chernin right, the sacrifice of pleasure meant even more to him than pleasure?

O n Yom Kipper sundown lasts longer than on any other day. That is because the ram's horn blasted so loud startles the sun, which must also make its reckoning. While it was getting dark, Kim Chernin walked about in the Moroccan village with the village girls instead of going to temple. When she arrived the little girls singled her out, they drew her away from her friends, made a chant out of her name, dragged her here and there through the dirt streets as if she were a new girl on the block. Later, Kim Chernin thought they might have detected the born-again body although Kim Chernin certainly did not leap up into the air, not once. Before it got dark she was taken to meet an old woman who was putting cow dung on a fire. The old woman wore a ragged shawl, had bare feet; she gave Kim Chernin a cup of mint tea. Then, she pointed to her heart, to each one of her breasts, mysteriously trying to tell Kim Chernin something Kim Chernin was not able to understand. Later, to make up for this failure Kim Chernin elevated the cup of tea into a ceremonial goblet.

As for me, goblet or not, I refuse to sip, no matter how many times memory offers. I think the old woman was trying to get Kim Chernin to fall in love. She wanted her to give up the farm to teach the children instead, who were not destined to know much more than poverty. Kim Chernin had better learn how to care for her own child before she runs off on a mission beyond her powers.

I refuse. I have no wish to live out the destiny she did not choose, nothing, not the old woman's entreaty, the pressure of a child's dark hand, the taste of mint that shatters through this memory will persuade me.

The next day Kim Chernin went back to the kitchen, where she was promoted from (mystical) dishwasher to a maker of vegetable fritters. She took the place of a woman who had taken the day off, to pick up her cousin from Chicago. The cousin was arriving at Lod airport, then going on to a conference in Jerusalem. The woman looked overdressed in a simple skirt, low heels, when she stopped in for morning coffee before the bus arrived. She was the cook's assistant, although rumor had it she was much better than the three cooks.

Kim Chernin did not mind being an assistant. She took her job seriously, spooned out the mixture of chopped vegetables, eggs, and flour into a large pan of smoking oil. At the first sign of a dark edge on the fritter, she moved fast, flipping and patting. She slid the crisp pancake out onto a wood slab covered with several layers of paper. There was an hourly newscast on the radio, announced with a double beep. Whenever that happened, someone went over, turned up the volume. Sometimes, although the news was broadcast in Hebrew, the born-again body (it learned everything at lightning speed) understood every word.

Kim Chernin did not want to go back to the hot sun, the silent workers, the bananas raining their lethal sap on the fragile avocados. She hoped the cook's assistant would fall in love with her cousin, run off madly with him to the family meat-packing plant in Chicago. Devora, who stopped in several times during the day to see how Kim Chernin was doing, told her the cook's assistant was ready to fly at the first possibility.

Devora and Kim Chernin were worried. This was the ninth day since the meeting at the *mo'adon*. (Watch out for three, nine, seven, thirteen. Memory is likely to arrange things in significant patterns that add up to nothing no matter how many times you rake through them.) Kim Chernin had still not found work.

She had always been fond of chopping vegetables. Now, because the born-again body took pleasure in mastering every skill, small decorative touches appeared. Kim Chernin's hands, which had lost dexterity when they were slapped away from the mother's breast, could now cut a consistent whole peel from an apple without losing the smallest coil. She could do it even with her eyes closed. She ran a fork down the skin of the cucumber, sliced fast, folded the slices into intricate, looped shapes, made tulip radishes, rose tomatoes. When the cook's assistant came back she ruined Kim Chernin's chances to work her way to master cook. But, said Devora, there was still hope. Right away, the first afternoon, the cook's assistant was already keeping an eye on the mailboxes. Kim Chernin and Devora agreed. If they were responsible for the mail, the mail would come before everything.

Meanwhile, Kim Chernin would have to put in her time in the chicken house. So far, no one had taken the job as a permanent placement. Most people worked there for a week or two before moving on to other jobs. Workers from other crews rotated through, gathering eggs, cleaning cages and windows, keeping an eye out for hens with broken claws. Kim Chernin, who in other respects thought of herself as heroic now that she had survived the fall of Theirs, spent a total of two hours and ten minutes in the chicken house. How she managed it that long, Simon could not figure out, but he had warned her.

He came looking for her during the morning coffee break; she was standing inside next to the door where she had been standing since she walked in. She had both hands pressed hard over her mouth and nose. The chicken house was a long, narrow rectangular shed, the cages stretched along both sides below small, high, filthy windows. The cement floor, covered with a wooden plank, looked damp and unhealthy. What she made of the feather dust, sour air, queasy droppings, stale seed mix, is easy to imagine. Kim Chernin, whose born-again sensibility now read the entire world as if it had been put there to convey meaning, knew she was beholding the phantom body in its caged inescapable confinement. Here was the macabre world ruled by Theirs, grossly insensitive to the sentient life of creatures. The hens had been raised indoors, several to a cage, forbidden all knowledge of the opposite sex. Out of this unholy circumstance they brought forth intermittently an otherworldly harmonics, part shrill cry, part lamentation. To Simon, who took her arm and dragged her outside, Kim Chernin, talking fast, running her sentences together, said the cages were detention cells. No, worse. The hens, forever deprived of lust and maternity, their eggs stolen the minute they showed up, were snuffed out when they'd produced their yearly crop of eighteen dozen infertile eggs. Their meaning had ended. Kim Chernin did not eat chicken again, not once, not even chicken soup, during the rest of the time she was on the farm.

Simon took her hand. It surprised him because it was so much smaller than the rest of her, the plump, greedy hand of a child. He thought the purgatorial cycle through which the hens passed was redeemed by the healing status to which they were in the end elevated. He went so far as to say that chicken soup, understood as the primary expression of Jewish maternal love, conferred upon the hens posthumously the maternity they'd been denied in life.

Kim Chernin said, "Give me a break. Are you kidding? You take this priestly tendency too far; you'll end up a bowl of maternal love yourself! If you can live with an atrocity like this, and you can, can't you, maybe I don't want to know you."

Simon said, "You do. You want to know me because I'm always ready to argue with you. If everyone saw the world the way you did, there'd be nothing to eat because everything would be too holy."

Simon kept hold of her hand. She walked where she wanted, he followed. It was thirteen days since the meeting at the *mo'adon*, she had still not found work. Past the laundry, where Devora was reading a letter from Dani. When the letter arrived several days earlier, Devora had slipped it unopened into the velvet case where usually only the afikoman is kept on Passover. Although she did not doubt Dani was coming back, if there were any bad news in the letter, she wanted it obliterated before she read it. The afikoman container must have done its work. When Simon and Kim Chernin peeked in, Devora was standing next to the ironing board, holding the iron above her head in her right hand, triumphant.

It might have been the hens in their cages, the worry about not finding a job, uncertainty about how and when her daughter would come, the way Simon walked next to her, a muscular thigh pushed up close against hers to the sheer delight of the born-again body, which felt the excitement running in fine threads all the way to the most favored places. That made it difficult for Kim Chernin to know if

the fields of millet and tobacco, overly bright in the midday
sun of a day in which for the first time autumn seemed possible, the cows roaming in large herds, running loose in the
unharvested fields, having grown wild and fat, were now or
back then, during the war that Simon was describing. The
Jewish soldiers had occupied the area. The villagers had fled,
leaving their cattle behind, their fields unharvested. The
front lines of the Jewish soldiers ran across their fields. At
night the villagers would slip down behind the lines and
gather in their tobacco. There were also Bedouin tribes, who
raised cattle, camels, goats. Most of the land up here had
belonged to Arab villagers until 1948.

The road reared up before them. Kim Chernin was
pleased to be walking on small legs, so much closer to the
ground than usual. Near the edge of the road, next to the
fields in which millet and tobacco had grown, she caught
sight of a bug at the tip end of a blade of grass. If she
threw herself down, stretched out her arms over her head,
closed her eyes and screamed loud at the top of her voice
Kim Chernin could roll all the way down into the wadi.
There was nothing up there in the mountains to bother the
air. In return, it allowed her to taste its carbon atoms, the
drying grass they carried. That day there was no wind.
The red wheelbarrow of rotting apples, from which someone had been planning to make cider, had given what it
could. To the born-again body the air tasted also of apples.

A utumn brought a clear, dry air. There were suddenly
cold nights. Kerosene heaters were distributed, with

the warning not to use them at night unless the windows were kept open. All over the fields, scattered profusely among the white rocks, red ranunculus grew out from the more rusted, disturbing tones of the red earth. There were also lavender crocuses, a stand of them grew at the foot of the guard tower where Kim Chernin, scampering up on small legs, observed in the grass below her, in the purple mountains, in the piercing blue of the Sea of Galilee, in the taut wings of a soaring bird, a perfect balance between light and dark. She, who had been unraveling, had come to rest.

Before or after that, she and Devora gathered wild anemones near the Arab village, where Simon took her to meet his friends, the village muktar and his family. Kim Chernin, who had learned from Simon five or six words of Arabic, smiled radiantly, let people look into her eyes, made a good impression. Therefore, she and Simon were invited back for dinner.

In that family, most of the food was cooked on a kerosene stove, although other people in the village had an outdoor oven. The wife of the village muktar served Kim Chernin a bowl of clotted milk, which left a mustache on her upper lip. The children climbed into her lap to wipe the milk mustache away. Kim Chernin saved her six Arabic words for the muktar's wife, who did not laugh at her accent.

The goat, roasted on the outdoor oven, tasted of cumin, coriander, and saffron. Kim Chernin's small body, although it had already started growing breasts, had maintained its pure, sharp sensations. Before dinner, Simon crushed chick-peas in a large ceramic bowl. Kim Chernin

had the impression no one thought it appropriate for Simon, a man, to be crushing chick-peas. The children
brought him sesame seed paste and oil. When the bowl
was full, while Simon kept whipping and stirring, the paste
rose up over the edges, the children shrieked, not a drop
spilled. At dinner, Simon and the muktar sat next to each
other, on folded rugs. Kim Chernin did not need language.
The born-again body drank in emotional undercurrents. It
savored the minor upheavals that passed between husband
and wife, flowed from the children in sudden rushes and
ritardanos, entered Kim Chernin as discrete particles of
knowing. She missed out on a few details, but then who
wouldn't?

When Kim Chernin went back to her room, she had
fried honey cakes wrapped in a soft blue cloth. She also
had a small wooden box filled with figs, which she shared
with Devora. Whenever Devora had a day off she went to
visit a Yemenite township near Tel Aviv to record their music. She got a ride down on the farm's tractor, hitched a
ride along the road from Tiberias, a camera and tape re-
corder hanging from her shoulder. She never used the
camera until someone asked her to take a picture. After she
knew them well they always wanted her to take pictures.
Devora had three copies made, one to send back to her
Yemenite friends, another for her parents, for herself there
were enlarged copies to hang up all over her walls. When
Devora had collected enough songs, she would write a
book about Yemenite music. She heard in it a high-pitched
longing for God, which was also a passionate longing for
the beloved. Devora could sing these songs in a small,

breathy, contralto voice. She had written down some of
the words, which turned out to be poems from Shalem
Shabazi, a kabbalistic rabbi from the sixteenth century.
Devora thought there were echoes of North African music,
even of Islamic musical traditions. In the Yemenite songs
sexual intercourse between woman and man was the sym-
bol of union between God and the soul. That is why the
poems were devotional and erotic, sexual and sacred all at
the same time.

The music on Devora's tapes was badly recorded. You
had to get through a whole layer of crackling, distance,
haze, before you could detect the erotic fever longing for
God. Kim Chernin could just make out the sound of
drums, which Devora said were really petrol cans. The
Yemenites danced to the music on festive and ceremonial
occasions. When Devora listened to it alone in her room,
when she had not heard from Dani, when it was almost
morning, she felt her suffering was also the Yemenite suffering for union with God.

Kim Chernin had made a few new friends. The pregnant woman had taken a liking to her. She let Kim
Chernin listen to the heartbeat of the baby, a faraway
sound, not exactly like the petrol drums, but throbbing
with the same longing for union. Up here, Kim Chernin
was loved and cherished; she would spend the rest of her
life there, if only she could find a job. Meanwhile, she was
sent here and there, wherever an extra worker was needed.
She was proud of her ability to master the various tasks,
cutting back in the garden, ironing sleeves in the laundry, making order in the storeroom where there were huge

sacks of grain marked with Hebrew letters. At dinner she ate with Simon, Devora, the man with slicked-back hair who was teaching Kim Chernin about the music Schubert wrote after Beethoven died. At Beethoven's funeral there were thirty-six torchbearers dressed in black. They walked on each side of the hearse. Schubert was one of them. The torchbearers carried white lilies, roses, burning torches, extinguished when Beethoven's body was lowered into the ground. From his deathbed, a year later, Schubert cried out, "No! it is not true. Beethoven is not lying here!" Schubert was buried in a hermit's robe, a laurel wreath around his forehead.

After dinner, in the *mo'adon*, Boaz and the young men from his crew played chess. She sat with them because her father had taught her the moves when she was eight years old. She never sat with the women knitting, who sat next to the coffee urn. Although they were not as beautiful as Devora, why despise them? Maybe they served as the women of valor, the *Eshes Khayil*, who in the shtetl would have earned the living, held down the store, rocked the cradle while the husband studied. On some nights The Bride sat next to Boaz. While she was there everyone spoke Hebrew. Kim Chernin closed her eyes. She took in the smell of anise cookies, the sound of chess pieces swept from the board when Boaz won an early game. At a table in the corner the three Israeli women who were friends held up a cup for Kim Chernin. "*Ma zeh?* What is it?" they asked? They held up a shoe. A photograph was produced, a pack of cigarettes, Kim Chernin named everything with a peculiar accent. She was soon able to say, "My name is

Kim Chernin. I live at Kibbutz Aralu. I am from California. I am a new immigrant. Yes, I love it here."

Here, in the longest ease Kim Chernin has ever
known (if one can trust memory to get something
like that right), if it were possible to end here, I would
have done all a biographer could do on behalf of an unruly
subject whose story will soon turn another corner, bringing
her back to everything she has come up here to avoid. If
I could set the mountain in a ring of fire, making it hard
to leave or enter, that is what I would do to keep Kim
Chernin from the kind of love she is calling down on herself. Unless of course the soldier is going to arrive with a
headful of nonsense, knowing by heart some entire passages from a twilight song of love and death, in which case
there would be no way to keep him out, he will walk
through fire, pledge eternal love, go down off the mountain, betray her. Nothing I can do, that's how it will go, in
keeping with some inevitable twist in the way things get
told, there seems to be no other way to register it. The
same laws govern the shape of opera, saga, epic, old tale,
weaver's fancy, memory, I guess.

There was a movie in the dining hall every Saturday
night. The tables were cleared away, folding chairs were
arranged in five rows, she and Simon and Devora always
sat together, although later that changed. The films were
usually spy thrillers. The kitchen boss was in charge of se-
lecting them. If there was one decent film the whole time

Kim Chernin was up there I see no evidence for it. After the film, Simon and Kim Chernin walked Devora back to her room, then Kim Chernin went to Simon's room. One night he sang, "These are my hands, my sister, these are the hands, my bride."

Kim Chernin, whose small body had been thatched and breasted by then, took his guitar out of his hands, put it up on top of the wardrobe, sat down on his lap. She unbuttoned his shirt. He closed his eyes. There wasn't a murmur from Theirs, no one to warn Kim Chernin not to play games with this man. He had a stomach like a corrugated washing board, although he never lifted weights, only the largest crates of peaches during harvest. She put her palms straight down on his stomach. Then she went back to her unbuttoning. Pants buttons are harder to open than the buttons of a shirt. He said, "That's far enough." She said, "No, it isn't. Now you do me."

If he had known time was running out, if he had known he wouldn't be able to keep her one minute after the soldier arrived, he would have done her too, he said so himself later. If that night he had unbuttoned the second-hand rayon blouse she wore under her navy jacket. If he had buried his face in breasts beginning to want kissing. Who knows? If only Simon had taken everything a little less seriously. If only the soldier had been posted somewhere else in the last minute.

Sometime during those weeks Kim Chernin had been given her permanent room. It was longer than her first room, a bit wider, had the same cement floor, a few shelves, a wardrobe near the door, a desk pushed up in front of the window. The window opened on the steep dry riverbed above the valley. From her window she could see swift-moving birds. Even Safad was visible. At night the Sea crept up through Tiberias was sent back by the guardians of the valley.

Simon had arranged for Kim Chernin to borrow the English typewriter from the kibbutz. She shared the sink in the entryway, the bathroom and shower with the braided woman from the laundry, who did not speak to Kim Chernin even once from that day to the night when trouble came, when someone tried to kill Kim Chernin. It would be winter then.

Devora was getting regular letters from Dani, they were full of news about his unit. The men in his unit had to run in circles in full battle dress in the rain, they marched thirty miles at double time, their tents were pitched where the rain came down heaviest to make huge pools of water.

There was some kind of protocol, Simon said. Kim Chernin had to try every one of the less desirable jobs before Boaz got her the best job on the farm, pruning trees in the orchards. When Kim Chernin stood stock-still in front of Boaz, not accepting the job, just considering, weighing up what would be expected in return, he put his wrists on her shoulders, his hands clenched in soft fists. There are people who do things like that and you don't like it. When Boaz did it, in his offhand, friendly way, smiling his boyish grin, eager to please, proud that he had arranged the best possible job, she accepted. If she liked the work, if she was good at it, her future at the kibbutz was sure. Even her enemies would not be able to vote against her.

When it rained, they got off early. If it was raining early in the morning, they didn't go to work. Then, she used the English typewriter, wrote letters to her daughter, to the man who loved her, who had given her the money to get here. She also wrote poems, in which the fat cattle roaming the fields of millet and tobacco were mentioned. Also the wind in the shutters, Dani's visit one weekend to the farm. He was driven up in an army truck on its way to build the security road along the border. The minute he arrived he took a shower (everyone could see the steamed-up window). Then, he threw himself into bed and slept for thirty-six hours. Although everyone knew this always happened when a soldier came home after weeks of training, the gossips were satisfied. Devora went into the kitchen to get bread and cheese and cucumbers, she looked pale, that could have been taken as a sure sign Dani hadn't only been sleeping, but it wasn't.

In the apple orchard down the road below the farm, Kim Chernin was given a small pair of clippers, a large saw (she slipped the saw through her belt), a high metal ladder. There were also large clippers with long wooden handles, but the crew had only three of those clippers to pass around. More were being ordered from America, the order had been made months ago, when the first members arrived at Araht to take over from a reserve unit of the army, which had been in charge of the farm since the other collective failed. The clippers had not yet been sent. With them, the work went more easily. You could cut down a good-sized branch with a single bite. With the saw, you would be at it for maybe ten minutes. Boaz made sure the large clippers got passed around regularly. Soon it wasn't only the young men from the security branch who loved him. He worked harder than anyone on the crew, most of the time stripped down to a T-shirt, although it was cold enough to keep Kim Chernin hopping. He kept everyone in a good mood, telling stories and jokes, there were always three or four radios blasting away from every corner of the orchard, the breaks were scrupulously called, someone, sometimes Devora, had always baked cookies to hand out to the crew with coffee. If the canteens started to lose pressure he arranged for new ones. Here, in the orchard, coffee was always hot.

Kim Chernin was strong since her long sleep (maybe the same regeneration would happen to Dani, he would wake from this thirty-six-hour sleep to find his body innocent, full of chaste desire for sensation, eager to give itself), able to lift a heavy ladder, drag it down the row of trees, climb without fear of the wind that could topple it, work from the top without danger, sawing, clipping the limbs of the peach trees precisely where they forked, so that the life force would flow into the limb chosen to bud, to flower.

Simha, as head of the orchard, reported to the joint meeting of the work committees. Kim Chernin was one of the best pruners on the crew. It wasn't only he who thought so. It had been said first of all by Nahum, their adviser, who had been pruning trees since he came to Israel in 1946, when the map of Palestine, drawn up by the Jewish Agency, already showed the whole of the upper Galilee, way up above Haifa, across the border of Lebanon all the way to the Litani River, in Jewish hands.

The apple orchard ran from the road to the very edge

of the border. The peach orchards were on the other side of the road above the wadi, the dried-up river valley. When the winds came down from the north, the trees shook. Kim Chernin smeared black pitch on the wound left by cutting away a large limb. She and Simon worked alone in a corner of the orchard, away from the radios, the hourly newscasts, American rock music.

One day before breakfast, she and Simon drafted a letter to the American Jewish Committee urging them to take up the cause of the Ethiopian Jews. Simon thought there must be a powerful lobby that could interest congressmen in a plan to transport the black Jews of Ethiopia to Eretz Israel. Simon was still looking for ways to redeem Zionism. He told Kim Chernin the Jews of Ethiopia did not practice Talmudic Judaism, he said their wandering had taken place before the codification of laws, their liturgy was in the ancient Ethiopian dialect Ge'ez. On Passover their High Priest sacrificed a lamb on the altar in the courtyard of the synagogue. If things didn't work out at Araht, he and Kim Chernin would go to Ethiopia to study conditions, to get things ready.

Kim Chernin went for the idea, a destiny similar to the mint tea that still wants someone to teach the girls in the village. Fourteen years later, when the American airlift from Ethiopia took place secretly, no one gave either Simon or Kim Chernin credit for having thought it up, although either would probably claim the impulse had been set in motion one fall day before dawn, when Kim Chernin climbed her ladder while Simon tossed down dried branches into the overgrown grass between the rows. I thought of them both yesterday, when Israel (after years of shameful juggling) gathered in its orphans just before rebel armies occupied Addis Ababa. Did Simon really know it would happen, sixteen thousand people transported by plane in thirty-six hours? Did Kim Chernin really believe him twenty years ago, tramping around near a dangerous border, when he said so? Did they wonder where the descendants of Solomon and the queen of Sheba would be settled? To Kim Chernin's mythological soul it might not have mattered; Simon already would have been brooding about occupied territories, he was like that.

Kim Chernin was happy. She strolled down the banked grass alley between the trees with her pot of pitch, she thought about asking Simon to lie down with her in the long grass across the border, just beyond the orchard, where a person they said could be shot just by going out there but Kim Chernin didn't believe it. She wanted to take off Simon's clothes, put her hands all over him, take up his hidden, sacred privacy. Her curiosities got the best of her. Now that Theirs was no longer there to censor her, civilization had not yet come down on infant proclivities, the men on the orchard crew wore their pants tight. If you looked where you were not supposed to, where you were not meant to touch either, sometimes there was a beckoning, perceptible presence not there in the way the women wore their work pants. Simon had better watch out, the born-again body knows no shame, he's headed for trouble.

People working in the orchard said they could feel the guns trained on them by invisible, silent watchers. Kim Chernin, frisky, full of fun, said they should all strip naked, except for their belt of clippers and saws, because sex was much better without love because love would only be a distraction.

There were two other women on the crew, a slim lovely girl from Finland, who lived in Kim Chernin's building with her somber Israeli boyfriend. The other woman (she was always trying to work with Boaz) avoided Kim Chernin, and the rest were men, most of them bunched up together away from the border near the road. The man who had been wearing overalls in the *mo'adon* (the owner of Zigefuss) worked by himself. Down here, in broad daylight, he had no interest in Boaz, never looked at him, rarely spoke to him or anyone else. He was so tall he sometimes didn't need the ladder, especially when they were cutting wedges in the lower branches, large triangular segments as entry points for the people who would harvest the fruit next summer. Is he the guy who will try to kill Kim Chernin?

Sometimes you pruned the trees to let in sun, cutting the coming leafage that would enshadow the ripening fruit. Sometimes you wanted to preserve shade, selectively cutting here and there to protect from the inclement sun. All this took skill. If you cut a small tree to let in sun you might damage the tree's capacity to put forth an abundant crop. Small details told whether or not to move forward with clipper or saw, the placement of a scar, the color of bark along the highest branches. Kim Chernin was good at the work because it was a form of love; the born-again body, growing into its desires, felt reverence for the growth and sacrifice that was the life drama of the orchard. Her work, she told Devora, was making love, a question of tenderness and precision, vigorous fast moves, lingering deliberations, cunning guesses about the true state of readiness, homage.

Devora said, "I wish Dani could hear you. Why don't you write him a homily on making love to trees? Tell him if he could learn a few principles, you know what I mean? He's a nice man, he is, really a very nice man, but you'd never know it when he's making love. Maybe he thinks women just don't come. I mean, if he's never been with a woman who does, how would he know women do? We think men know more than we do. They're the ones who keep pestering and mostly the women are saying no. So, it never occurs to us. A guy might be kissing you for the first time he's ever kissed anyone, pretending he knows what to do but he doesn't because in spite of the fact they call it instinct it can't be instinct because no one just knows instinctively what to do. You know what I mean? I never knew one man who just knew what to do if what to do was make a woman happy. Why does Dani want a virgin? So she wouldn't know he's got ten thumbs? She'd think it wasn't meant to be the way she thought it was meant to be? No one holds out for pleasure. The minute you don't get pleasure, you start wondering why you were expecting pleasure in the first place. If men go on marrying virgins, no one's ever going to notice men don't notice. Not even noticing? Could you imagine even one woman in this world who didn't notice? I put his hand there, you know. I just put it there, but he pulled it away, so I put his hand here, I pressed his hand, not very hard. If you did that with a woman, she'd figure out that breast wants to be squeezed.

"You write Dani a homily about making love to trees. When Simon makes love to you, Simon will know what to do. When Simon sits next to you at dinner he notices every move you make. When you want a piece of bread he's already grabbed for the basket. That means Dani could know. It isn't just being in the army, it isn't just being a man; he could be what Simon is, but is that a reason not to marry him? My mother says sex doesn't last anyway. The men keep doing it but it's not the same, my mother says it's an urge they have. Some urge! I think men do it because they might be lonely, desperate, they're feeling helpless but they don't want to know they feel, especially helpless, especially not a soldier. So now lonely, desperate, helpless has suddenly become an urge. Most men I know, they would rather believe they were fornicators, adulterers, lechers, than just admit they want to creep into your lap and cry their eyes out, sometimes.

"Face it, the army is not there to train great lovers of women. Women always fall for soldiers off to war, but a soldier is in the opposite direction of a lover, any sensitivity he might have has to be beaten out of him. All that running about with full battle gear in the rain. So cute in their tight pants. They get into your bed. A head in a suit of chain mail. Thirty-six hours. I sit there, I'm trying to figure out what it takes to not notice. It takes for sure not having any curiosity. It takes maybe no real liking for it the way women like it when we do. I think Dani was making

love to his unit. To all the guys there. To his mission as a
soldier. He gets it over with, now he's asleep, tomorrow
he'll be getting up early. Men do not live much of their
lives with women, maybe their skin is born tough, maybe
it doesn't make them wild when someone strokes it, I have
never seen one man begging to be touched more, when
they want you to do things that usually you don't do, they
want you to feel they've made you do it, they've brought
you down to that, it's always something to do with something other than just liking it, isn't it?

"If a woman is everything a man does not want to be,
how could they possibly love us? Why should they want
to make us happy if all we are is the leftover of what they
are not? My mother says, 'Only bitter people generalize.'
Am I bitter? Why? Because I've had three broken hearts,
that should make me bitter? You know how long thirty-six
hours are? I mean, if you're measuring by how long it takes
someone to wake up? Not that my heart's broken. In the
Yemenite songs the longing is the best part. No one really
hopes for union. Union with God? I came to the conclusion, it's that way here too. Love means you fling yourself
in the mad hope someone will be there to take you in.
Don't hold your breath! Longing means the longing has to
be for no one being there, otherwise if they're there,
they're there, why would there be longing? When I was
waiting for Dani to write, that was sacred. I would have
died, I swear it, I would have died to have him.

"So you write Dani a homily on making love to trees.
You tell him, you have to start by noticing. Tell him it
isn't natural not to be curious. Tell him from me you can't

make it with a woman if you don't know the woman's there."

This is a good place for Kim Chernin's favorite theory. It makes sense here, after Devora has trailed her lament through the orchard. I'm not trying to say Kim Chernin was not listening to Devora. She must have been listening. Why else would she have been thinking about the first time she figured out boys did not like being boys? While Devora opened her heart, Kim Chernin drifted off to speculations she'd been patching together since she was twelve years old.

So, boys did not like being boys. She based this observation on their need to be constantly making remarks when she walked down the halls with her girlfriends, calling obscenely after them, trying to get their hands on them, following them home from school, drawing pictures of them on the backseats of the bus with exaggerated tits and buttocks. What were they up to? What were they after? Were they angry at girls for having remained girls when the boys were forced to give up that privilege?

Some of these thoughts must have come to her only later. They were the sort of thing she liked to write about in cafés, on paper napkins. The napkins could be shoved in between the pages of books she was annotating, she liked to fold them intricately so you could follow the train of thought, with its clauses, parenthetical comments on earlier comments on sentences that arrived where they were going with considerable digression to sudden insights that astonished the writer, who drew heavy underlines, numerous exaltations. When I find them crumpled, smoothed out, laid flat in some earlier attempt at memorial order, I think she would have been better off writing on lined index cards where the ink would not have spread into thick lines, wavy blots on the absorbent paper. Still, if Kim Chernin was content to leave the things in back pockets, never using them to get a doctoral thesis, not even a book out of them, why should I bother? I mention them in passing because they keep flapping through her memories, about as appealing to me as a street-soiled newspaper.

Much of this napkin writing had been inspired by a reading of Freud's essay on fetishism. She had not brought the essay with her to Israel, she knew it by heart, having read it at least thirteen times in an effort to figure out if Freud was kidding. She suspected him of a subtle form of Jewish self-irony with a Viennese twist. He had of course not meant seriously what he said about little boys experiencing shock and horror when they got a peek at their naked mother, figured out she didn't have a penis after all, assumed she must have been castrated and that the same terrible fate could befall them?

To the degree men feared castration, Kim Chernin had written only a few days ago on a napkin from the dining room, that fear was a disguised form of a wish, an expression of men's hidden desire to get rid of the penis that made it impossible for any boy ever again to share in the fine glory of the primal mother. The boy's horror at that moment of differential gazing had to be understood (she noted in small letters with a chewed pencil she carried in her shirt pocket) as an unbearable mortification, his first knowledge he would grow up to be what his father was, a being not well planted on this earth, deprived of roots to the earth's fecund doings and knowings. Men did not primarily fear women or hate them, Kim Chernin thought, or imagine the natural inferiority of women. Men simply never had been able to recover from the shock of not being destined to be mothers.

Kim Chernin thought she (and Devora) probably knew more about men than Freud because she had slept with more of them. He knew them as fellow thinkers, colleagues, letter-writing friends, as sons, patients, husbands, fathers of patients. He had probably never been to bed with a man, watched him undress with hidden angry glances down there. She did not pity them, Nature was harsh, her decrees could not be questioned, those forever excluded from carrying life's mystery between their legs would have to accept their limitations.

As Devora talked, Kim Chernin imagined a time when there were only mothers with their babies, a closed sphere of groping hands, skin surfaces, the wet and the dry, long gazing, pinpricks, scented talcum dust, the slippery, sunbaked savanna of the mother out of which all later genders, separations, abandonments, differentiations would arise.

Did Freud really not know men were haunted lifelong by the loss of their own mother-body? He must have known how in that moment of fateful gazing there was lost forever the boy's own earlier sense of his breasted body, momentously swelling and curving, in which the seeds of first selfhood were scattered, embedded?

It turned out there were no signs of this knowledge in

Freud. No indication that this first comprehension of difference must have been influenced by the tribe to which you belonged, the mother's age, the weather zone. Probably Kim Chernin had been influenced in this napkin writing by the impressions made upon her by her gentle, poetry-reciting father, her fierce mother. Those biographical peculiarities taken by themselves would not make her ideas more (or less) universally valid than Freud's, I suppose. He too must have been born from a particular mother, a certain father. When Kim Chernin was small, one day hurrying home with her mother through the streets of the Bronx, she had believed the wind was her mother. Her fear had been cut through with longing and awe. She could not imagine her father as a hurricane, it would not have been possible.

Kim Chernin felt sympathy for these haunted, brave creatures who had gone on to discover sonnets, wild odes, lands at the edge of the known universe to make up for their first deep grief never transcended, this harsh fate to woman born, yet never woman. She knew how many women held themselves back from similar ventures, for which they were by nature so strongly endowed, hoping to leave men a small sphere all to themselves in which they too could be creative, triumphant.

When a man looked at her when she walked into a café, she saw in his eyes the yearning for his own lost female body. That is why he used a language of possession, felt he had a right to the woman's body, took it sometimes by force, imagined his entitlement. In the way her father had loved her mother, with sensitive unflinching devotion over a lifetime, Kim Chernin saw the way out for men. But first they would have to forgive women for having made them different, with fewer persistent miracles of milk, blood, babies. On the whole, Kim Chernin did not think Dani would be capable of this solution.

I myself might hesitate to take on Sigmund Freud without a consistent psychoanalytic training, a close, careful reading of the texts in their chronological order. Hopefully, I have not added anything to this napkin philosophy of Kim Chernin's youth. Kim Chernin's analyst pointed out how thoroughly Kim Chernin hid her own penis envy beneath this neat reversal of Freud's text. He had not convinced Kim Chernin, who did not in the least convince Devora, who probably wondered what Kim Chernin was talking about, why indeed she was even talking when Devora's (sweet, shy) heart had just been broken open.

At the Roman ruins people gathered shards of pottery, beamed their flashlight into the shallow curve, threw pebbles into the crumbling well. Because it was old, outside the farm, close to the Arab village, perched perilously above the wadi, by late summer visits from the farm had fallen off, no one but Simon and Kim Chernin went there in autumn.

Kim Chernin was sure the place had been built up from historical layers of outlawed doings. She thought it was one of the high places where Canaanite divinities had been worshiped in sexual fertility rites. She wondered if sex was different when desire came up from the need of the whole creation to be renewed by the fiery meeting of egg and seed.

Simon was sitting against the dirt bank next to the cave. Facing him, her legs crossed over his, Kim Chernin sat staring him right in the face. Busy with her Canaanite ruminations, she had been listening vaguely the whole time he was telling her his vision. Mostly, Kim Chernin had been thinking, if Simon could make it through the marching column, Kim Chernin might really come through her troubles too.

Simon avoided her eyes. She was a falcon, she probably resented him calling her back from her flight. Simon got to his feet in one quick spring, pulling her up with him. He went over to the well, kicked it hard three times with the tip of his work boot. He had thought, because Kim Chernin was here, he would cry, because she would be his friend, understand his vision, stay with him forever. Kim Chernin put her arms around his waist. She stood behind him, her chin digging into his back. Once or twice in her life Kim Chernin had the good sense to remain silent. This time, it would have been better if she had not.

Usually when a man carries a woman in his arms, he gives the impression he could drop her. Simon set Kim Chernin down next to the cave on a plaid blanket without missing a beat. If she didn't love him because of his vision, he still had one chance left. Her skin was pink all the way down from her neck to where he put his face because she liked that. She threw the blanket off when he wrapped it around them. Kneeling over her, he noticed how young she was, eleven or twelve years old, nipples up before he kissed them. Tomorrow he would tell her again about his vision. Tomorrow she would not be thinking about her daughter. A letter had come in which the daughter said she had forgotten how the mother looked.

Simon had noticed how Kim Chernin balled up her hands when she wanted anything more than anything in the world. That had happened when she was getting time off to go down to the kibbutz in the valley where her daughter might go to school. In that school the children all shouted at the same time, demanding her daughter's name. (Her daughter's name was Larissa.) One small girl in red pants had already been selected to look after Larissa when she came. When Kim Chernin told Simon she had balled her hands into fists, that was because she felt everything so intensely she didn't know how to keep it inside.

Kim Chernin was curious about him, especially there. Excitement turned her eyes dark green, usually they were green with flecks of yellow. She wanted to see him as if she had never seen one before. Her hands fluttered over him before she took him. In his excitement, he noticed a drop at the tip, she went for it.

She said, "We are sea creatures. Salty."

He had large hands, they did not cover her breasts.

She said, "Someone's been teaching you things. What a pity. I'm here for the first time, groping."

He was kneeling, holding himself up over her with his arms spread on either side. She was looking at everything, fast here, back there, the way you would if you thought who knows when you'd get another chance? The sting of sharp grass cut into his fingers. Starting now he would start to count. If his arms shook, if his body threw itself at her, he would think terrible thoughts, the forced march if he had to, to hold himself back for the perfect timing. But she, she was coming to meet him, was wanting him before it was time, too easy, took no skill, that way anyone could, she didn't need him to, one moment just as good for her, no precisely right moment to enter because he knew her so well, because he loved her. . . .

I stop there.

(A few hours later) when Simon came up to her room, he did not think he was angry. Even young men know love is not something you get because you deserve it.

Kim Chernin was at her desk. She was working hard on a letter to her analyst, she had not heard Simon enter the room. He turned her chair, put his hands around her waist, lifted her straight up against him. At first she smiled, then narrowed her eyes.

She said, "Not this, Simon."

He said, "I waited on purpose. Now it's too late?"

She grabbed his hair in her fists. She said, "Put me down. If there's something to say, I'm not going to say it up here, am I?"

He walked her over to the wall next to the wardrobe. When he put her down he was up so close she was pressed against the wall the way the volunteer had been with Yosif one late night when Simon was coming back from patrol during the first hard weeks before he had begun to invent the woman in a straw hat who would be there in summer. There was a passage in the Zohar, about the light God made at the beginning of the world. The woman in the straw hat would have some of that light, a spark. Because of this spark Simon would recognize her.

Yosif was a skinny, wiry guy, ready to volunteer for the army. At home in Alaska he had dark hair, up here it had turned red because he worked outdoors all day in the sun. He never fell in love; if he wanted a girl, he swaggered. Simon had seen him up against the chicken house, his pants dropped down around his ankles, his small thighs bunched up in hard muscles, giving it to the girl who had laced her hands around his neck.

Kim Chernin said, "You're wasting your time, Simon. I don't want love. I told you a thousand times I don't want love. You want me to break your heart, that's what you want from me."

Simon pressed closer. He closed his eyes, although he had always been planning to keep his eyes open. He put his hands all over her. He said (gasping), "I thought you liked this?"

She said, "When I say so, you're going to stop. You hear me? Right now. I'm telling you. Stop."

Simon stopped. He let go of her. Shaking hard, he turned away fast, pulling her arms around his waist the way they used to when they were friends.

He said, "What I told you I never told anyone else. I waited to tell you from the moment I saw you. Why you? It's nothing to you. No one could make love to you the way I could if you wanted me to make love. It's all rubbish, isn't it? If I walk out of here, you'll never see me again."

She said, "Simon! Don't you dare. You're my best friend. You were right the first night, I was wrong. Who said we were meant to be lovers?"

"I was right? Right? Right about what? I waited so I could know, so I would know you, so it would be perfect, for a man it's easy, I waited so it would be perfect for you. It would have been. I would have known exactly. Exactly. Exactly."

He pulled himself away to start for the door.

She ran after him. She said, "You're upset because for me there's no exactly? That's why you're upset? I told you I'd end up with someone like you. The one man in the world to drive himself crazy because a woman doesn't need him to be a supernatural lover? Come back here. Come on, why are you glaring at me? I'm not making fun of you. Come here, you're slippery as an eel. I can't get my hands on you. Don't be a fool. Where are you going? What's the rush? There's time."

There wasn't. That was the end of it. Simon pushed her away, walked out of her room, down the stairs. The army truck was pulled up near the dining hall. It was almost dark, almost winter. The tall man talking to Boaz (who had been in the army longer than he had) was the long-haired soldier.

If memory has been tampering with the facts, if it has made the soldier arrive three days early to get him up to the farm when Simon walks out of Kim Chernin's room, don't blame me. All this happened. Names and faces have been changed and the name of the small collective farm on the mountain near the border. If this was an invitation to license, I apologize.

At dinner, Devora says, "Have you seen the soldier with the beautiful face?"

If Kim Chernin has been waiting for these words, she gives no sign. The basket of bread does not fall. Her hands do not shake. The most I would allow is the hair rising on the back of her neck. Before the dishes are washed, other women have mentioned the soldier with long hair. There has not been another soldier up here whom anyone even noticed.

A soldier is beautiful in uniform. It takes much of his individuality away, gives him back slightly larger than life. No longer frail, individual, unique, he is one who defends a border, preserves the land with his sacred offering. One like this, whose warrior lineage goes all the way back to the house of Abraham, would certainly be very appealing to Kim Chernin. (I do not defend her shameless mythologizing of the heroic.)

Safad is an easy distance away. If they fall in love it won't be any different than for Devora and Dani, the musician and his girlfriend stationed on a kibbutz in the Sinai. In a country that can be mobilized for war in three hours that's how it is. When he comes to visit he'll run fast up the steps to her room, throw open the door, run like crazy to the desk, pull her down on the floor with him. He's the sort of crazy boy (why should she stop inventing him because he's there?) who won't take a shower when he leaves because he wants to smell of her. Maybe he's a virgin. Not that he will fumble around or won't know what he's doing. He lives at home with his parents, shares a room with his grandmother so his sister can have her own room. When Kim Chernin goes to visit his parents' flat he will stand in the kitchen with his arm around his mother's waist.

After dinner Kim Chernin goes back to her room. She

goes fast, still not willing to believe she has cooked up a real man out of dream stuff. What if the soldier is less than the man she's made up for herself? What if he sleeps for thirty-six hours? What if she's stuck with him because she summoned him? What if he has hands that fall on her out of his absence or because they do not know she's there? Out there somewhere, roaming the farm, innocently looking for the woman who conjured him up, is the soldier.

For Kim Chernin everything has become urgent, avoiding him, encountering him, picking the time, waiting for the right time, not dying of curiosity to set eyes on that face never clearly glimpsed in its dream language. Devora has seen him first. This, although innocent, is a transgression for which Kim Chernin may never forgive her. Soon, when the kitchen boss tries to dislodge Devora from her room Kim Chernin will not go with Devora to the hearing. There may have been extenuating circumstances. I think Kim Chernin should have gone anyway.

Some of the nights up there are real dark. Some memories are filled with howling dogs, but that night the dogs are quiet. Fanfullah drowses between the paws of his protector. Zigefuss hunkers near the kitchen although no one would ever give Zigefuss scraps. Kim Chernin tells herself she is looking for Simon. She swears she did not know Simon was in the *mo'adon* knocking over chess pieces. A young man with an uzi on his shoulder climbs down from the guard tower behind the children's house.

Stop there.

You cannot trust memory. It wants to make things worse than they were, for the sake of a good story. Memory is an instrument crossed by so many purposes, no one has ever figured out how to read it. Memory is not for amateurs. I've made it my life's work. For Kim Chernin to get involved in hanky-panky the night her soldier arrives, with another soldier, a complete stranger? Not likely.

Pretty soon Devora shows up at Kim Chernin's room. She says the soldier spent the whole night at Boaz's table in the *mo'adon*, playing chess. She says he beat the pants off everyone. She says he doesn't show off, he studies at the Technion in Haifa. He's going to be an engineer. He's very tall, says Devora.

Devora is excited. You can tell from the way her upper lip doesn't meet her lower lip when she's talking fast. She has a tendency to repeat herself. She mentions several times that he speaks English. Devora's Hebrew is not what it could be. She does not seem to realize this is Kim Chernin's soldier. Or maybe he has mistaken the woman for whom he came up here? Maybe he has already fallen for Devora?

Devora says Simon came into the *mo'adon* late, when everyone was about to go to bed. He pushed Boaz out of the way (unlikely), sat down across from the soldier, chose black. Devora says he closed his eyes, made a few quick moves, slapped his hand down triumphantly on the table. The soldier studied the board, shook his head, urged Simon to go on playing. Simon swept the chess pieces off with a flick of his hand.

The soldier came out of it with dignity. He wouldn't say Simon had won. He was willing to set up the board exactly as it had been. Simon said no one could set up the board exactly the way it had been. The soldier proposed another match. Simon flung himself away from the chess table. He was holding the rook in his left fist. Devora kept an eye on him.

He must have missed Kim Chernin, who was coming back from the guard tower, circling back around the infirmary, looking into the laundry. He ran into the soldiers on guard at the gates, pushed past them, went off down the road out of sight. They caught up with him in two minutes, for security reasons.

In the annals of gossip this night was set down as the night Simon had been drinking. For Kim Chernin, it was the night she managed to avoid the soldier, to make herself go on living in the wild hope of someday meeting him.

As I've always said, (love) the whole kit and kaboodle grows out of despair. Doesn't it always?

W hy should I make sense of the things she does? If she wants to avoid him let her avoid him. My job is to collate memories. If I step in, that is only because her memory gets on my nerves. I am compelled to sort through dream shadows, real events, condensations, codings, marginal jottings: the memories of a person who in her own time never bothered to distinguish wish from shadow from dream from fabrication from miracle. (The miracle of seeing before what comes about after. Or making a man of clay out of whole cloth.)

Up there, people worried about eggs. Whether the dairy would be put in, how late the woman with three earrings had talked outside the *mo'adon* to the man who limped, if the explosions near the border were from shelling or from the army blasting to make the security road. Usually it was the security road, but some nights the neighboring kibbutz was shelled. They wondered if the rumor was true about terrorists in the caves, if Simon had been drinking, how much rain fell, if Dani was ever going to visit Devora, if someone had been stealing medication from the infirmary (they had been), if the nineteen-year-old from Massachusetts who argued a lot was really going to marry the thirty-year-old woman from Mishmar Haemek. At dinner the musician with slicked-back hair talked to Kim Chernin about *Die Winterreise*, in which you could hear Schubert's unflinching, desperate knowledge of his forthcoming death.

Mostly they were a down-to-earth, hardworking folk, engaged in practical tasks, sixty people thirty years old and under, Kim Chernin thirty-one, wearing rough clothes, intent on building a collective future. If you looked closer, you might have noticed they were beginning to have a common, slightly faraway look to them, as if they were all secretly dreaming behind closed doors. Because Kim Chernin already had this tendency, living on the border pushed her farther than she would otherwise have gone.

The next day she took a good look at the soldier when he jumped up into the truck to talk with his men. I don't know when this happened. Does it matter? It might have happened when she was returning from work, had gone into the kitchen for yogurt. Maybe she was called in as substitute for the cook's assistant who had gone off to Jerusalem to spend the night with her cousin in the King David Hotel. When a memory has something urgent to record, the edge of a splinter will do. It does not bother with context. Kim Chernin may have been standing not quite in the doorway where she could see without being seen. If she has to discard him, better not arouse his interest.

He has the lean grace of something not yet conscious of its beauty. A long neck carries his head thrust slightly forward, jaw and chin brought in with a sharp line. Wide mouth holding something back. A cry of joy? terror? If he is the one whose life is about to be changed, would he know that? His eyes have an eager, silky, unprotected look. He wears his belt low, marking off hips and thighs from the long torso turned in that moment slightly toward Kim Chernin, who thinks it is the slightly hollow place below his eyes that is breaking her heart, maybe she already sees the shadow loving her will cast. He has brown hair, parted in the middle, falling long with a slight wave on either side of a dark, sensitive, supremely intelligent face.

This soldier's mother, whom he resembled, was a Sephardic Jew from Syria. His father's family had been in Palestine for generations. His paternal grandfather had been a career officer in the British Army. His mother's mother sat most of the day at the kitchen table telling his mother homespun stories she had told ten thousand times. Even if he had never met Kim Chernin, this division between two families would have made itself felt, it would have had to, sooner or later. He was twenty-one years old, had been born on the fifteenth of May, ten years, eight days after Kim Chernin.

If this is the man, Kim Chernin has removed his boots, one at a time, to kiss his high-arched foot. When she couldn't sleep, he carried her up and down her room

in his arms. He has come to know all about the rape in the
cellar, the man in the park, the baby carriage from which
she handed out leaflets with her mother in the Bronx when
she was not yet five years old before her sister died. There
is no way to interrogate him about these fine points of
knowledge.

The soldier is leaning against the slats of the truck,
his right arm stretched out leaving his chest exposed, as if
he has nothing to hide, no small vulnerabilities to protect.
Kim Chernin recognizes the way he moves his head forward in a quick, slight gesture, then sharply back to get his
hair out of his eyes. She observes his tendency (also familiar) to bring his hands together authoritatively in front of
his chest, thumbs up, palms pressed flat. She had not expected him to crouch down the moment he moved, to
lower his voice, to speak confidingly with his soldiers.
That means he has a will of his own. She is gratified to observe the men's respect for him. She cannot get used to
him out there, no longer hers, empty of everything with
which she had filled him. If she stepped out into the sun-
light he might not notice her.

If he did not want the woman who had dreamed him
up, if he wanted Devora who was prettier or the girl in the
orchard who followed Boaz around, Kim Chernin would
have made a fool of herself.

Now that he has jumped down out of the truck, now
that he is coming toward the kitchen to make arrangements for his men's midnight meal, will he even glance at
Kim Chernin?

I am tempted to yell at the soldier, "Don't look, don't
lift your eyes, don't acknowledge her. She has no claim on

you, she did not give you life, did not invent you. If you
happen to match up with her unruly figments, that is not
your fault. You carry no responsibility. She's nothing to
you. Leave it at that. Go back to your girlfriend, it makes
no difference if you are or are not engaged to her. Do not
hand over that (very) innocent boy to this woman."

Dov Aviad walks up to the kitchen door. His eyes are
darker than they were a few weeks ago. Up close his face
is younger, features newly set, the kind of young male
beauty that cannot last beyond its single (deadly) season.
I sometimes wonder how his life would have been if he
had cut her off there and then. If he had been even a bit
coy, not wanting to show the power she had over him already. I know her, she would have been cut to the quick,
that's all it would have taken, the love affair would have
died right there.

That day, by the kitchen door, the woman he looked
at could pass for beautiful (I imagine a look of concentration serious to the point of rapture). He looked back, hiding nothing for three whole seconds before they both
turned fast to clothe themselves.

What can you do in three seconds? Take a breath of
smoke? Not even time to blow it out again! Put
on lipstick? An ice cube clinking against a glass will take
more than three seconds to settle down. Not many people
can endure three seconds of gazing with a perfect stranger.
When that happens, when neither breaks sooner than the
other, both are in for something.

Kim Chernin thought nothing in her life, not even the birth of her daughter, matched those three seconds for their savagery. Did they ever take place? Did she dream them up like so much else? No.

She keeps the windows open all night in spite of the cold. When she was little, she had expected her sister to come back as a bird. When the family moved to California, she wondered how her sister would find them. Now the sister has to make her way over the sea to the small room on the second floor in Kibbutz Araht.

She got up before it was light to write a letter to her daughter. She was planning to have coffee with the orchard crew before starting down in the truck. She loved the kitchen in the early morning, the sinks and stoves gleaming, the stone floor scrubbed clean. The mugs were mostly chipped, beige and off white, too hot to hold in your hands. She usually wore the same work pants for several days, then threw them into the laundry, where they would go through an ordeal so violent they came back several shades lighter.

With the letter she encloses a picture so the daughter will remember how the mother looks. It is a picture of Kim Chernin on the back of the truck, in shorts and sandals, squinting joyfully into the sun during the period when Devora was still taking pictures to send to Dani. Kim Chernin writes three more letters, to her mother, who has not approved of this trip to a land taken from Arabs. To the man who loved her, who gave her the money to come. She tells him she will spend the rest of her life in Israel. She does not invite him to visit.

She takes a shower (it is still dark). Washes her hair,

dries it over the kerosene heater. The soldier is out there somewhere, roaming about, innocently looking for the woman who has called him. Maybe she will drag the covers from her bed, twist them back and forth in her arms. This would be the behavior of a madwoman, not someone recently born again into her body.

In three seconds all that has been brought to an end.

Kim Chernin has been shunted into the ambiguous status of the older woman, a mysterious role through which Theirs will make her way back. Because Kim Chernin has fallen in love, her brief fling with the born-again body has just come to an end.

Kim Chernin picks up the pair of wrinkled knickers from the kibbutz that failed. She remembers the day they were discovered in the laundry by Devora. It took place before the going down of Theirs, before the brief fling of freshness that missed its chance because Simon was waiting to become her perfect lover. She tries the knickers on. Tight across hips and thighs, they look good with long socks folded down over the top of the rubber work boots.

Running down the stairs, she takes in the entire farm. It will never look the same. Someone has just seen it who one day will never see it again. Maybe he has waited the whole night outside her building, will take the stairs three at a time to take her in his arms. The owl that flies through this memory never existed. The air is wet, something nameless must have been weeping.

Devora has no reason to wake up early. If she's not awake the whole night crying her eyes out, she can sleep until breakfast. She sleeps soundly the day after a letter arrives from Dani, the rest of the time sleep is a perilous undertaking. Today she is expecting a letter, or tomorrow. She sleeps curled up with her back to the wall, tangled black hair spread out in anguish on the cover. Devora, a fatalist in love, will be true to Dani until the end. That was decided the moment a letter did not come from him yesterday.

Devora says, "Let's hope your soldier likes to write letters. Let's hope he doesn't have a wife hidden away in Haifa." Her voice is husky, tearful, affectionate, worn out. With those legs, visible from beneath her red flannel nightgown, she wouldn't have to worry about perfect beauty.

Kim Chernin, her body heavy with memory, has lived the longest stretch of waiting she has known in her life. She is no beauty and it is still dark.

When they drive back for breakfast Simon refuses to ride with them. Kim Chernin jumps out, runs back down the road where a nanny goat with filthy withers is trying to get into the orchard. They have been clearing new ground for planting. The earth breaks practically violet. Simon is staring silently at her with a haggard, melancholy gaze. She had forgotten how young men could be sometimes.

The soldiers are housed in barrack rooms near the laundry. They are never up by breakfast. Boaz has his arm around Kim Chernin's shoulders; the girl who likes to work with Boaz comes along on the other side. The Bride sometimes does not show up for breakfast. She has migraine headaches. In front of the dining room Boaz stops to scrape his boots on the thick blade, a few inches high, that has been worn to a silver sheen. Kim Chernin makes it into the dining room without knowing she has seen the soldier.

Kim Chernin does not eat eggs, bacon, fried bread, tomatoes. She hates stewed prunes. She sticks to the fresh bread the driver had been down to fetch at the Arab bakery. He is the same guy who dropped them off, picked them up at the orchard, the man with a slight limp who might be falling for the woman with three earrings. Kim Chernin looks up just in time to see the soldier come into the dining room. She gets up fast, goes into the kitchen.

In there, she is up to her old tricks. She starts washing pots. She carries a sack of barley in from the storeroom, hefts it up onto the counter. She tells the story of Red Riding Hood in abominable Hebrew, goes out the back door fast when Boaz calls her. He uses her name. The soldier is standing close to the truck.

Now, he can repeat her name, make her come at his bidding, maybe he will make her love him more than she wants to love. Love means you hand yourself over without reproach to whatever happens because (like children) you believe in the laws of destiny. You are out to prove they exist by falling prey to them.

In the orchard Kim Chernin clips her palm for no good reason. Simha, the head of the orchard, has to patch it up with the first-aid kit. During the time it takes to climb down the ladder before setting out through miles of obsession to the next tree, a conviction grows that Simon is keeping an eye on her. She can never catch him at it.

These trees must have been planted only a few years ago; they have the look of something not yet fully grown. Delicate in their branching, one can only guess how they will look when they mature. They make her sad, here on the border where shells could fall on them.

When Simha calls the break, Kim Chernin tries to sit with Simon, some yards off from the rest of them. He is huddled up in two jackets and three sweaters, visibly shivering. She sits down, leans against him with her back the way they used to. He moves away.

Now that it is almost winter, by evening there isn't a soul out on the farm. There is talk of a moon coming up later than usual. The dogs are getting restless. Kim Chernin thinks there will be a high wind bringing down the ghosts who hang around the ruins.

There: she is running fast from Devora's room (a letter had arrived). She is swinging around behind the buildings for a last quick view of the Sea before it is smudged out for good this time. He is leaning against the building, looking down at Safad. This coincidence, which could have happened to anyone (sooner or later in the course of a day you run into everyone on that farm) seizes her with a terrible power. It is the last blow. If she doesn't watch out, she will throw herself into his arms. I'm not kidding. She could have started crying that minute.

He and a buddy have invented a weapon the army is going to use. He doesn't need Kim Chernin. He is twenty-one years old. When she tells him she's known him before, he will believe her. When she says she made him up he agrees. She will say she recognizes him for himself, sees him as someone else, knows what he might become, wants to make him that, sees herself in him as she might be if he loved her. What she feels for him cuts across the history of her loving. She will not complain, no matter what happens. Why should it matter? They have not yet exchanged one word.

He has the look of a man about to set out on some desperate crime. Had he called her name? No, he had not.

The Bride has come out for a breath of air. She is wrapped in Boaz's heavy street coat, a striped scarf over her ears. She is sitting on the children's merry-go-round, smoking a cigarette. She looks up curiously at Kim Chernin, who is out of breath, wild-eyed, running from the first love she'd ever felt in her life no matter how many times she'd thrown herself at love before.

T he next day he is sitting at her table. When they walk out of the dining room it is late afternoon. He takes her hand.

I think, *If he does not want to love her for the rest of his life, he shouldn't have done that.*

The Bride is sitting on the merry-go-round, smoking. Lost in her calculations, she does not pick up her head when they walk by.

They lean against the wall outside the window where the musician is playing over and over again the song where the traveler who has set out on his winter journey meets up with the hurdy-gurdy man.

When she turns to look at her soldier, to see him the way he is apart from having dreamed him up, his unprotected innocence makes her wince. She cannot see past the man she has invented. She can never reach this soldier. If there is tragedy in loving him, that is where it will fall. She cannot escape the man she called, no matter how much she wants this one instead.

Dov Aviad holds her left hand in both his hands against his chest.

"I never expected a woman like you. A woman like you cannot be expected. But I had known there would be something good when I came to Araht."

"I'm not good," she says.

In his grandmother's village the older son of a poor family died unexpectedly. His widow was twenty-five years old. According to custom, she would have to marry her husband's only surviving brother. He was a boy of thirteen. Everyone expected it to be a marriage in name only until the boy grew up. But then it turned out this boy had been passionately in love with his brother's wife for years. It was a scandal through the whole village, but that's how it was. Passion or not, good for him or not, he married her.

Kim Chernin says, "Was it good for him?"

Dov Aviad does not answer. Maybe he has forgotten Kim Chernin. During his silence the wind crosses the border, picks up speed, hurls itself at them. He says, "Was it good for him? In my opinion age is not important in such matters. In stories of this kind you are never told the ending. I used to ask my grandmother, 'What happened?' She always said, 'What happened is what happened.'"

She says, "Do you know how old I am?"

He knows. He asked Boaz, Boaz told him.

He says, "My grandmother is always sad. She says life

is sad. She says you don't find out, not until you live ninety years, life maybe is not worth living."

Kim Chernin says, "Sad? She says life is sad? In ninety years that is the worst she has to say against it?"

He says, "People think children don't know about death. It's not true. When I was small I dreamed my grandmother fell off her branch. I got out of bed fast, I went running to see if she was still breathing."

Kim Chernin says, "I used to think my sister would come back after she died. I didn't know if she would find us when we moved to California. I wasn't sure birds could fly that far."

He says, "I knew you would be on that side."

She should have said, "What do you mean, 'that side'?"

I think she might have wondered how he knew he could take her hand when they left the dining hall after three hours. They talked the whole time about *Death in Venice*. A film playing in Haifa then. He had a copy of the book sticking out of his shirt pocket. When he came up to her table for lunch, that was the first thing she had noticed. Then, she noticed his hands.

She says, "You can't know people unless you've already known them. If you don't recognize them right away you never will. Most people can't make sense of that."

He says, "My father wants me to make a career in the army. My grandmother tells my father he's a fool. She doesn't say it to his face. She says it to my mother when he comes in the room. This makes my mother unhappy. If I go in the direction of my father, I could live my life not recognizing. I'm studying to be an engineer."

She says, "You won't work one day of your life as an engineer. You won't kill anyone either."

He says, "I knew an American girl, she could not understand how Israelis love their country. American Jews can't know this. Even if a thing is against your soul you will do it for your country. When I am unhappy I go to the beach. I go when it is almost dark. Sometimes I have thought it might be needed for something to happen, to save me."

She has just met a man who believes your country can ask anything of you, even your soul. She will try, I know her, to persuade him his soul comes first. She will go at it day and night. She will never understand how his love for his country makes him his own man, not the soldier she dreamed up months ago at this very spot that first night with Devora.

Kim Chernin leans up against the wall. She looks down at Safad, to which it is already known she will lose him. She says, "I don't think you will think you were saved."

Is she laughing at him because he is talking too seriously about himself?

She isn't laughing, she has no sense of humor.

He imagines he can cross through her room without waking her. That is because he is young, does not yet know much about women who lie awake all night listening. He stands on one leg to take off his sock. In that position, reaching forward, the boy he was until recently is visible. That means when she was setting off for the first time to travel in Europe he was seven years old, in the second grade, knew how to read and do math, but had wobbly handwriting. When he straightens up, after the second sock, to unbutton his shirt and trousers, he is even more than the man she hoped he might be.

He is not wearing an undershirt. In this, memory is probably mistaken. Dov Aviad suffers from the cold. His mother's family is hot-blooded, given to anger, highly emotional. Dov Aviad likes heat. If he had been outdoors since nightfall, patrolling the farm on a winter's night, he would certainly have been wearing an undershirt.

Without his boots and socks, khaki shirt and trousers, the soldier is naked, he wants her. It is possible to see the rise and fall of long muscles in his arms when he adjusts the rifle on the desk. Then, he changes his mind, checks the clip, suspends the rifle by the leather band on the back of the chair.

She wishes she had a body equally beautiful. She is older, that makes a difference; even at his age she was not as beautiful as he is. She has to work hard for her slenderness, such as it is. She wants a body beautiful enough to make an offering. She wants to give a body beyond reproach. She directs a targeted scorn at hers, knowing by heart every disqualification. No way can it match the exaltation he inspires. There is infinite longing in her fingertips, flooded with the wish to throw themselves on him. She wants to touch him with long, slender fingers, no other fingers will do, first there then everywhere else.

If she is his first woman, he probably would not be walking over to her bed so slowly. She imagines he would tremble, throw his arms out. It would be a gesture of warding off. Aren't men like that the first time?

She has her eyes almost shut, pretending sleep so he can wake her. The soldier takes a long time to cross a room that is not seven feet wide. During this time Kim Chernin goes back to Masada. That is because, since he left the desk and chair, where his rifle is hanging, he has been walking toward her since the year 71. Then, he was on his way to a high, fortified rock, where she was waiting for him. Before he got there, the story was out about the Romans and the breached wall, the fire and the suicide. From that time until now, steadily, without losing faith, the soldier from Masada has been walking toward her.

I want to shout at her. *Cut it out. Wake up, open your eyes. Figure out who he is here in this room where you are telling yourself you were always older than he was. Always, in your incomprehensible suffering, so much more beautiful. And how long this time will he be able to keep you?*

His hands are cold. He puts them on both sides of her face. If she looks up now she will see all the delicacy of this young boy who wants to be saved by her. He has already told her what happens to his buddies when they go into the army. He has said the first time they come home on leave, they are still the same men, a bit older. The second time, the jaw is tighter, the mouth more taut, but they are still recognizable. Then comes the next time. It happens to all of them. The boy he knew all his life docs not come home. He searches his friend's eyes, he cannot find his friend in them.

With awe, reverently, Dov Aviad folds back the blanket. He thinks of Acteon in the moment he set eyes on the moon goddess. He is afraid he too will lose his soul before he has begun to grow it. Therefore, he must make Kim Chernin bury it inside her. There it can be kept safe if he should happen to misplace it. Because this is what he wants from her, it is far too easy to enter her dreaming.

Just now, as he puts his head against her breast to study her breathing, she is thinking about David, the barbaric king on whom the Jewish people lavish so much uncomprehending pride. She wonders how he felt the night he went up to the roof of his house when he saw the woman bathing. Did David feel what Dov Aviad is feeling?

His hands enclose her waist. They move on, find welcome. Kim Chernin wonders what sort of night it was when David went out onto the roof of his house. It was probably a hot night. Then a breeze from the courtyard. Why was Bath-Sheba bathing? Had she taken off her jewelry? Maybe she was wearing a coiled snake just above the elbow? She had abundant auburn hair, coiled up at the back of her head.

Did bathing mean bathing in oil? Was she outdoors because of the new moon, was it a ritual bath, one of those Canaanite doings? Was she dragged away from sacred observation, dragged to his bed, flung down on the covers, spread open, taken?

David loved men, he loved Jonathan, he was far less Jew than pagan, dancing naked when he could to harps and psalteries, timbrels and cornets in his linen ephod, yearning for the sacred priestess of the earth goddess, for whom he was perhaps intended as mate?

They have six weeks. They are almost never out of her room. When she gets back from work he is waiting for her, lying on her bed stretched out on his stomach with a book. He reads *Death in Venice* several times. Then he reads *The White Goddess*. When she takes her shower he wanders in after her to read aloud. He likes to embrace her when she is still wet, then the pages of his book get crinkled.

They become the kind of lovers who like to talk while they are reading and making love, their arms or legs crossed together, someone's head on someone's shoulder as it gets dark before she gets out of bed to light the kerosene heater.

When it is dark he takes off to join his soldiers. By three or four o'clock in the morning he will be back, with rifle and lantern. In the morning she is up before him to catch the truck driving to the orchard. Then, little by little she is no longer living the life of the farm. It goes on without her, as if she has already left.

The one who has never loved before has nothing to fear. He comes into love the way he said he would go to war, holding nothing back for love of his country, having no idea what could happen to him, because he hasn't been to war before.

Silky, eager, unprotected eyes. When she looks up

from reading, these are the eyes that turn to watch her when he tells her, again, how he has seen his friends go into the army, guys completely different from each other, womanizers, some great athletes, several musicians, some of them had been studying philosophy, the first time they came back they were the same guys, only their hair was shorter. But the next time, maybe it was only a few months later, when he saw them on leave, they weren't there, none of them came back. He wonders if that will happen to him too. Has she ever seen anything like that? Eyes dying?

He was not King David. He was not the boy from Masada. He was good enough the way he was. If she had known how to reach him, take him in, she might have been able to help him. If she had known him, even a little, he might have kept calling and writing after he went back to school. He might have kept coming up to visit on weekends when he didn't have to study. He would probably not have had to fall in love with someone else who saw him as he was, twenty-one years old, doing all this for the first time. A young guy worrying about what would happen to him when he had graduated, had spent his summer traveling, or on the kibbutz with Kim Chernin if she was still there, still wanted him. Maybe the ten years would not have mattered.

She used to look at him all the time. She kept trying to see him. She stared at his mouth, trying to make it his mouth. Even twenty years later, he cannot be distinguished from the dream soldier. I saw a picture of him once, a memory of a photo sent when he first went back to Safad, in his uniform from before he'd grown his hair long.

Maybe he just was an exceptionally beautiful young

soldier who can't be remembered any other way even by a snapshot.

The six weeks he spent with Kim Chernin have a ghostly shape, edge of a splinter again, without context. And they are better than what comes after them. Every memory of those weeks is saturated by her fear of losing him when he leaves, goes back to a life she cannot imagine for him without her, in which there is no place for her unless he can bring himself to tell his mother he is in love with a woman ten years older, who has a child, who lives on Kibbutz Araht, who can be no part of the future his grandmother and mother and father and younger sister need him to make possible for them, the brilliant only son of a poor family, all of whom in their tiny flat grow absolutely silent when he is studying.

Every time he lies down next to her at three in the morning, he has to decide whether to enlist in the army for active service, in which case he will be out of the army in two years, if a war doesn't come to kill him. He has no idea a war is coming in two years. Or, he can sign up for four years as a desk officer.

Every time he walks into her room toward morning, if he weren't going into the army, if he had been born somewhere else, he might be wondering why Jehovah created trees and grass before he created the sun and stars. If he weren't going into the army, he might learn all about the original mother, who made the skies before her son got busy with grasses.

He says he could go into the intelligence service, he's good with languages, he doesn't seem to know torture is used against the enemy. Can he imagine these hands, with their long, tapering fingers, their tendency to worship the woman he loves, beating a man because he will not betray his brother?

Young men of twenty-one are not easily tired. That is why, according to the most ancient wisdom, they are well matched with women in their thirties. The youth of this young man is a pleasure. It tends to make them laugh a lot, after the exaltation of the first half dozen times. He has to throw his hand over her mouth to remind her she is not in the court of King David. Here, the walls are thin with envy. Even muted, her laughter reminds him of a mulberry tree. She says it reminds her of cucumbers. He says her laughter is very sad.

At three in the morning he stands next to her bed until he wakes her. Then he seems to know exactly what she wants him to do. If he did it right she would be kneeling on the bed in front of him. Then, because of the difference in their height, that is what she wanted.

Some of this was possible to do over at the window. There he can point out Safad but he doesn't. He knows he will be leaving in a week; he does not wish to remind her there is a world outside this room.

Toward morning, when he is asleep against her breast, she dreams the war thoughts of his land's blood guilt. If she does not lose him because he forgets her, he will be ground down in these battles she lives through for him, because she is trying to save him. She wants a man who would give up his country for love of her, for his soul's sake. When she is afraid to lose him, it is not because she knows he is his own man who will not put a woman before his country. It is because her sister died young. And so love can only be an old tale full of sadness. His forgetting, his going down from the mountain, his getting caught up again in the world of his old life has nothing to do with him. It is simply the way things happen.

One day they visited Acre. For hours they sat on walls built by the Crusaders, in a confusion of light above the harbor. During the war of 1948, after the fall of Haifa, Acre was flooded with Arab refugees who stayed on when the people of position had fled to Lebanon. The refugees lived in hard conditions, sleeping in the streets, in the coffee shops, the town of twelve thousand housing more than forty thousand. If Dov Aviad knows this story, he doesn't tell her. They go into a café, where the tables have been stacked against the window because it is winter.

Kim Chernin tells the Arab boy she wants an ice cream. He looks at them sharply, laughs to himself, carries a table out into the streak of pale sunset in the courtyard, turns on the music loud, brings her a glass dish of chocolate ice cream she eats with a straw.

If they had asked him, the boy could have told them the story of Acre. The flight of its inhabitants set off by the mortar harassment of the Israeli Defense Forces during the last week of April 1948. A week or so before her eighth birthday. A couple of years before he was born. Those who remained in the town experienced, from their side, the birth pangs of the Jewish homeland, fear, filth and hunger, unemployment, desperation.

During dinner at Dov Aviad's family's home in Safad no one mentions the war of '48, when his father was posted to the Sea of Galilee. The grandmother tells stories in Ladino. If she has guessed Kim Chernin's age, ten years, ten months, ten days, does it matter? Only good girls come to have dinner with the family, she tells Dov Aviad.

When Kim Chernin is leaving, his mother puts her arms around Kim Chernin. She kisses Kim Chernin on the forehead. "As if I were your own mother," she says.

All the way back to Araht in the bus Kim Chernin cries with the soldier's arm around her shoulder.

Then, there is only one last night. Therefore, that night belongs to the earth mother, who drinks seed. Kim Chernin loves to tell stories about the earth mother, how she could never get enough of it. If you keep one eye open, even if you are madly in love, if you look over your shoulder at exactly the right moment, when you already know for certain it's going to happen, you will catch a glimpse of a cumbersome, shadowy figure, no great beauty, braids on her head, just passing through, keeping an eye out.

Kim Chernin says the pleasure in that moment, for both lovers, is strangely intense. That is why the Hebrew kings, the warriors, the common people kept falling back to the worship of the earth mother.

Because he was skeptical, Kim Chernin decided to show him. Although it was done only to her, although she didn't touch him except on both shoulders, he felt in his own body what was happening to hers. Later, when the soldier had gone home, when he wrote to her, he told her his body had wanted to open as if his body were a parched earth and there were rain coming.

They have made a fair amount of clutter in the room. Sheets and blankets, pillows, a few difficult texts with cryptic letters, his handkerchief, papers that fluttered down

from her desk, he managed to button his shirt, she unbuttoned it, she throws his shirt against the shelves where
there are a few books, the ones she has brought with her,
Freud and company, the prophetic version of the Old Testament, those he had left for her. He does not leave *The
White Goddess* or *Death in Venice*, with which she is already
too familiar.

It is dawn, anyone can see that. She has promised,
saying she wouldn't lay a hand on him once it was dawn.
She looks into his eyes, saying, "Then you did, then I
did, then you put, then I put." Before too long she gets the
one singular sacred she has expected, that tribute, like no
other.

When it is over, the soldier cries. He is standing on
his long legs, his chest is smooth, he has no hair on his
chest, his army shirt buttoned wrong, partly unbuttoned.
He cries because suddenly, without turning away, without
putting his face in his hands, without putting his arm over
his eyes, he understands that after all she might lose him.
And so he cries her tears because, he says, she has already
cried too many.

Someone has gone through these memories setting
whole scenes on fire. At times it has been like walking
through a house in which only the fine, small things have
been done away with. I have shards, fragments, incriminat-
ing ashen possibilities. To remember has become a game of
make as make can. But the life of the farm, the work in
kitchen and orchard, the regular Saturdays of films, after-

noon visits for tea, the workaday world in its daily exac-
tions, all that is perfectly in order.

Have the memories been done up to give an illusion
of coherence when coherence was no longer possible for
Kim Chernin? Are they a false stage, a protective contriv-
ance? Or is the deception increasingly malevolent?

I had imagined if I worked with caution, carefully
weighing the merits of each forgetting, transposing, con-
densing, hiding from oneself, dreaming things up to make
things better, the lost memories might be smoked out of
hiding. Whatever happened up there, Kim Chernin did
not come out of it in good shape.

Certainly, her relationship with the soldier came to an
end. I have spent hours trying to sort out who the other
woman might have been. Devora was always a candidate.
I've already mentioned, when Devora was forced to move
out of her room, when a hearing was held, Kim Chernin
did not accompany her?

On the other hand, the relationship with the soldier
seems to have gone on after he left for Safad. There were
calls, letters, hours spent waiting by the telephone booth
near the laundry. Sometimes, Devora is waiting with her.
That has made it seem unlikely the other woman was
Devora, unless there was a time before betrayal, then a
time after.

There are certain obvious clues, the soldier showing
up on the farm in civilian clothes for example. This suggested a time after his reserve duty. On the other hand, in
the memory of their visit to Acre, when they are sitting in
the café, he is leaning toward her across the table in his
uniform. They only went to Acre once, so far as I know.

But I have also glimpsed them in a small, dark shop filled with barrels of olives. Kim Chernin is tasting Greek olives. She seems to prefer the fat black olive from the southeast corner of the Peloponnesus. She takes a bite, thinks it over, reaches up to put the rest in his mouth. So far, everything is perfectly clear. She is eating Amfissa olives from the foothills of Mount Parnassus, Dov Aviad has bought a small, paper-wrapped package of olives grown on the island of Thasos, his grandmother's favorite. That is why I think this is a memory of the same day Dov Aviad and Kim Chernin went to visit Dov's parents. Twenty years later it is still possible to smell the curing oil, fennel, freshly squeezed lemon juice, the garlic marinade in which the Nafplion olives had been marinated. But if they were on their way to visit his parents while he was still on reserve duty, why is he dressed in civilian clothes? A small detail, setting everything into question.

Kim Chernin did not survive long after she left Israel; whatever happened up there between her and Dov Aviad, it seems to have been the blow from which it was no longer possible to recover. I have thought it worth my while, as one who came after, to probe these memories. The death of Kim Chernin cannot be a matter of indifference to me.

Would Dov have bought his grandmother's favorite olives if they had not been on the way to visit his family? He looks young and dazed, his hair is not as long as it will be later when he comes up to the farm for weekend visits, he is always gazing at Kim Chernin, everything happens to him for the first time, he tastes, he sees, he sits on the Crusaders' walls, as if his life had begun a few weeks ago when he first set eyes on Kim Chernin. He is the sort of man who loves once in his life, this is the time, it won't happen again. Everything about him, his grace, his upright bearing, the brooding intelligence he fastens on this woman, all make it unthinkable he will not still be in love with her a few weeks from now. But that is what happened.

In the stories Kim Chernin told Dov Aviad the heroes tend to forget when they go down off the mountain. It happened to Siegfried when he left Brunhild. It happened to Tristan, when he returned to Cornwall. The world, ambition, his recovery from the old wounds made it hard for him to remember the woman who had healed him. If Kim Chernin had tried to make sense of what happened with Dov Aviad, these are the stories she would have told herself.

But how has it come about that one day Dov Aviad is no longer calling her on Monday and Wednesday nights at the telephone by the laundry? What has happened, now that his letters are no longer arriving in the late afternoon every day the way they used to?

If it is not Devora, who is it Dov Aviad comes to visit when he still comes up to the farm? In one perfectly incomprehensible memory he is running with a letter in his hand. Sometimes he is in uniform, sometimes in light brown civilian clothes, then it is Kim Chernin who is running, back from the orchard, in muddy work pants, clutching the letter.

Who ran? Why were they running? Was it before or after he left the farm? If he is breaking off with Kim Chernin why should he be crying?

In another attempt to arrange a consistent story I

grouped the memories by certain formal qualities. There are memories in which people make stylized gestures. The memory of Dov arguing with Boaz fits in here. These memories have a tendency to repeat themselves. Boaz and Dov Aviad are standing by the merry-go-round in the children's playground. Boaz pushes Dov hard against the shoulder. They are talking fast, Boaz seems to be shouting. The memory plays them with urgent expressions, absolute silence.

Other memories flash by so fast you can't recollect them the minute you were about to figure them out. Some keep throwing out first this detail, now another. But the details in themselves are meaningless. There are bits of discourse, a maddening, repetitive speech between voices that have grown shrill and husky from saying the same things for twenty years.

Some of the memories take place behind the glass door of an old-fashioned shower. You can see people moving on the other side, lifting their arm, putting their foot up against the wall. But who they are, why they are doing what they are doing, remains indecipherable.

No matter how many times you try to stare the memory into transparency it remains opaque. The memory of the night someone tried to kill Kim Chernin is like that. Someone is breaking in the door to Kim Chernin's room, pounding, kicking. Through a crack in the door a knife flashes. But everything takes place behind darkened glass.

Once, during a strenuous period of notes and transcription, I caught sight of Simon standing on the bottom step of Kim Chernin's staircase, barefoot, without a shirt.

It is nighttime, it must have been very cold. Simon is

bent forward, a knife in his hand. I have refused this memory. Why Simon? Why now? If I myself do not want to imagine Simon this way, how much stronger would have been Kim Chernin's wish to eliminate him?

If he is not wearing a shirt on a winter night, he must have come running from his room because something has just happened. Has the soldier suddenly come back up to the farm after breaking off with Kim Chernin? Did she go out to walk with him by the guard towers the way they used to? Who is it Simon was after? The soldier? Kim Chernin?

In the memory of someone breaking in Kim Chernin's door, the memory in which the knife flashes, Kim Chernin is in her room. She is leaning against the window, watching the door crack, she is in a state of incredible lucidity.

To be lucid in a moment like that, when the next moment you might be dead, speaks to a trouble akin to madness. If she had died that night there would have been no one to reconstruct the story. As it is, twenty years later, there is little I can know for certain. The door cracking. And now Simon, on the stairs, clutching the knife.

Maybe Kim Chernin and Simon had begun to go up to the Roman ruins again after the soldier left for Safad. Maybe the soldier ended the relationship with Kim Chernin because of Simon. Then, the relationship between the soldier and Kim Chernin might have started up again after a brief separation. The triangle may have been cobbled together of those three. What do we know about Simon that makes one thing or another impossible? If he was sitting on his bed one night with his guitar, if he was writing down his story about Kim Chernin, if he heard the soldier drive onto the farm, heard him run past on his way to

Kim Chernin's building, Simon might have jumped up, grabbed his orchard knife.

But in that case why is Kim Chernin alone in her room when the door is being shattered?

There is also a time during which Simon has disappeared. Was it before or after the night with the knife? The security branch has been out searching for him. They are afraid terrorists may have kidnapped him from the ruins. They have even looked for evidence of him in the caves. Bitter suspicions have fallen upon Simon. An official sent out from another kibbutz has questioned Kim Chernin in the infirmary. He wants to know about Simon's friends in the village, he asks if Simon confided his plans to Kim Chernin, if Kim Chernin thinks he may have crossed the border into Lebanon?

Kim Chernin is not intimidated by the interrogation. This is a memory of shrill, repetitive speech. Kim Chernin says, "If I knew anything, would I tell you?"

Later on, if it is later on, Simon has returned. He goes about through the memories wrapped in several blankets, covered with a sheepskin, walking about through the snow without seeming to notice where he is going, definitely lost, infinitely shaggy.

Somewhere, I knew, there must be a thread that ties together Devora going alone to the hearing, Simon disappearing, reappearing, clutching the knife, the soldier running with a letter, weeping. I thought I had it all worked out, a double triangle linking Devora to the soldier, Kim Chernin to Simon, the soldier once again to Kim Chernin, Devora for a time to Simon.

Then a new figured emerged. She'd drifted through before without carrying much significance, smoking on the merry-go-round, coming out onto the landing outside her room to watch the dogs circle the chicken house. I imagined she'd come through, the way fragments often do, with maddening persistence that eludes all efforts to decipher meaning, because there is none.

But she was important. Undoubtedly, she was important.

Certainly, it makes sense to bring Boaz into the triangle. His quarrel with Dov Aviad, for example. I would imagine Sena, The Bride, has entered the triangle through Boaz. Sena, probably because Boaz asked her to help Kim Chernin, came to her room one night to suggest a plan for bringing Kim Chernin's daughter to the kibbutz.

In the memory of Sena at Kim Chernin's door a stylization has occurred. I can see them shaking hands, Sena taking off her suede jacket, then she does it again, as if there were something intensely meaningful about taking off her jacket. In my opinion the repetition has nothing to do with meaning, it seems a gesture thrown up for the purpose of warding something off.

There was a time (it seems) when Kim Chernin, Boaz, Dov Aviad, and Sena used to borrow the orchard truck, leave the farm after dark, drive down into Tiberias to eat hummus and olives in the rundown Arab café where Kim Chernin once sat writing in her notebook before she came to the farm. I think it was Sena who saved Kim Chernin the night Simon pulled a knife. What else can it mean that she is fumbling in the darkness, struggling with Simon over the knife?

In the café, when they get up to leave the table, Dov Aviad holds the light brown suede jacket for Sena. Kim Chernin stands by the door with Boaz. She is running her fingers through her hair. It may be a cold night, all this is happening in winter, Boaz looks back over his shoulder, Kim Chernin is not wearing a coat.

Therefore, whatever happened later, in the beginning Kim Chernin and Sena became friends.

The memory of them on the merry-go-round is pleasant, there is no difficulty about what is happening here. Smoking, talking with their heads bent close together, plotting to get the daughter to the farm, counting over the members who would vote for, against her, conspiring to win over a crucial vote, Sena said Boaz would take care of the security and orchard workers. Even the law-and-order man would vote for Kim Chernin if Boaz told him to vote for her.

Eventually, I put together quite a few memories of Sena and Kim Chernin both wearing winter coats. Several times there is the memory of the night two wild Afghan dogs got into the farm, were seen walking with their heads bent, one behind the other, around and around the chicken house. Simon comes through, wearing a filthy robe, barefoot, sitting on the floor in the infirmary with his arms around a small boy's shoulders. Devora has broken off with Dani, that means the soldier might have fallen in love with Devora, but I think he fell for Sena.

There is a moment when he and Kim Chernin are in Kim Chernin's room. He is wearing black cotton trousers, a black and yellow print shirt, he is wearing suede shoes, he's started to grow a beard. I guess he's been coming up to visit on weekends for months by now. Sometimes I catch a glimpse of Kim Chernin waiting for him by the orchard, scanning the road for the car that will come around the corner fast. She walks a few steps down the road, turns around, paces back again, maybe she's crying.

I think the sobbing one hears all through these memories could be Devora, who has given up her work in the laundry. Devora has fallen ill; the doctor says it is a flu. After she goes back to Jerusalem it will become pneumonia. Everyone thinks Devora is sick with love, therefore they despise her. Everyone is glad to know love never works out, even when it befalls a beautiful woman.

They will have been glad about Dov Aviad and Kim Chernin too.

Dov Aviad and Kim Chernin are in her room. He is reading something from the typewriter. This is one of the silent memories, with exaggerated gestures.

Then, he has gone out of the room. Kim Chernin stands by her desk, waiting. When he comes back he has Sena with him. Sena walks right over to Kim Chernin, she takes her by the shoulder.

All three are talking at once, not a word comprehensible. Now Dov stands to one side, he seems to want them to make things up, he looks urgent, out of his depth, stricken. He throws in a word but Kim Chernin is intransigent, unforgiving, inconsolable?

Has she never been betrayed by a best friend before?

She looks old and haggard. Dov goes out of the room, Sena talks in a quiet voice, from the expression on her face her voice must have been quiet even before memory shut it down.

Then, Sena looks back over her shoulder. Does she think Dov Aviad has come back into the room?

I had not noticed before that Sena was beautiful. This woman, who must have recently fallen in love for the first time, shows a face cut through with desire. There are also marks of guilt, sorrow. I think it is the sorrow that has made her beautiful.

She is married, she has been Kim Chernin's friend, her protector. She has no business falling for Kim Chernin's soldier.

If that is what happened.

Sequence is impossible; before and after comes as a self-revising refusal to let the story be known. That is probably why the soldier is sometimes dressed in uniform, sometimes in civilian clothes when he is running with his letter to find Kim Chernin in the orchard.

If he dropped Kim Chernin when he fell for Sena, that would have been because down there on the city of solitudes when he went back to the room he shared with his grandmother, he would have felt too small for the role with which Kim Chernin had invested him. He can believe in himself only in her presence. That, I think, is what he has been trying to tell her in his letter. That is why he has been running, crying.

When he is away from her he knows she will stop loving him, when she wakes up to discover he is only a boy trying to decide if he should go into the army for four years at a desk job or sign up for active service and if a war comes he will probably be killed.

I know her, she has been telling him practically from the first night he came to her room with rifle and lantern that when he goes home she'll never get a letter from him. She has been telling him he won't call on Monday and Wednesday nights, that when he leaves the farm, that will be the last time she sees him. One way sooner or later he'll go for a younger woman, his mother will never allow him to keep Kim Chernin. He is the one who has to lift them all up out of the crowded flat in Safad.

I understand why it had to be Sena, someone so close to Kim Chernin she almost was Kim Chernin, as near to Kim Chernin as another woman could get, because I don't believe the soldier ever stopped loving Kim Chernin, he was the sort of man who loves once only, if he got himself caught up with Sena, that would have been because she was life-size but Kim Chernin from the first moment had always seemed to him larger.

Before he went back to school he used to say, "Could I be with another woman after Kim Chernin?" He always used to refer to her ceremonially, in the third person. That meant for him she was larger than life. I see her more as a creature. I third-person her to ward her off in case she figures out how to get back from the grave to possess me.

If he got mixed up with Sena it was because he could write to her in a language he knew, in Hebrew. That might have been the letter Boaz found that started the fight between him and Sena when he slapped Sena in front of the dining hall while Kim Chernin was watching. It could have been that letter that finally brought Dov Aviad into the quarrel with Boaz. It doesn't matter if I can't hear a word they are saying. I know Boaz is shouting about betrayal. From the look on Dov's face he agrees with everything. Dov has a beard by then, the dark shadows under his eyes by which for a long time Kim Chernin remembered him. With his long hair, that haunted expression some people find appealing, at school other students have been telling him he looks like Jesus. They haven't intended a compliment. He hasn't heard one.

Every fragment, every ashen chard in every single one of these memories is crossed with betrayal. If Kim Chernin had been able to cry she would have cried her eyes out. But the tears are always from Devora, alone in her room, unable to get out of bed, despised by everyone, no longer even visited by Kim Chernin.

P eople die of what they cannot learn. Yes, they do. Kim Chernin died of not being able to learn that you cannot make people up out of whole cloth and expect them to go on loving you when you are no longer there to invent them.

That's what I think.

It was Sena who saw her off at the airport with a box of chocolate from Dov Aviad's mother. She gave Kim Chernin a photograph of Dov Aviad with a beard. In spite of everything he wanted Kim Chernin to remember him. Sena tries to reason with Kim Chernin. That's the impression I get. Kim Chernin walks up and down through the crowded waiting room, stubborn to the last, refusing to forgive Sena.

There is no last time she saw Dov Aviad. There would have been no reason for a last time, she expected to see him again, to be asked to forgive, to be told how much he still loved her in spite of everything.

He would have been expected to explain all over again how she is too large, beyond him, he cannot bear to feel the way he will feel when she sees him stripped down one day when she discovers he is not the man she invented.

These things have been repeated in a shrill voice for more than twenty years now.

When the plane is called, Sena tries to embrace her. Kim Chernin moves away fast, once or twice she looks back over her shoulder. Sena watches from behind the barrier, then she says something to the guard, he shakes his head, she goes past anyway, she is catching up with Kim Chernin who is watching a soldier meticulously punch his way through the box of chocolates looking for hidden knives.

I don't know how long Kim Chernin stayed in Israel after she left the kibbutz. One night, somewhere, she and Devora are sitting up on Kim Chernin's bed weeping; they are holding on to each other, one more desperate than the next, Devora's long hair falling over Kim Chernin's shoulder. Devora would have forgiven Kim Chernin for her neglect, Devora was like that.

So it couldn't have been Devora who took up with the soldier, it must have been Sena. Sena is still waving good-bye although Kim Chernin has already crossed the bleak, small space between this country she dreamed up when she was a kid, and the short, desperate life that is soon ending.

Look back, Kim Chernin. You will never see this woman again.

It must have been too much all at once, the loss of the dream of the farm, the collective she was to have seen grow up around her, the children whom she would never see born, the new baby she would not watch grow up near the border. I think he was born a day or two before Kim Chernin left the kibbutz.

In Scotland Kim Chernin stays in a house across the stream from the thatched house in which her friends David and Margo live with their five children. That would have been Boar Hills, the place to which Kim Chernin had been invited before she left for Israel. Most of the time Kim Chernin sits at a table near the window, writing.

I think she went down to the sea toward morning, it would have been bitterly cold, a wind up over the water; she was not wearing a jacket, why would she have thought of putting on a jacket?

She was barefoot, why would she notice the stones along the path?

I don't think she walked out to sea. I think she walked up and down on the stretch of sand between the rocks along the shore, without her coat, not having eaten or slept for days, how would I know how many?

Maybe that's when she went through the memories

shredding, burning, ripping, tearing, setting up false witness, probably already planning to deceive me.

I wouldn't say she died of shame. To her it would not have been cause for despair to be betrayed twice over. She never doubted love would lead to something like that if you followed it far enough back to its oldest story, the father who betrays you in the primal beginnings. No one goes much farther than that.

I think she kept walking until she wasn't walking any longer. The tide would have come in about then. By late morning the sea often covered the rocks where she had been walking. If I had been more clear-headed I would have looked back right away. I would have fixed the spot, tracked down her footsteps through the sand. I would have bid some kind of farewell to Kim Chernin. I found it cold coming back from the beach without a jacket. Then came the joy, known in that pure form only for that moment, she had gone down, had gone forever, the inconceivable had happened, Kim Chernin was dead.

I was puzzled by the salt on my lips. I did not wonder why Kim Chernin was gone. Maybe she had come to the edge, everyone has one. I was stumbling up the rocks on legs I did not inhabit. Ankles, wrists, all articulations could at any moment fall asunder. I could be strewn about on the path, unceremoniously scattered. It took an effort of will, even a ferocious concentration to hold me together.

This body I had inherited, its unknown histories, swollen hands, maybe she died of a broken heart. She was the sort of woman who dies in her youth, even if she is already too old to die young. Maybe this body had already housed innumerable lives. Small odd jumps, angulated twistings, tremors, shakings, a tide of drowning in my ears, someone's sorrow clinging to me. She died when one new love was no longer just as good as another, when sequence was broken, when Dov could not be replaced by any other. That broke her. Yes, that broke her. When Kim Chernin walked herself out on the edge of Boar Hills, she must have known she had been worn out by love. Why not? That happens.

I, who came after, irrelevant, the survivor, held on as I could. The passage of cold through cold shoulders. Fingertips uncertain about life. Far off an almost forgotten terrible knowing. That was hunger. Maybe it is forbidden to call love that cannot be answered. Maybe the lover is not allowed to love most her own transformation. Kim Chernin believed love was beyond law. Maybe she was mistaken.

A purple tide ebbed from my fingers. I did not debate these matters then. Life resists when it is reawakened. Maybe there was no border left for Kim Chernin to cross. Unless death is a border? Can one fling oneself out against death as if that too were a transgression?

Back then, coming up from the sea where she had walked herself to death, the rocks cutting my feet, it is I who have to recognize the man with light brown hair coming down the path toward me.

There is a look of recognition in his eyes. I go into his arms because I figure out he must be the man who loves her. I am in his arms, it is safe here. It is I, Kim Chernin is dead. I am wearing her green knickers, the work shoes she had taken with her from the farm, although she should have left them.

Yes, I go into his arms as if I had done this before. He seems satisfied I am the woman for whom he has come. He has a beard of soft, silken blond hair. It does not scratch my cheek when he bends over. He is very tall, a slender man on long legs, but he does not remind me of the soldier.

I look back once while we are walking away. I do not see Kim Chernin. The tide comes up by then, his arm hugging me so close I can scarcely walk. He smells good, I think I will like him when I get to know him. It was for his sake I set out to assemble Kim Chernin's memories. I didn't want him to find out the Kim Chernin he had loved was lost forever.

He is talking about Kim Chernin's daughter, whom I remember. A little girl named Larissa, whose memory Kim Chernin had not taken away. Why would she? Wasn't I intended for Larissa's mother?

A woman from the post office is waving. She is calling to Margo, saying she has found us, we are here on the path back from the sea.

A little girl is running toward us. Is this Larissa? I thought Larissa had been a blond girl. This one is dark. The post office woman calls her Jessica as she swoops past to throw herself in my arms.

I know who she is. She is David and Margo's oldest daughter.

If Kim Chernin had held out until summer she would have seen the soldier again. He came looking for her but I had already gone back to California in her place.

He stopped at the post office to ask about the philosophy professor who had five children (this story was told to me later by Margo). The two eldest were in the post office, they took him home, at the door he told the tall man with graying hair who he was, was given a place to stay in the garden, a made-over shack cold even in summer, although he had a paraffin heater, a down sleeping bag.

Dov Aviad lived with David and Margo for several weeks, talking about Kim Chernin. In the fall he was going into the army. He had signed up for two years of active service. He didn't know it then but war was coming in less than a year. If he had known, he would have signed up anyway.

Nothing ever came of his relationship with Sena, who had a son two or three years later, before Boaz got involved with one of the volunteers who came up to pick apples in the summer. Sena divorced him. I have never heard of him since.

I guess Dov Aviad had come to talk to the last people who had seen Kim Chernin alive. Or maybe, after she died, he could imagine himself large enough to be loved by her?

She imagined human beings acted upon by impersonal forces, whose influence roved out beyond individual will, personal decision. This (this) seemed to exalt her. Let this be her epitaph.

She could love, cast off, love, abandon, in the name of self-knowledge. As if the beloved were never more than a wandering fragment of the self, as if human intimacy required no further accounting.

A savage view, if you ask me, no wonder she died of it.

If Kim Chernin had seen me walking back from the sea, she would have called me Theirs. It would never have occurred to her that Theirs would go down along with Kim Chernin. She and Theirs were the two sides of the coin, toss them up, twisting and turning, they'll fall together. I, who survived, have inherited their dilemma. You'll see what I mean when you read Kim Chernin's letters.

Kim Chernin should have had a chance before her death. She should have told her own version. I, who came after, would have preferred to know sooner what I found out when I read Kim Chernin's letters. If someone else finds a new voice hard to get used to this late in the story, imagine how I felt when the letters turned up twenty years after I thought Kim Chernin had shut up for good.

When I set out to make sense of Kim Chernin's memories, I was prepared to laugh at her, take her just seriously enough, keep an eye out for the traps she set me. I never imagined I would lose the sense of humor that has been my distinguishing trait, setting me off from Theirs and Kim Chernin.

It happened when the soldier fell in love. Suddenly the string of disasters she'd set in motion no longer seemed a laughing matter. The minute he showed up I could no longer take her peccadilloes lightly. You think you know who Kim Chernin's lover was? You think you know to whom she had been writing day and night before she walked herself out on the coast of Scotland?

Oh yes, Kim Chernin has had the last laugh. Just listen!

The
*D*eath of
Kim Chernin

❦ ❦ ❦

Written from Boar Hills,

Scotland

FEBRUARY

1972

February 4th
Early morning

Beloved!
        Yes, You, Mine!
    In spite of everything.

Five days ago they woke me just after midnight with a summons from the big house, a telephone call from Israel they said, you were calling me in spite of the hour, you must have known what time it was here. Because you wanted me back, because you demanded I get on the next plane. What would have happened if I had come? Would you have changed your mind by the time I arrived? If I had a phone in this cottage you would have called me day and night for the first days. You knew I would have to be summoned, no matter what time of day or night, the house boy would have to be sent for, sent running to me, I would have to come in my farm boots and work pants, in the blue sweater you gave me before I left, the only clothes I still have because I wouldn't put on any others to

213

say good-bye to you. The rest is gone. Let it go. I don't want them to find my clothes, or my books, or the pictures of you or your letters, or have you forgotten how you started to write to me before I ever thought to leave the farm?

You called me five days ago, I whispered into the telephone, you couldn't hear me, you told me to shout, shout with the people of the big house lying awake in the room next door? Shout that I would come back, yes right away, that night, the next day?

"See," you shouted, "I am saying it in my own language, I want you to come back. Doesn't that prove I mean it?"

This time you should have sent me a letter. If you did not dare to call, why this disembodied voice that has already grown shrill from repeating itself? I play the tape to the end. I wind it back. I start over.

You used to say to me, "I wonder how long it will be before you stop writing to me?"

I, stop writing to you?

You said it before we had any idea we would have to part from one another.

You said, "From the first minute I saw you I could imagine myself forced to say good-bye to you forever."

No doubt you have forgotten that?

Or suppose we chose each other in order to suffer. To feel what we said was forbidden. Why forbidden? So that all along we could prepare to renounce each other?

It was you who wrote to me before I left. "Your hand tracing the line of my hand is beautiful with a beauty not of this world."

You wrote to me in Hebrew; it was a pledge you meant every word.

I see you standing in my room, not once only, without your blue sweater, buttoning your jeans, barefoot on a late winter afternoon, by the open window.

Did I tell you to come to my room? If I had come to your room would I have read to you from Ecclesiastes? Would I have pushed you against the window, bent back your head, laughed down into your eyes to tell you I would never see you again?

And now you wonder why I seem confused, why I am still waiting, why I never believe you when you say it is over. Is that how love ends? Is that an ending?

One day, you were sitting across the room from me, I remember you were sitting on my bed beneath the photograph of my daughter, with a half smile like hers, the same look of having seen too much too early, as if I had made you, too, suffer by leaving you. Then it happened that I walked over and dropped on my knees.

I had already told you the story of the owl. I had seen it one day when I was out walking in the woods near the waterfall in Tamalpais (you pronounced Tamalpais with a stress on the first syllable, as if it were an Arabic word).

I had been out walking, the owl took me by surprise, on the tree above me, on a low branch in broad daylight, over my head. All my life, I had told you, I had felt this longing to fall on my knees. You said, "Because you feel the same way about me you felt about the owl?"

When I used to kiss you, in the days when it was you who came to my room, you would draw away from me, you would say, "I think you would be content to kiss me like that forever." One day, when I pulled you down next to me on the bed, when I embraced you roughly, you said, "I feel as if you want to possess me." You said, "I like it."

You lived in the building next to mine. From my window I could see the windows of your room. All night I willed you to come to me, to cross the few feet of space between our buildings, a blanket wrapped around you, or in the red nightshirt so I could undress you.

So I stood there. Why not? You had become the one whose touch awakens, puts to sleep, acts upon, calls up, lays to rest, the one without whom, without whom is unthinkable. One day you said to me, "It is beautiful. Our love is beautiful. We are two women who love each other. That is all."

The heater had an amber coil, we kept the window open because of the paraffin, you seem to want me to forget the kind of twilight that suddenly breaks you.

Now you say, in that new harsh repetitive voice of yours, "Why are you always talking about pain? Before I met you I never suffered a day in my life."

I suppose that is what forgetting means.

Shall I forget too? Shall I forget those months before I left, before you came to say good-bye because you were sending me away?

If you are the person who has forgotten that woman who was in love with me, who was that woman?

February 4th
Evening

I went across the bridge with Jessica. She was born the week before Larissa, in the same hospital in Dublin, in a room next door to the room where I ended up. When they were both seven months old we took them to Cornwall, left them in their cots dug in high up on the rocks while we climbed about below them.

I always knew if I were desperate these were the people who would take me in. Does that mean I am desperate?

I know, it makes no difference to you whether or not I am desperate. Therefore, why should it matter to me?

We crossed the bridge that leads to the field where the bull scares Jessica. She wants to run across the field but her father has told her to walk slowly. From my cottage, you can see their cottage, down to the bank, across the field, over the bridge. Just after dawn there will be smoke starting up over the rooftop, that is David up early getting the twins ready for school. Then he rides into Saint Andrews on his bicycle to teach at the university.

Half an hour later Margo will be fussing about with Rachel, who is always eating. It is Jessica who comes over here every morning to fetch me. If I could settle down, keep myself inside my own skin, keep my thoughts from racing, stop thinking about you, I would have a home here. Larissa could go to school with the children, carrying those sandwiches Margo makes on home-baked bread.

This morning I went away from here, I went back to you. It happened at the bridge when we stepped down into the field where the bull is pastured. I noticed the field was covered with frost where I was crossing the space between our buildings the day it snowed. I took two steps toward you, you were coming to look for me and we weren't even lovers then.

I have been thinking about the day I left the farm. Devora's father drove us down to Jerusalem. I knew there was no hope of seeing you again, you had already read to me from Ecclesiastes. The snow had been melting for days. There was a red flower growing up out of the snow. Devora's father got out of the car to take pictures.

I got out of the car, I looked down at that flower you had pointed out to me when we were walking together one afternoon. I thought of tearing it out, suddenly the horn sounded, I looked up, you were there, waving to me in spite of him sitting in the backseat beside you. I saw your face moving away from me, the saddest face I have ever seen, and then you were gone.

I am afraid to lose you because after you maybe nothing savage will exist. Maybe I will forget myself the way you were afraid I would forget you every time you left my room.

Suppose I were there in my room, suppose you looked at me with that hard, cold, suspicious look I can imagine on your face when I listen to your tape. Do you remember it was you who came to Sarid after you sent me away from the farm? I had given you up, you had asked me to give you up. So why send me away? Because you were terrified of the way I looked at you. Terrified of what?

"Kim, one day you will wake up. Then where will I be? Writing you letters you no longer read? Calling you on some telephone where you will not be waiting? You are asleep on your feet, no one can come ten steps close to you without being turned to a dream. I feel it happen to me if I walk into your room. The power of your dreaming turns me into something only yours. As if I had not the power to stay myself against your dreaming. I don't like it."

I already had a dream soldier, I didn't want you for dreaming, no one can come ten steps close to me without being turned to a dream? I wanted you for the acre of red earth that walked with you wherever you went, that is what I wanted in the beginning, and for the way the new barn grew up between your hands when you described our future at community meetings. I wanted you for the rooted person you were, set down hard on this earth.

I know who found out. I know because I saw him watching me in the orchard, never taking his eyes off me, he watched us when we walked into the same room, he saw everything we hid from ourselves. He was already my enemy that first night in the *mo'adon* when he argued for law and order, when he couldn't get his eyes off Boaz. If it weren't for him, would we still be at Araht together? What was there to lose? Our position in society, your good name?

We are not the first, somewhere others are surely together, maybe a dozen miles from here, on their own small farms in the highlands. Maybe in small flats on a side street in Tel Aviv? Why not in Jerusalem? Otherwise, I tell you, we are going to die, you slowly, year by year in the arms of a man you do not love, cannot admire, in a world where you will not study what you might. I cannot bear to think of you withering away on a kibbutz that will not thrive. How could it thrive without Simon, without Devora, without me there? It will grow larger, you say, it will have its own swimming pool someday.

I play the tape back, punch it to silence, listen to your voice echo along the stone walls. I can make you speak at top speed, as if you were desperate to say everything before I turn you off. I can slow you down to a drone, as if every word had to be wrung out of you. You say I was careless, I was selfish, I overcame your resistance, you talk as if I were a magician, practicing spells.

Was it thoughtless of me to go away? When I went to stay with Devora's family in Jerusalem I could not find my way about the streets. In Jerusalem, among steeples and minarets, along the walls of the city, I looked for you. I must have known by then what would happen. I knew the woman I loved did not have much time left.

I have come back out into this world where I cannot find my way from one street to another. I did that for you. Even here, in this Scottish village, there are not more than a dozen houses, a small post office with a grocery store, some half dozen paths that lead past stone cottages out to the sea.

I left the kibbutz, I went to Jerusalem, I left Jerusalem because the streets had begun to break down. I went to Sarid. Devora came with me because she did not think I could travel alone.

We stayed in a small guest house. In the middle of the night I woke myself with weeping, Devora came over to hold me in her arms. Why weren't you there? In the morning I knew I could not remain. The kibbutz was too large, I couldn't sort out the paths between the fields and the gardens, so I was leaving, Devora's father came to pick her up. She took my things, threw them into the back of the car. I was walking behind her, I kept my gaze fixed on Devora's feet in their blue sneakers walking through the dust ahead of me.

Suddenly, you had taken me in your arms. You were there, you had come from Araht, hugging me as old friends might, embracing me for the first time in public.

We got into the car, Devora's father drove us to a school on Mount Carmel where Devora's sister was at school.

Do you remember that girl? On my last day I will remember not you, not Dov, not Simon, not Devora, not the path to the ruins, not the valley or the black sheep grazing. In my last hour I shall hold steady before my eyes that girl Miriam and how she came running, in leaps and bounds, skips and hops, straight into Devora's arms.

We got the impression she was a small, less beautiful version of Devora, alive in some way no one can be much older than she was. Devora and her father were standing at the bottom of the steps. She jumped up to fling her arms around her father's neck. She took them both by the hands, whispering in a conspiratorial voice about the girls she had invited for the day's outing. She glanced at us in the backseat, reassured we weren't coming along.

We wanted to spend the day in her room. She sprang into the front seat, chattered at you in Hebrew, linked her arms through ours as we went fast down the hall toward her room, calling out the names of her friends as we passed them. When she left, slamming the door behind her, we had nothing to say to each other. We stood a few inches apart, her quick spur of light had made us believe we too had a future. But this was the room of an ending, the last place we would ever be in private, together.

We had that day, six hours, we had three hours left. We sat side by side on Miriam's bed, a few minutes to go, listening to our silence. You leaned over to kiss me, a young head peeked in the door, I jumped away from you.

My fear, when you had lost all fearfulness, that on the last day I would ever see you I would not hold you in my arms.

You laughed. You no longer cared what people thought. In the car again with Devora and her father, taking you to the bus, you put your arms around me. You whispered in my ear. I sat still, counting the seconds until I would never see you again, as if we were only enacting what had been long ago foreseen, intended.

It was not our last meeting after all. I had told Dov not to see me off; I had said good-bye to Devora on the street before her parents' apartment; I got out of the taxi leaving my bag behind with your pictures and those letters you had already written before I left the kibbutz. Maybe I hoped, someday, driving about on a wild course through your country, your past might catch up with you.

I had learned to look at nothing but my two feet placing themselves one in front of the other. I had learned to count my steps to measure the space from here to there when suddenly you were there with your arms around me. It was the second time, it lay down a hope, an expectation. Perhaps I keep myself awake day and night, trying to achieve that pitch of desperation in which you appear to take me in your arms.

That day you held my hand in public. We walked up and down in the airport waiting room, our arms around each other. I offered you a chocolate from the box Dov Aviad's mother had sent to me. You said, "It has gone even beyond chocolate." We looked at each other trying to figure out which one of us would call the other back, refuse to let the other go. You threw your arms around me, kissed me on both cheeks. "They'll think we are sisters," you said.

I kissed you on the lips. "That is how sisters say goodbye."

Neither of us laughed, you stared at me as if you dared me to do it again. I did.

It is I who have loved best. For days and days I have lived without you, I have forgotten nothing. I know who I was when I loved you. Think what you like: this fact is for me an immense, enduring pride.

February 8th
Midnight

During the first days in Israel I thought, what a terrible destiny to be the birthplace of a Messiah. It was still warm, small insects buzzed around the lights. At night one had to keep the windows closed or by morning be covered with bites. I learned to read with my head under the covers, holding a lamp close to the book. That was before you had returned. When I arrived at Araht, you were absent; I had no idea you existed, no one spoke to me of you; now I am exultant about that time when, without knowing you, I might have been waiting for you.

Did I leave Dov for you? Hadn't Dov already left me for his studies? You think I am bitter about Dov? You think I never forgave him? I forgave him. Love did not. You stepped into the place he had left, love acknowledged your presence. We were all at risk. Anyone can stop loving tomorrow; Boaz could walk out on you the minute you glance over your shoulder. You risk nothing with him because you do not love him. No one is responsible for the lover. Don't blame me because Dov Aviad can't sleep at night; maybe what Dov Aviad needs to know he can only learn by being wakeful.

Love is supposed to bring you back to what you were before. Before what? When I met Dov Aviad, his knees started shaking. For that one moment he will be in my debt for a lifetime.

By then you had already come back. We had met each other, our meeting was in no way memorable. I thought you beautiful and cold, the cold visionary. You thought me arrogant. I made friends, I went to work in the orchard, I became friends with Boaz. People came to have tea in my room in the afternoons. At night, after I'd gone to sleep, Dov Aviad would come, set down his rifle on the table near the window. I never gave a thought to you then, and you said to yourself, seeing me laughing and talking with the others, "She's not for me."

Later, you told me you had seen me laughing. Then you grew afraid, as if I had the power to make you tell what you had never planned to tell anyone, ever, as if I had made you tell what you had not yet confessed to yourself.

Who were you then? If I could figure that out I would stop writing, go to bed. If you are not that woman, if you were always only this person you claim to be, what did love want with you in the first place?

"Kim," you say, "it is late. I have gotten out of bed. I cannot express to you my feelings in writing. Maybe I cannot express to you my feelings at all. Maybe it is impossible to put into English the feelings I have only in Hebrew."

There, I recognize the woman who loved me. In that voice, weary, determined to put into English what can only be felt in Hebrew; there too, when she says, suddenly tender in an afterthought, breathing out a breath of cigarette smoke, "I suppose one could love or hate you with the same intensity." There, clicking off the tape machine, coming back, softening slightly, "How's my English?"

Don't you wish to know what to make of this love, why have you taken this easy path, calling it madness, how can you rest not knowing what is asked for, what is promised by this love? The word *madness* has no meaning. Unless it means the capacity to understand love, withheld in any other condition.

When Dov left Araht, when the letters came, when the phone rang down by the laundry, the beautiful soldier was wrapped back into his dream garment. Once he was gone, had he ever been there?

Dov left Araht, he went back to his studies. His reserve duty ended, why didn't he leave his studies for me? The night you walked into my room Dov was at work fulfilling his obligation to his family. Of course I don't blame him. I ask only, where was his obligation to love?

I know you understand these things although today you are determined to forget them. Something tragic and lovely brushed over your childhood. You have told me how in childhood something would break you during the twilight, an intolerable anguish.

After you had been discharged from the army, when you were in love with Yigael, after you had quarreled with him, you waited for him to come back. You waited even after you knew he was never coming. You shut yourself in your room, you studied English, you stopped eating, you prepared your exams. Then, there were dark circles beneath your eyes. Days, weeks, months passed, no word from him, you knew he was not coming. Still you waited, you passed your exams, now you could attend the Hebrew University, in Jerusalem. But you could not tear yourself away from that longing, that hope that was no hope, that waiting that was never intended to end. I ask you, What were you waiting for? Weren't you waiting for me?

We were already marked in childhood for each other, that's what you said. We were pledged by a sacred vow, between our fathers, who must have known each other as students and promised their son and daughter (still not yet born) would one day be united. When you told me the story, did you already guess you would turn me into the yeshiva boy driven mad by loss and desire, the dybbuk who comes back from the grave to haunt you?

Why were you sent away as a child to another kibbutz? Did you ever know your father? What about your mother? Your foster mother was an angry woman. She would grab you by the arm, throw you out of the house. The neighbors would look out, they would see you sprawling in the dirt but of course no one said anything. That grief you felt then, the outrage, the desperation, that sorrow, the longing you would not admit, that was the course your love would follow, straight out, then right back to its source.

When I went to visit your foster family they showed me pictures of you as a child. Everything you were to become as a woman was already in your face. Those luminous eyes, that secretive smile, that questioning expression that cannot keep its sorrow hidden, a vulnerability only I have seen. But I am wrong. There was no trace yet of the mastery: no sternness, no preeminence of will, that came later.

When you came to my room you shrugged off years of willing yourself to be what you are not as easily as you took off your coat. The first night, when you had come to discuss Larissa, you already told me about the little girl who used to sit in the barn to sing to the cows. One day you had noticed tears in their eyes. You thought they were crying because of your songs. I guess you were very young then. Because later, when your foster mother told you, scornfully, the cows had eye infections that year, you were still young enough to believe her.

When you loved me I was the promise of everything that had been forced into hiding, all that would have been you before it had been slashed down. I was the life you never dared dream up for yourself, you who had never been off the kibbutz except to be in the army, for whom the city was a sudden violence. You now wanted to leave the kibbutz, leave Boaz, take me with you to Jerusalem.

I turned you into a dream? That's what you tell yourself to get rid of me? That time when you walked across the room to where I was sitting on my bed to stare at me with a haughty expression; did you know what you meant when you slipped out of your sweater without one word, without ever having done anything like it in your life before? That sudden disclosure, that forbidden nakedness was, I tell you, your surrender to everything you might become. To the past, to its old, lost possibilities, to the sensibility and suffering of your childhood, its mystical brooding at the edge of possibility. You gave more than your body; you gave more than you knew you possessed. Have you forgotten that too? You said, "When men see me like this they take in their breath."

I must have intercepted your offer of yourself to yourself.

You once accused me. You said, "I think you are only in love with my body." We both knew that was nothing but pride, a way of establishing you were a woman with slim hips, much taller than I was, with longer legs, larger breasts. Tonight I am standing in the window, trying to turn myself toward the east, toward you, the sky no longer dark, a clear sky, the winds silent. There is a breath too mysterious to speak. I have known it since childhood, a call, a summons, the muted voice of the messengers calling us back to the beginnings. You have known it too; that knowledge was our bond.

February 10th
Evening

I have been out walking with the children all day long. The twins, Benjamin and Emma, ride in their large pram, facing me. The pram was given to Margo by the woman in the manor house, the one you woke up with your telephone call last week, when you demanded I come back to you. The children and I went down by the short path to the sea. There are oak trees in the meadow below the manor house. I kept my eyes on the twins in order not to notice the way the bark of the trees was shredding into luminous threads. There is something disturbing about that.

I have been remembering the night you first came to my room. I don't like to remember how, until that night, you did not like me. By then, we had been living together on the kibbutz for several months but we had scarcely spoken a word to each other. Boaz was away from the kibbutz for a few days, he was taking a course on new weapons.

You knocked at my door after dinner. At the time, I was trying to bring Larissa from America. In her letters she was beginning to forget me, she couldn't remember the way I looked. She was afraid another mother might come back. If that happened, how would she know? I had come to a meeting of the farm's education committee. You had dropped in to see how things were going. What I said was translated into Hebrew but you addressed me in English. That was your way, I thought, of letting me know I was inferior. I remember how cold your eyes were. I knew you were my enemy. I thought you would soon remind me there were no children Larissa's age on the kibbutz. But later, someone told me that after I left, when the kitchen boss made disparaging remarks about me, you defended me passionately.

I heard a knock at my door; I was reading, I had not expected visitors. By then Devora rarely left her room, she was in mourning for Dani, who had not joined her at the Yemenite wedding. The Yemenite family had come all the way on foot from the south Arabian Peninsula to Israel. By then, Simon no longer talked to me. He went around covered in sheepskins, old blankets, constantly shivering. I saw him one day sitting on the floor in the doctor's waiting room, refusing to go in before our village neighbors the way the rest of us did, his arms around the little boy with swollen eyes who came up from the village twice a month when the kibbutz doctor showed up on the farm. That was the first day he never talked to me again.

You, visiting me? Before you came I had been planning to race out to see if someone, coming late from Safad perhaps, had brought back a letter from Dov. That night, Devora and I had met by chance by the wooden boxes, several hours after dinner, although the mail had been delivered for the day.

You, visiting me? You were very formal; we exchanged courtesies, I invited you to come in. I remember the way you took off your suede jacket, laid it out carefully at the foot of my bed. You sat in the chair in the corner in front of the window, your hands folded together in your lap. I sat at the edge of my bed. Soon all of this would become habitual.

You wanted me to go to your kibbutz, to speak with your cousin about bringing Larissa to live at Araht. You assured me your cousin would help me, she was an expert in children. If she gave a positive opinion about Larissa, no one in Araht would dare go against it. You seemed sure she would give an opinion in my favor.

You had come to my room the first night Boaz was not on the farm. You had come to visit me, as if you were already arranging things to keep me there. That is why I doubt you are the victim of my dreaming.

The first night you came to my room everything that would happen was already present. Did I knock at your door? You, the arranger, must already have known you would turn me little by little into the beautiful soldier.

That night I could not figure how I came to be talking to you. From time to time I would look up at you. I told you why I had left my daughter at home. I told you about the doors slamming, the light plucking at flowers in the rose garden. You listened without saying a word. You sat without breathing, entirely still. For that alone I could love you forever. You had a cigarette in your left hand, you didn't light it. That is why I trusted you with my secret. You.

Because now, in a quick rearrangement, a sudden dropping away, someone else was sitting where you had been sitting in the chair in the corner next to the window. She looked like you and yet not a bit like you; her expression was more provoking than yours, sadder, more weary. She was staring at me intently, as if I had just come around a turning in the path when I was not expected. She was older than you, I noticed that distinctly. Then, in three quick waves, your face was done with itself. First, the haughty expression went down; then the provocative sorrow; now there was someone curious about me, eager to show herself. Something had broken you open. Something I said?

You said you had been lonely as a child. On your kibbutz everyone talked about you. You went about by yourself, you wore boy's clothes, you rode your bicycle. When the other children in your group were asleep you woke up terrified at night. Later, you had a friend named Roni, a funny-looking little boy who liked to draw. When you said the name Roni your face became ecstatic. Who was this Roni? You were looking off into a distance, as if remembering the one night in your life you had been happy.

My happiness did not come from the way you talked, sat still, from your hands still folded in your lap, the cigarette in your left hand, still not lighted. It was knowing you would stand up, walk out of the room, return to being the other, come back to me here in my room, where someone unnamed would have taken your place, the secret sharer, and she would love me.

You think in that moment I should have remembered the soldier?

When we said good night, you put your hand on my shoulder. It was before I opened the door, you put your hand on my shoulder. That was the first time. You said, in a low, soft voice, "Before you came, I had been so lonely here."

At that time I didn't know you and Roni had come to the farm together, both recently discharged from the army, comrades not lovers. Maybe you married Boaz after Roni left because Boaz spoke perfect Hebrew, had been in the army, marched fifty miles to Jerusalem. You were lonely, I hadn't arrived. I wonder how things might have been if you'd let yourself know I was coming. If you had waited.

The next day I knocked at your door during the rest period. I had returned from the orchard, showered, put on clean work clothes. I always had a pile Devora had ironed. I knocked timidly. *"Mi zeh?"* you said. Then you repeated in English, "Who is it?"

So you knew who it was?

You were lying in bed, reading. You had been expecting me. I saw that you were naked. Your body was covered with a sheet. You had the electric heater on, the window wasn't open. You looked up at me the whole time I was talking. I stood with my back to the wall. Because I had spoken to you the night before, because I knew you better than anyone had ever known you, I had come to tell you how I felt about you.

How did I feel?

I remember the smile on your face. You said, "It is because *you* are feeling like this Kim that I am not feeling this way myself."

What did you mean?

The whole time I was talking I could see you were in love with me. It was in your bare arm stretched out holding the book, the tilt of your face upward, the shadow from which your eyes peered out in their luminous indiscretion. I saw you for the first time with your hair down over your shoulders. A revelation, almost nakedness. There must be places in the world a woman would not be allowed to wear her hair like that, not even waking, not even first thing in the morning. After that, workday or Sabbath, you never wore your hair braided again. Were you already aware that, between us I was to be, the beautiful soldier, the doomed yeshiva student, who one day would become your dybbuk?

In its pure, first form our friendship lasted for three days; we walked out under the guard towers, we sat on the children's swings planning for Larissa. When we walked out of my room one night you put your cheek playfully next to mine. For each of the three days Boaz was away you walked down to the orchard to walk back with me for lunch. Simon came along behind us, in three work jackets and a dirty scarf. We went up to the Roman ruins in the afternoon, you used to think Simon was around there somewhere, watching us, keeping an eye on me. Now we know who it was. We talked in an undertone, shivering under the wet and wildness, we had dinner together, sitting at the same table, both of us strangely excited, you the aloof, the solemn, the unapproachable, making everyone laugh. After dinner you came to my room, took off your suede jacket, set it at the foot of the bed, went to sit in the chair across from me. Then the other would show up, shyly, laughing self-consciously as if she'd never had a friend before. If it had stayed like that, if you had hidden the desire of the secret sharer, I would be sitting in my room tonight, across from your room, writing a letter to Larissa. You might be standing behind me, reading over my shoulder, would perhaps add a note, telling her to learn the Hebrew letters. You would write my name in Hebrew, then her own.

One night Boaz returned. You apologized for not being able to spend time with me. You said, "I know you will understand." Why should I understand? I was standing near the dining room with a letter, I heard your voice inside, Boaz and some others had arrived through the back door, through the kitchen, you must have run forward to meet him, your voice eager to please, guilty. I had a letter from Dov Aviad, he was worried because I hadn't kept our phone date near the laundry. It must have been a Monday you came to my room, the first time I forgot to get my call from Dov Aviad.

We never chose to mean more to each other than we meant the first night. What we meant that night could not have been chosen, it was so small, practically invisible, the way love has to be or one would run from it. We lost each other before our friendship began because it was never friendship. Tonight, in this stone cottage you will never visit, I find that so sad.

I went to your foster parents' kibbutz. I met your cousin, we walked about the farm together, we went to the children's classroom where I played with a freckled little girl who threw herself into my arms, then bit my ear hard to make it bleed. Your cousin brought me to meet your mother and father. We had dinner together in the dining room, I was introduced as a member of Kibbutz Araht. After dinner we went back to their rooms for tea. I asked to see pictures of you; they brought out a large album. For more than an hour they left me alone, turning pages. Then, when they came back, they seemed to know I had come, not merely on official business but as your friend.

That's when I found out what you had offered me. I learned then what it means to be sitting with founders of an established kibbutz. If things didn't work out at Araht I would come to live there, your father said. I would find work, they would send me to study, I could have your old room. My daughter would have children to play with.

I slept in your room that night. When I lay down, I could feel the warmth of your body, its heavy curve into the mattress. It was the only night I ever spent with you, the first sleepless night on your account. The next day, after lunch, your father and cousin walked with me. Your cousin gave me a package of crumb cake, your father kissed me on the cheek. He had been singing all the way past the gardens on the way back to the road. "As if I were your father," he said.

I came back to Araht with presents for you. Chocolate, a package of American cigarettes. You saw me when I got off the bus. You told me later you had wanted to withhold yourself, to make me suffer for you.

You came to greet me, you walked straight out of the dining room, you must have been waiting for the bus. We were more than an hour late. We went back to my room. You loved chocolate, your father told me. He said, "Nothing can be so bad for Sena that it won't be better with chocolate."

In my room, you said, "I have to go. Boaz is expecting me." Then, you tossed your head and laughed. "So what," you said, opening a bar of chocolate, pushing a piece between my lips. "Let him wait."

From that day everyone noticed our friendship. Everyone seemed, in the beginning, to be happy about it. They were always giving us messages for each other. People spoke to me about you. They said, "Sena needed a friend like you. Before you came she was thinking of going back to her own kibbutz." You are not a woman people easily love. You are admired, respected, the sort of woman who refuses office, cannot put aside authority, determines silently the direction of the farm, while everyone else is strutting, talking. No one up there, not Boaz, not Roni when he was there, knows you as I do.

February 11th
Morning

I t was winter when we met, late December, wind at night, the mornings very cold. In the afternoons, when you came to visit until he told you not to come anymore, I lit the heater. Neither of us turned on the lights. You said to me, "I go out of the real world when I come in here."

Love grows up at the crossroads. No one is to blame. Not you for me or I for Dov or I for Simon or anyone for Devora. Two roads meeting where a choice has to be made; if you go back, if you choose the known, the familiar, love follows you for a time like a murder of crows, then deserts you. I can't speak for Simon or Devora, but you and I will not meet again, it will be your choice, you will prefer to excommunicate me, the only known way to get rid of a dybbuk. And therefore, I will always obsess you, even after you never speak my name again.

I have not eaten or slept for weeks. That is the old way to love. You scoff at it, you who threw your arms around me one day when you came to my room. You said,

"I dream you went away last night, I dream you were going about in the world by yourself, with big sad haunted eyes. When I didn't see you today I waited every minute until you would come back or not or maybe never."

In those days we did not hold hands. Our friendship was confessional: everything secret, hidden, must be told, endured together. It went on for weeks, embracing briefly only when arriving and leaving, sitting across the room from each other. Two women speaking like this are already throwing themselves recklessly toward what they have never been, could not have imagined until that moment. I find that love is so large; I stand on my own shoulders to reach what you began to be for me, across the room, in your daily transformation. It would happen the minute you stepped in the room; sometimes it would come over you on your way up the stairs, taking them two at a time the way Dov used to. If you knew what you were like then, your lips parted, folding your hands in front of your lips, trying or half trying to hide your desire, if you had seen the woman I saw then, her desire, you would not be able to forget her. "Sena's medieval beauty," Devora whispered one night when we huddled in the corner of the *mo'adon*, during a community meeting. Since then, especially these last days, I see you with a sprig of white lily in your hand, the flower of unwelcome annunciation, looking suspiciously at me over your high cheekbones through narrowed, reproving eyes.

On New Year's Eve there was a party in the *mo'adon*. The whole community was in a feverish mood. I was wearing Devora's batik shirt, a pair of embroidered bell-bottoms she had found in a pile of old sheets. You had on a blue sweater, a tight skirt. All the men were looking at you. When I told you, you said nothing, but your eyes said, "So what? Isn't it obvious I dressed this way for you?"

You stood most of the night at the side of the room, watching me dance. When I came over, you took my hand; we held hands behind the folds of my shirt. You refused to dance, you wanted to watch me. Boaz was drinking with his friends from the orchard. That was the night he first talked to Hiram, who came to the party with an army knife in his belt. Was he expecting an invasion from our neighbor village? He wasn't drinking, he stood behind you, watching Boaz, his hand on the hilt of the knife. Maybe he was already thinking up what would soon happen.

Boaz came over to get you to dance. You refused him. Hiram watched you refuse him. Boaz grabbed you by the hand. He was drunk, he picked you up in his arms, this time he lifted you up above his head. Then he staggered, he almost fell. Everyone could see how angry you were. It was terrible for everyone to see you like that, ashamed, furious, saying nothing. He set you down, walked away, leaving you alone to hold my hand for the rest of the night. Other men came to ask you to dance. You refused. "I'm here with Kim," you said, an explanation requiring explanation, never given.

That was the first time we saw them together, Boaz with Hiram bending toward him, he could have been whispering, he might have been telling him something in a low voice for the first time, once only; then Boaz looked over, he looked at you fast, then at me, the two of us together. From that moment, December 31, 1971, we had only two months left.

Each time you become more than you were a moment ago you are involved in a transgression; that is what happened that night after you and Boaz went back to your room. I couldn't sleep, I walked about in the twilight, Simon walked with me. He hadn't been to the party, he didn't say a word. Each time we went past, you were at your window, looking down at us, smoking.

That was the crossroads, an all or nothing, all of the past against your whole future. To go on from that moment you have to betray the past. If that night you watched me until morning it was because you thought I was carrying your future. You didn't need me; anyone would do. You only needed to love. That impersonality in love, is that the crime of which you accuse me when you say I dropped Simon for Dov, Dov for you, you for the next one? Love is not a sublime glue that sticks you forever to this one, to no other. Love is not an enduring attachment, why should it be? Sooner or later someone gets cold feet, runs back to the old slippers, the faithful dog by the fire.

Because you were forbidden I imagined you would last forever, because the day finally came when we went to see a film in Safad. We sat in the back of the truck, on the hard, narrow benches. We were looking at each other constantly. You were cold, you shivered and huddled close to me. The others were in the front. That was the first time I had you alone to myself away from the farm, without Boaz and Hiram, his watchdog.

When we were driving back to the farm you said, "Why don't you ever show me your love?" I remember leaning very close to you, to whisper. That is not what you wanted.

You were there to offer yourself, I to receive you.

We went back to my room; we sat, as always, opposite each other. You asked me again, "Why don't you ever show me how much you love me?"

Show you?

You came over and sat next to me on the bed. You put your arm around my shoulders. For the second time your cheek rested against my cheek. You had been chewing cloves. I sat awkwardly. The next move had to come from me, you had done all you could. It was I who had to put my arms around you, bend you back, put my lips to your neck. I did nothing.

That was the first time you began to reproach me. You did it with your eyes, saying nothing. They fixed themselves on a distance over my shoulder, where you seemed to be looking at some certainty I had not yet glimpsed. If I happen to recall you the day I am dying I will remember you like that, vulnerable, not knowing what to do next, biting your lip with shame, your hand forgotten on my hand against my thigh. If things had been different you would have pushed me down on the bed, then it would have been easy.

Without a word, you swing your jacket off the bed, step out of the room. The next evening, after you have spent a day in bed with a migraine, you make the same approach while I sit quietly on my bed.

You have to leave. It is close to eight o'clock. I see you gather yourself together. By the time you have zipped the suede jacket, there is no trace of that earlier presence, sitting with her head bowed, long hair hiding the shame, bent over her knees on the bed next to me as I do nothing. I do not even put my hand on your hair.

When I walk out of my room it is cold; I hear the telephone ringing down by the laundry; no one else, not even Devora, is expecting a call. Simon comes up behind me to walk as far as the *mo'adon*, still silent. When he turns he crosses the path with Hiram, who must have been on guard duty that night. I haven't seen him all day in the orchard. What has he been up to, skulking somewhere, making sure you are in bed with a migraine, walking in a circle around the chicken house, following me up to the ruins when I go alone in the afternoon?

I walk in quietly to the meeting. The color comes up in your cheeks. Your eyes do not flinch but everyone can see you are remembering the woman with her head bowed over her knees ten minutes ago next to me on my bed.

Right then, we might have known we would not grow old together on the small farm near the border. If I had known I would pay with our future would I have stepped back? Never! If I could keep you near me through a comradeship of days and nights in place of what we have been through, would I choose it? Never!

The next day you were assigned to be my teacher. This did not happen by chance. You will instruct me in Hebrew. I will come back from work two hours early every day for lessons. "If you don't watch out," you say, "by the time Larissa gets here she will know Hebrew better than you do." Boaz has no objection. He cannot object to a collective decision, even if Hiram insists you have arranged it.

One day, repeating my lesson for you, stumbling over the impossible alphabet, you say, "I understand now why it is not good for the teacher to love the pupil too much."

February 11th
Afternoon

I am perfecting the way to come back. I am working on it every time I go out of the cottage. So far, it works when I go over the bridge with Jessica. Something in the light, suddenly one sees, chestnut tree, two-hundred-year-old shade, boys tossing crumbs up into the air, crumbs falling. An aspect to things. As if it had happened over and over, as if one had seen it exactly like this over and over. Chestnut tree, two-hundred-year-old shade, the crumbs falling, the boy running away from the birds. Is that it? Between one step and the next, suddenly, in broad daylight, at a turning of the path, near the far gate, in the meadow? Something comes through. Moments, in which whatever is not usually apparent, becomes apparent. One sees what is there. It begins with stillness. Things slow down, become weighty, rooted. The light gets to you. In and for itself gets you, cuts away, surfaces, resistances, gets under the skin, awakens.

You saw me going from one to the other, from Devora, whom I threw over for Simon, whom I left for Dov, whom I abandoned for you, whom I would forget the minute someone new came on the scene.

If that sequence was anything at all, it was the Impersonal moving on, shattering attachments for the sake of going farther. It is only the lost love that lasts. Dov's for me, mine for you, Simon's for the lost homeland, Devora's for that simple man who slept away his leave with her. And yours? Yours, the only love that has pulled itself out by the roots.

I suppose it is absurd to think you might have come here with me, might be sitting by the fire Margo has just built up behind my back as I write to you at the window. No doubt you're right, ten months from now the sight of you entering a room would not make me weep. There would be no savage grace in your hand falling along my shoulder. I would take you for granted when you set down a pot of breakfast tea on the plank table where I am writing. Maybe you would ruffle my hair as Margo has just done, reminding me to come for lunch, promising to send Jessica to fetch me.

Maybe I wanted you for that unexpected Canaanite wildness, possible only at the border, in that collective in its first year not quite what the founders who sent us there had in mind for the small farm near the border. Maybe they hadn't correctly calibrated our youth, the sixty of us thrown together in our isolation, our ignorance of our neighbors, the lure of the borders. When you came to my room, you spoke a language not quite English, some odd throwback, densely, unashamedly poetic.

There was the story of the dybbuk, then you remembered the River Keshot, the wide deep river of knowing; you didn't wonder then what you were saying, sitting next to me on the bed, your head on my shoulder, that long dark heavy hair of yours falling straight down over my breast.

How strange you were then, my beautiful one.

"Woe and woe," you said, wringing your hands, bent over my lap with muffled laughter, "We have the idolatrous instinct, that's what we have. Because of us maybe one day Araht will be punished? The members will be driven out? Araht will exist no longer?"

Then, you lift your head, you draw back the hair out of your eyes. Your upper lip is delicate; it curves in a fine bow. You say, "Why don't you ever touch me?"

"I never knew you wanted me to touch you."

Your eyes are hooded, darker than they were before you started laughing. But my hand is already on your breast.

Because you have said these words, I have become the one who may touch the breast of a woman. Five weeks after you first came to my room, you have made me into the bearer of unthinkable rights. Merely by wanting me to want you I now can want, touch, take to myself, the original body of love.

Is this a moment when you imagine I would think of the soldier? Suddenly, I am one of those privileged to desire as he was privileged to desire. I, until now the one who bestowed, am now receiver of this raw blessing.

Because it is love, because I am baffled by my transformation, I do not know if you want me to go on touching you. Then for the second time you laugh in my face.

But what will happen? Which one of us knows what to do next?

I brought my lips within a breath of your breast. I did that.

On another day I kissed you for the first time. You were lying next to me in your suede jacket on the bed. These things were awkward at first, two not knowing how to go farther. It is you who came to lie down next to me on the bed, thinking I must be asleep after the afternoon shower. If you did this, why do you turn away when I, after thousands of years, turn back finally to kiss you?

Next day you come foolishly; you can't sit still, you tease me for being too slow, too fast, always awkward. You wander around picking up books, turning over Dov Aviad's letters, stand at the window with your back to me, jeering, "Maybe you only love me for my body."

"Go find Boaz," I say, "tell him for me you're not worth the trouble."

"I'm the trouble?"

"Some people would rather start fights than be in love."

"Some people have no idea what love means."

"You mean me?"

"You know what will happen, the minute you have me, you won't want me. If I give myself, you'll throw me out. I'll end up begging you to come back. Only I will never, I won't do it. I'll get rid of you first."

That night you sit in the *mo'adon* next to Boaz. He and Hiram are playing chess; neither of them pays attention to you. Boaz is absorbed in the game, Hiram glances at me furtively over his shoulder whenever Boaz bends over the board. They have an hourglass; when the sand runs down, the turn goes to the other side. I don't take my eyes off you. Let the kitchen boss stare if she wants to. The three of them are knitting, endlessly knitting. Simon is wandering around barefoot in the snow. Devora is crouched in her room learning to transpose desire in the Yemenite way into longing for God. I don't take my eyes off you; you never glance up, not once.

That night, from the window of my room I watch the darkness of your window. After an hour or so a light flares up, you are there, lighting a cigarette, still not looking at me. I put my hand flat against the glass. You smoke, you bend your head back, lost in thought. You never glance over at me, not for two hours. Then you go back to bed.

The next morning I bring you a letter. I stand at the door to my room until I see Boaz go down to the orchard with the others. The truck drives off the farm, Simon is huddled by himself under an army blanket, his hair matted and snarled. I run down the stairs, cross over to your building, race up the stairs to your room.

I knock, I wait. You say softly, in that low voice you know how to use, "*Mi zeh?* Who is it?" As if it could be anyone else.

You are still in bed; I come to sit next to you at the edge of the bed. You reach up to embrace me, the covers fall back, you are wearing a rose-print flannel nightgown. Later you say you are happy I have seen you like that, now I know you have not made love with him.

Now I know!

I am dressed in work pants and boots, a heavy jacket. I have a knife and clipper at my waist. There is the languorous femininity of you in bed. You have fear in your eyes, you are afraid I am ending things. You grab the letter out of my hand, "Don't do anything, Kim, not before we have a chance to talk. First we will talk the way we do, you know how you are, always going to wild conclusions. So what if yesterday I was afraid? Does that matter?"

Sometime during the day you manage to give me a letter. It is written in Hebrew, I can't make out a word. Was it in the mailbox after lunch? Did you slip it into my hand under the table? Did you have Boaz give it to me when we were on our way to the orchard, as if there were nothing to fear from him?

During the day I take your letter out of my jacket pocket. I am working that day across from Simon, who never talks to me. You know I will not ask him to read me your letter, even for me that would be going too far. At times, trying to decipher the letters, I think you have written the letter I always waited to receive from my sister, telling me she was going to die.

In the afternoon when I come for my Hebrew lesson I run fast from the orchard, clutching your letter. You laugh when I come in breathless, you know exactly why I have been running. Every time I show you I am desperate you are at ease, relieved, without doubt, a believer. You offer to translate your letter, I refuse, I am angry at you. "I had to write in Hebrew, you'll see why. You'll know why when you know what I am writing."

I cannot forgive you the long silence last night at the *mo'adon*. Today gossip stops every time we enter a room. You of all people have grown oblivious, daring people to imagine what no one can imagine.

You lean across the table. You take me by the shoulders. "You will listen," you say. "I will read to you."

I put my chin in my hands. I was stubborn like this too, when anyone tried to tell me my sister had gone away to school, when no one said she was dead, when everyone pretended she'd come back someday.

"When I'm writing to you, I don't feel that I have room for anything more than this obscure pain which fills me and all my body."

I'm like that too.

"Kim, isn't the fact that I'm writing in my own language a proof? People keep disturbing me from writing and waking me up from this special sleep I'm sinking into when writing to you. I wish I would be able to translate what I wrote exactly because if I miss anything I might lose something more dear than anything else in the world. Your love, the beauty between us, the expression of your love and mine, the tenderness and the beauty in such an expression."

It is late. The time for the Hebrew lesson is over. I have to get back to the toolshed, where we are cleaning the clippers, sharpening saws, polishing knives. I take the letter from you. I fold it carefully into the breast pocket of my muddy work shirt. We say nothing about later but we both know you are coming.

I hurry with my shower after work; I don't want you to arrive when I am in the shower. I want to dry my hair over the heater, I will wear musk beneath my arms. When I walk back into my room you are there. Before I can step back you take the towel off me. When you touch me I am shaking so hard, your hand, then your arm, then even your shoulders start shaking. You say, "I have never been shaking like this in all my life before."

I know you will not dare to remember this.

It is I who unbutton your jeans, you who wear nothing beneath them, who are naked under your sweater, who are lying naked to my nakedness next to me in bed.

February 15th
Afternoon

Why not let love go where it will, end where it must, if it must end? Because we are women the true face of love, its hazard, its impermanence showed itself only that much more acutely. Ten months from now you might have turned into my dearest friend. Suppose we found out we liked one another because we both cook fast. I might grow a sense of humor, you might discover an affinity for English tea. When we walk out at night your hand, always larger than mine, might suddenly have grown smaller.

How do you know what would happen if you get on the bus this morning with a small bag, drive down to the airport, arrive here unexpectedly? If you stop at the post office, they will tell you where David and Margo live. You can ask for the family with twins, with five children, for the American woman living in the cottage. A little girl with a squint will take you to find me, she'll run away fast when I hear your footstep over the bridge, throw open the window, shout your name ten times running. Sena. Sena. Sena. Sena. . . .

I don't ask you to come to me, I have never asked.

How could I ask you to entrust your first steps in the world to me? What do you risk? A marriage that will end anyway? A year, two years from now you will walk out on each other, he because he cannot forgive you for never having loved him, for marrying him because you couldn't have Roni, for loving me more than you loved Roni. You'll walk out on him because he's going to show you by habit how violent he is.

There was a time when I might have said you belonged to me. What does that mean? You could come in the afternoons, sometimes early in the morning before I was awake if Boaz had been out on night patrol. The sense of a stolen hour remained, but your fear of transgression no longer existed. When I think of you your hair is always spread out over my body, over my breasts, over my thighs, as if you have wished to drown me in you so that you can be certain I will never leave you.

Then, your fear comes back; now you too are aware of the gossip, although most people still cannot believe what is impossible to believe of you. Zach, who lives next door to me, up the other staircase, his wall papered against my wall, watches us whenever we are together. When you come in, you always whisper. Then, you bring me a small radio, you never say a word until the news, the music, the incomprehensible chatter covers up even our whispering. You have noticed the friendship between Boaz and Hiram. We both know it has grown up because of us, because of what Hiram tells Boaz about you. That is his way of expressing the desire you feel for me. He builds his closeness to Boaz with a glance, an intake of breath, a passing look, a look of surprise (fake), a transparent, veiled suspicion.

Boaz does not fully believe, that is clear from the way he walks with me between the trees in the orchard. Hiram cannot penetrate his vanity; Boaz will not believe the heat is on between you and me. Then of course there is Dov Aviad.

Some weekends he comes up to visit, driving fast in his father's car. For a time the four of us spend time together, we have tea in your rooms, we drink sweet Carmel wine sitting on the floor in my room. There are the ways we let each other know we belong to each other, gestures too subtle we think for men to notice, expressions we are certain they cannot read. When women love they no longer follow the codes men have cobbled together. It must be their sense of possession that sets us free, some million-year-old rage that makes it easy in moments like these for you to betray your husband, for me to keep what is happening from Dov, while everyone is beginning to know something. Hiram stands guard, interrupting us in the *mo'adon*, when we happen to be alone in the dining room together, coming upon us in the grain storage room, when I am helping out a day in the kitchen, when you have come in unexpectedly with a message for the kitchen boss. Zach, his ear pressed to the wall, there is no way of knowing if he hears what you do not want him to hear when you press your hand over my mouth, hard.

Then, Simha begins to limit the time of the Hebrew lesson. There's too much work in the orchard he says, although it is the slow season of cutting back, smearing the wounds with black pitch. Simha watches closely now to make sure I am back to work on time. Therefore I am constantly running, up from the orchard to you, back down to the toolshed, back to my room to shower before you get there on any day Boaz has a security meeting, or is off the farm on kibbutz business, the only days now when you take off your clothes.

You say, "Time is running out. Can't you feel it? I knew the first day I set eyes on you I would say good-bye to you one day forever."

You live now as if you know this will be the last ten days, the last week, the last time you kiss me. You begin to quarrel with Boaz; you never mention me, he will not yet bring himself to know what everyone else is finding out. In the orchard, he works next to me, across from me, behind me, climbs my ladder to help me down, goes with me on errands to the shed in the upper orchard, shows up suddenly to help me carry tools. One day he tells me the story about the gang rape; I refuse to believe him, I am not afraid of him. In time I will have to be afraid. He can keep you from me, he has that power. How he has come to have it I don't understand but I know he will use it.

One night there is a movie on the kibbutz; you are sitting in front of me, next to Boaz; you turn to look back at me with a brooding, measuring gaze. Maybe because of your hooded eyes, the impression they give of following into the distance what has already been lost, this gaze is intercepted. First by Hiram, then by Zach, then finally by Boaz who sits up straight in his chair, folds his arms over his chest, looks over your head at Hiram as if giving in, surrendering. I am aware of these currents even if you are not; you look at me in the flickering darkness. Devora wakes up for the first time in weeks, looks at me sharply, with interest. Just then, almost an hour into the film, Simon walks into the room, swinging the door behind him, breaking the tension.

After the movie Boaz and Hiram go off on guard duty. This is their night of love, they will stalk and investigate, rifles across their chest, they will cross back beneath our windows. Tonight a desire they will never recognize starts its slow turn into violence. They will invent intrusions down by the lower farm, where the wire has been cut near the chicken house. They will plan raids on the border caves, where they will snake up from behind to take captives. Meanwhile they will cross back behind our buildings, where you are sitting with me on the bed. We know something has happened that can now not be reversed, the something you have always expected, you who brought it about with a single look of desire.

That night, you say you want to belong to me. What do you mean, belong to me? You don't care about your work, the farm, the new barn, the children who will be born, you don't care about your marriage. For the first time you say, "You know I love you more than Boaz. Doesn't the fact that I'm saying it make you believe it?" I have no idea why you are trying so hard to convince me. I have always known it, I have always believed it.

You are shivering in your suede jacket; you put your face in your hands. I try to draw back your hair, to breathe against your cheek, to whisper reassurance. You shrug me away. "I hate it when you touch me like that. Then I think maybe there is something in your love, something heartless."

You are fascinated by the Mandelbaum Gate, through which some years ago there was the single passage between Jerusalem and the Old City. You know all about Ha-ram al-Sharif, you have studied history at school, where David set up his altar. But no one mentioned David's pagan ways, his nakedness, his love for Jonathan, his dancing. "My sister says she will leave the kibbutz someday, Roni says he will study art in Tel Aviv, I know a girl from my group who went to Paris. I would be nothing without a kibbutz. Even as a student, what gift do I have? Because I speak English, I'll study literature? Because I study literature I'll live in an apartment alone, with neighbors who are not comrades, only neighbors? Some people have only one world which for them is possible; this is my possible world. I can't explain to you, you are a wandering person, always here and there, moving from apartment to apartment. Your poor daughter! If we don't bring her here, what will become of her? Will you ever go home? Maybe you will just drift on, you and Simon, sooner or later he'll forgive you, he still wants to save you, off you'll go to another kibbutz when life here becomes impossible. You know why I want to help you? It's not because of you. It's because of your daughter. The daughter of a mother like you needs a kibbutz. You know why I sent you to my so-called parents? They will take you in when you have nowhere else to go. Somehow, I don't know how, you made a good impression. When you go there to live, when you don't want to live here anymore, when you are tired of me or the kibbutz throws you out, I'll be able to see you when I go visit."

"I hate it when you talk like that."

"You never know when I am joking. You have no sense of humor. Sometimes I think you are not even a Jew.

A Jew without a sense of humor? On the other hand, who would think you are an American with your crazy kind of talking?"

Crazy, because I think you should love me? Crazy, because I don't understand why you married Boaz in the first place? Crazy, because I am not terrified when you want to belong to me? "You want to belong to me? Good. I accept you."

"You are not joking. That is the trouble with you. With such things, you are never joking."

That night you write to the therapist you had seen as a child. They had been worried about you at the kibbutz, going about alone on your bicycle, wearing boy's clothes. The first year you sat with your back to him. You never said a word. The next year you turned to the side. He too said nothing. Sometimes he read to you. In the third year you turned to face him.

Because of this letter you go away from the kibbutz a few days later to speak with the therapist. He is in private practice now. So after all, our love has taken you to Jerusalem. I wait for your call next to the laundry; by dark it has still not come. I must arrange to get the truck to pick you up from the road. Dov Aviad calls although it is not Monday; he is surprised when I answer. He admits he calls all the time to know the phone will be ringing somewhere close to me.

I can't stay on the phone. What if you are trying to call that moment? You will have missed the last bus, I have to arrange for the truck to get you. He says, "I have the impression I am losing you to Sena. My grandmother tells me there are some people, for them friendship means even

more than love. Maybe it is this friendship you have with
Sena?"

"I'll call tomorrow. I'll explain everything tomorrow.
I'm waiting for Sena. What if she calls and the phone is
busy? What will she do? Stay alone on the road in the
dark? I'm waiting to arrange the truck."

"I don't think you will call tomorrow. If you call tomorrow, I don't think you will explain."

The minute he hangs up, the phone rings. I am standing there without a jacket, in my heavy sweater. The wind
cuts through as if I am meant to understand there is now
no way to warm myself. Love knows when it is about to
break with its own impossibility.

You are standing beneath a light, on the outskirts of
Safad, very young and forlorn. I have brought a sandwich
for you to eat. You say to me, "I can see you are a mother
after all."

Finally, we are back in my room. You are sitting across
from me. You have not taken off your jacket. You have not
embraced me when we walked inside.

"You don't have to tell me," I say. "I know what has
happened."

Your therapist has advised you never to speak to me
again. He has told you I am a dangerous woman. He has
said Boaz is a decent man, why shouldn't you be happy
with him? He says your wish to belong to me is nothing
but the confusion you felt when you were a child, when
your foster mother threw you out of the house. He says, if
you go on with me you will end up like you were then. He
reminds you, you used to sit with your back to him, without talking.

That night you swore to me you would never take his advice.

By the following morning, Boaz had found my letter to you. He found it, not in the drawer with your sweaters and scarves, not among your papers, not with your underclothes and socks. He found it in the last page of a book you had slipped under the sink in the foyer, behind the box of wash powder, covered with brushes.

We met by chance the next morning when I went to work. It was very cold. The moment I saw you I knew. You came up to me with a look of sorrow on your face. That is the face I remember, as if you never had any other expression, no yearning, no desire, no smile of half hiding, nothing stern, aloof, unapproachable, no visionary zeal, nothing tender, only your hooded sorrow, the fatalism, your resignation.

It was not Boaz, not your therapist, not your life on the kibbutz, your dreams of its future driving us apart; it was not your fear that I would stop loving you; it had nothing to do with your desire to belong to me. You wanted to suffer for me, that was the only love you were able to imagine. You wanted to lose me, to have me torn away, to send me from you because that was the only love you understand. You are the architect of all this, not the kibbutz, not marriage, not Boaz, not even I in agreeing to leave because you had promised Boaz never to speak to me.

"You know me," you added, with a broken voice, "if I say a thing, I do it."

But that same day you came secretly to see me. I was working extra hours in the kitchen because I did not want to go back to my room after work. Simon was sitting on the truck outside, whistling his Egyptian love songs. He had developed a habit by then, everyone noticed. He'd pick up a melody only so far, then break it off. He'd start another, annihilate it. I saw him through the screen door, he had started going barefoot by then, his feet were swollen. You came into the room behind me, dragged me by the hand into the storeroom, pushed the door shut behind us. You stood in front of me, you put my hands on your breasts. You said, "I'm not the sort of person who is going to cry about this. If I have to give you up, I give you up, we both knew it would happen sooner or later."

A few days later Simon disappeared. We didn't hear from him. The security branch was sent out to find him. They thought he might have been kidnapped by terrorists. Dov Aviad came back. While Dov was there you kept away from me. Dov came to me late at night the way he used to; I was always awake, crying. He would put my head in his lap. "You don't have to say anything, you don't owe me an explanation. Boaz told me he doesn't want you with Sena, not to see her, not to speak with her. Maybe he's in love with you. Now he hates you. He wants to keep you from Sena only to hurt you. And Sena agrees."

He says, "Now you will mourn for her, you will go away into your pain. Already when I put my arms around you you are not there. I feel you slipping away. Soon, you will not answer my letters. When I come to see you, you will lock your room. And what will become of me then? I told you that I had difficulties in finding someone I could talk to. Two weeks before reporting to the reserves I met the girl who I mentioned once or twice to you, the pianist.

And really she was something special. We used to talk over the phone a lot, and really in a way got very close. Last week I met her, and believe me, it was like drinking water after tasting wine. And that was exactly why I was afraid of you. After you, every girl in the world automatically is at a loss. And to find a younger version of Kim Chernin is something impossible. I knew it and felt it from the start, and now it's just the truth."

"If you want that girl, you can have her. I'm not holding you back. You think she's so special, why bother with me?"

"Maybe I think highly of that girl, but I don't love her and you know it. Maybe I was wrong talking about her, but you know I don't think of you as a real woman. For me you are something above that. And I just couldn't realize that you could become jealous."

"You couldn't imagine I could become jealous? Would I even have this friendship with Sena if you hadn't gone away, gone back to Haifa, gone back to your special pianist?"

"I don't deny I feel resentment toward our relationship. It is true I can't see a future for us, but I don't bother thinking about future relationships. I just know I want you."

Do I make him say these things because they are things I want you to say? Do I torment him because I cannot reach you? I don't believe you gave me up because I am a woman. I believe, if you ever love anyone again, you will give him up too, even if it is Roni, because giving up is what you mean by love.

Now that I am gone, Dov Aviad calls you every day. You comfort Dov Aviad. He cannot go on without me, just as I cannot go on without you. You would not believe how cool your voice is when you say this; the contempt comes through, although you say you feel pity for both of us. Of course, there is no longer any reason to pity you.

February 17th
Late Night

I hope you don't think I am writing all this for you? I write to testify, to exorcise, to commemorate, to call up, to savage, to set down. What does all this have to do with you?

It was you who taught me the sixty Biblical names for Jerusalem. Then, I was able to call you "My City, My Holy Mountain." I would call you Hephzibah. God's name for Jerusalem. It means "my delight is in her."

So what?

Simon had been staying in the Arab village up the road. Of course, it never occurred to us to look for him there. We couldn't imagine friendship between ours and theirs, we hadn't imagined Simon would turn to them when he was desperate. When he came back, his face was pale, rapt, almost transparent, as if the weeks he spent lying on a mattress wrapped in blankets had turned him into a wandering rabbi. The minute he came back he started writing letters to me again; in the orchard he talks end-

lessly, calls me his sister, says nothing will ever come between us. His love for me has grown pure; it comforts him
to know that someone like me is in the world.

Someone like me!

Things move fast now. You and I have set in motion
the disintegration of our small time together. I think it
started the moment you looked at me in public with pure
desire.

Devora decides to go back to Jerusalem. She will stay
with her parents until she finds an apartment. Kibbutz life
is not for her. She wants to study Yemenite music and culture. She has written to a friend of her father's at the Hebrew University in Jerusalem. Everyone seems to know I
will be leaving shortly. How can I leave? Where will I go?
Why will I be leaving? You will not want me to go. You are
the most powerful person in this community, you will keep
me with you. How could you go on without me?

On the weekend Dov comes back to the kibbutz. He
has driven up like a madman to intercept a letter he wrote
to me the day before. He finds it in the mailbox, put in
there by you who come to my room whenever you argue
with Boaz. Dov crushes the letter in his hand. He runs
down the road to the lower orchard. I am not there, we
have been burning branches up by the village. He runs up
the road, back onto the farm, goes to my room, up the
road to the ruins, where he smells the smoke, runs on
down to the orchard to find me. But I too have been running. I run across the whole orchard, through the rows of
bare, clipped, wounded trees, smelling the pitch, toward
the toolshed, where Dov is out of breath, in tears, panting,

bending over, clutching the letter in which he has said good-bye to me.

If I am leaving soon, maybe this is the last time I will ever see him; we go into the toolshed and stand together against the wall, next to the rake, the shovel, the broken barrel where the apples were stored at the edge of the orchard only a few months ago. He holds me as if he knows the letter has ended things between us, although he has ripped it to shreds, renounced it.

Love loves desperation; Dov and I come back together as if you had never come between us. It could be the first night when he came to my room with his rifle and lantern. I know you want me to express contrition, Simon coming to pieces, Dov unable to go on without me, your marriage nearly broken, probably you think I should take responsibility for Devora too, as if she would have found the way to work things out with Dani if I hadn't been there to set a bad example. If I hadn't come, maybe she would have made peace with the kibbutz, found a way to stay on there.

I express no contrition.

One day Boaz slapped you hard when you were walking out of the dining room. He walked away fast, you went after him, pulled him by the shoulder, turned him around, slapped him twice, first your left hand, then your right, turned on your heel, walked straight over to me, so let's not kid ourselves about violence.

I won't recant; I haven't talked you into anything. I don't name it one way or the other, I wouldn't dare. If I don't stop where you expect people to stop, if I don't bolt, take to my heels, run off, plead for the sake of my daughter, don't blame me! You have been from first to last as free as the day you came to my room, to offer me Israel, the kibbutz movement, your influence, your family, your cousin, her connections with Oranim, an entire home-grown future I couldn't have had without you. If that wasn't love, you name it!

In the toolshed after a time Dov holds me at arm's length, both hands on my shoulders, both of us crying because of the letter that never arrived. After the showers, before dinner, he set out to find you. You hadn't spoken to me for four days, given me any sign, no letter, no glance, no acknowledgment when we passed through the kitchen to throw our plates into the sink. Mostly, you kept to your room, the explanation was migraine, you never lit a cigarette in your window at night, you came in late for dinner, disappeared before I would have a chance to brush up against you walking out of the dining room. So Dov went out to bring you to me, indifferent to Boaz's anger.

Dov finds you on the children's merry-go-round, in your Chicago coat, smoking an American cigarette. Boaz is pacing out a slow circle, his hands shoved deep in his pockets. He springs to attention, lunges at Dov. Dov grabs his wrist to stop him. He is on an errand of mercy; he is not afraid.

When you come to my room you sit in your chair by the window. You accuse me, in front of Dov, of not loving you. "Did you try to talk to me even once during these four days?"

Dov goes over to the typewriter and reads some

words I must have written to you. Never mind what they were. I probably said, "I want to worship you."

Dov goes outside; he leaves his jacket with us, it is still bitterly cold although we have already seen the red flowers in the snow. We know that he will be back soon. You throw your arms around me, you are holding me so tight I can't stop you. We hear Dov's footstep on the stairs, we fly apart, the door opens, he comes back to us.

Maybe that was the last hour for me and Dov Aviad. After that things happened fast, the time came when I could not face him. There were nights when you still came to my room, furious with Boaz. Other nights you wouldn't let me touch you. I said, "Sit close to me, I want to talk to you. Turn the radio on. I promise, I won't touch you."

You said, "Now I think you are very corrupt."

"I see that you don't want me to touch you. I see that you are afraid of me."

"I want you to touch me."

When Boaz was on the kibbutz, you were afraid. You said there was nothing to fear, but you jumped up when Zach walked up the stairs on his side. You ran out of my room whenever you heard the security truck come back into the farm after dark.

One day we visited Oranim, where Araht would send us both to study psychology. We visited the library, where three women were at work, their heads bent close together. You pulled out a book, began reading to me in Hebrew. One of the women looked up, stared at you, then suddenly smiled. When we went into the main building a secretary recognized you, stood up to greet you. She said,

"I congratulate you on how beautiful you have become, Sena."

Outside, in the children's zoo, there was a large cage with an owl. When we went past, you grabbed me playfully by the shoulder. "Not here, Kim, on your knees, I warn you."

A girl recognized you and said, "Sena, I didn't know you could speak English so well."

The beautiful old woman you had known as a child, who took your hand and mine when she showed us around, showed us where we would eat, where we would take classes, where the bus would come to fetch us to take us home to Araht. As if there were no obstacle, no impediment to any future we might dream up together.

We went to visit your foster parents. The minute we got there you took me to your room. There was a heavy, green curtain that pulled in front of the door, enclosing the porch. You closed the curtain over us, picked me up in your arms. "You see, I've arranged everything." You lifted me off my feet. You were much stronger than I was. "I've been waiting to do this all day."

Count the days.

Later, your parents walked us past the barn, out to the road. They were singing; it was your father who was singing, quietly, as we walked. They waited with us on the road until the bus came. Your father said, "Now you are our daughter."

On the bus you put your head on my shoulder. We pretended we did not know Hebrew. When two young Arabs addressed us, we answered in English. You rested against me even when you heard them talking about us. You heard them say we were sisters.

We drove back through the valley, our eyes closed, your head on my shoulder. When we waited in Tiberias for someone to come down to get us in the truck I gave you my jacket to wear. No one came for us. We walked through the town, we saw men playing pool in a large room with a bright light. We had made it to the city together, we had tramped about in our future, we had been away from the farm for a whole day, the lifetime of a butterfly, whose wings fluttering in California cause snow to fall at the North Pole. You were wearing my jacket. We walked on down that long boulevard where I had walked alone those months before, waiting for the bus the first day I came to Araht. That night, in my jacket, arm in arm with me, you said, "I am married to you now. Nothing can part us."

February 19th
Early

I hear voices.

All the way down to the water the trees are bare. Smoke comes up out of the chimney in the last house before the sea. Yesterday, we all worked in the garden. Rachel, with an apple, a chunk of stale bread, a fistful of cheese, sat in my lap. Seth pushed the wheelbarrow up and down between the rows of cabbage, even when it was empty. The twins sat in their carriage, staring at everything with their round eyes. Only Jessica worked, pulling weeds in a perfect circle around me. Margo said I would sleep that night. David brought me a cup of tea, rubbed my hands between his. But we all knew, it was doing no good. I was drifting away, the tea, the circle of weeds, Margo crouched next to me in her long woolen skirt, even the children could not save me. I wanted to get back to my cottage, back to my letters to you, to the voices reminding me of a place, high up on a mountain, where someone had loved me.

Then our time together was you in tears. Or perhaps it was I who cried. It was raining, the snow had melted, there was no work in the orchard, Boaz and Hiram were prowling around somewhere, plotting whatever it was they were plotting. You were in danger then. Boaz threw you around your room, you threw him to the floor. Hiram knocked at the door; Boaz told him to go to the devil. He picked you up, threw you on the bed; you kicked him so hard he bent double. You were out of there in two seconds; two seconds later you were with me. That was the first time you asked me to leave, to go back into the world, to your parents' kibbutz, to Oranim, to Jerusalem with Devora. You couldn't stay away from me if I stayed at Araht. You couldn't stay away even for two hours. I had to leave, I would destroy you.

One night when it began to rain I was walking back from Devora's room, where she had been packing. I saw you and Boaz running together, your arms around each other's shoulders, covering your heads with a coat. You were laughing, you ran past me, you didn't see me.

Another time I was sitting in the dining room playing the piano. You came in, sat down next to me, touching my knee. You put your arm around my shoulder. You said you could imagine sitting like that with me on a late night when we were both old women. Boaz and Hiram came into the room. Boaz had been looking for you all over the kibbutz. He said nothing, he walked past us. We both saw the look in his eyes.

When I agreed to leave, you could say good-bye. That is why I agreed to leave. Then, because it was the last time, you felt no remorse. You were no longer afraid of Boaz. You threw your sweater against the wall, threw off your jeans, threw yourself down to throw your arms around my knees. Your hair covered my feet. So after all, I think it was you weeping.

Suddenly, we heard footsteps on the stairs. We both jumped up. We heard a knock at the door. Was it locked?

"*Mi zeh?*" It was you who were speaking, on your feet, holding yourself upright, in that authority you can pull out for any emergency. Finally, after a long silence, "It's Hiram, let me in."

We are hurrying to get dressed. I pull on my sweater, you are quicker than I, we hear him scraping his feet.

"Is Sena there?"

I have finished dressing but I have had no time to put on my boots. You are sitting in the chair, fully dressed, you have a roguish look that will give you away. I sit on the bed, I ask Hiram why he is looking for you. He opens the door.

"Boaz is going all over the kibbutz with a knife." He notices that I am not wearing shoes. He takes in the ex-

pression on your face. It seems to give him enormous satisfaction, as if we had finally brought a climax to his suspicions. Since neither of us moves, he says again, "Boaz is
going all over the kibbutz with a knife."

I say, "And you are planning to protect her?"

"It's you he's after. Not Sena."

He has an excited, feverish look; he and Boaz have
been drinking. He runs his hand through his hair. He
looks very handsome that night, his hair combed smooth,
straight back, his face struggling not to show his excitement. He says he has been trying to reason with Boaz;
both of us smile.

You leave the room with him, glancing at me once as
you walk outside, perfectly in control of yourself. The
minute you go out I lock the outer door to the building. I
come back to lock the door to my room.

I wait; I can hear someone shouting outside. Your
voice comes up through the open window. The heater is
burning down; there is a stench of paraffin. I hear Simon's
voice. Everyone is shouting in Hebrew, Boaz is shouting,
Hiram is egging him on. There are footsteps up the stairs;
it is impossible to say how many.

Someone is hammering at the outside door. Pounding
with fists, throwing himself against it. Someone is trying to
drag him away from the door, the pounding begins again,
the door flies open with an incredible loud crack against
the wall. Boaz is screaming in English, the two of you are
shouting in Hebrew, Hiram somewhere in the background
cursing.

You say, in English, "If you lay a hand on her I will

never speak to you again. You know me. If I say it, that is what I will do."

There is a long, long silence. I listen to all this as if it were not happening. I am perfectly calm. You are there, you will protect me. Now the pounding starts on my door, on the door to my room. Boaz is hammering it with his fists, throwing himself against it. There is a loud cracking sound, the door splinters, another tremendous heave, it buckles but the lock holds. Through the crack I can see you struggling with him. He has thrown you to the ground. You shout, keeping your voice muffled, "Boaz, I am warning you." Through the opening I see the flash of his knife. Still, I know you will not let him harm me. I am calm. I stand with my arms folded. He is shouting, "I am going to kill you. I am going to kill you. Do you hear, Kim Chernin? I am going to kill you."

The crack is getting larger. If he keeps this up, he will kick through it. I rush over to the wall, knock on it, calling to Zach. I tell him to come at once, Boaz is breaking in the door, he has a knife. I hear Zach leave the room, go down the stairs, I hear him come back up my side of the stairs, then he is running down, up his own stairs again. I hear him enter his room. He comes over to the wall, whispers, "Hiram is there. I can't get past him."

"Go get help," I insist, trying to keep my voice calm. I don't know why I am trying to keep my voice calm. Maybe it has just occurred to me that Boaz has finally won, his violence will prove that our love leads inevitably to violence.

Suddenly it grows quiet. Somehow you have managed

to grab the knife, fling it outside. You run after it. Through the widening crack in the door I see you moving fast; I think you are running away to leave me alone with Boaz. He is pacing back and forth in front of my door. There is a sound of running feet. I hear your voice; you are shouting to Simon, Hiram is shouting. The three of you have made your way under my window. Simon has the knife, he is barefoot, he isn't wearing a shirt, he is crouched low one hand held out in front of him, the knife clutched close to his chest, stalking Hiram, backing him away, leaving the stairs clear for you and Zach and Zach's Finnish girlfriend to run back inside as Boaz starts kicking in my door.

The next morning everyone knows something has happened; no one can believe it has happened to you. You are walking around the kibbutz with your head high, aloof, above gossip. Boaz stays in his room for three days; you bring him dinner. Dov Aviad calls on Monday at the telephone near the laundry. You pick up the phone, you say Kim is leaving the kibbutz, Kim is going to Jerusalem with Devora. Reluctantly, when he insists, you give him Devora's number.

Then it is the last day. You are reading a letter you have written to me in Hebrew. You have read to me from Ecclesiastes. Now there is nothing to look forward to anymore; what you have given you have taken away. For your sake I am going back into the world, I am leaving our mountain.

Devora's father comes for us; you stand beside me at the car while I put my knapsack inside. Someone calls you, you embrace me quickly, say something to the kitchen boss. You too are leaving the farm that day with Boaz. You are going to visit your parents. We drive down the mountain. There is the red flower. I've forgotten its name, so perhaps, after all, I too am capable of forgetting.

At the airport, after they have looked through the chocolates where there are no hidden bombs, when I am walking away from you to the plane, it occurs to me you could come with me, push your way past the guard, get on the plane with me. I could take you by the arm to make you come with me, talking about that cottage in Scotland you would never let me mention because you couldn't resist it. The bridge over the river, the bull in the field, the path to the sea, the bare trees, the smoke coming up out of the last stone cottage before the sea. The wood turner and his wife who live down the road. Margo and David who want me to drive into Edinburgh with them, to see the doctor.

I see clearly, as never before, into another world. I see pure light. This is the light, from which after a time the universe will be unfolded. I think its name is Shekinah. I am standing by a pool so deep and pure, azure and silver cannot suggest its beauty. This world is on fire and now there is wind.

I know you will not finish these letters, I never intended them for you. I don't care if you stamp them out, hide them better this time from Boaz, throw them in the garbage. Maybe when we met we were both beyond the crossroads. You wanted me for a friend, I wanted you for a sister, we became lovers. Was that the same thing? You have turned back, you have gone back to the everyday. I shall pass through a more severe gate. It would mean much to me if you knew I made a choice. This too is a strength, this not stopping, this going on to where it all leads, to what love makes of itself when it is not abandoned.

I told you about The Messengers? They come every night, toward morning. I think they want to help me sleep. One of them whispers in your low voice. She wants me to believe it is you, over the terrible distance. Let your long, dark hair down over my breast. Now I shall sleep. It is promised.

The
*R*eturn

❦   ❦   ❦

LATE FALL

1991

Of course it makes a mockery of my life's work. What else would you expect from Kim Chernin? I always thought there was malevolence afoot, deliberate deception, to say nothing of memory having its own reflex of withholding. If this is the story Kim Chernin set down, so be it.

I'd rather believe Simon was holding the knife to keep Hiram from getting upstairs. If Boaz tried to kill Kim Chernin how close did he come? If he had broken through the door a minute or two sooner, before Sena got the knife from his hand, if he still had the knife when he kicked through the door, what would have happened to me?

Sena in love with Kim Chernin? I'll give that some thought. It makes no difference to me if Kim Chernin was in love with Sena. I repeat, it makes no difference. Sena, on the other hand. She had before her eyes the evidence of Simon. She knew Kim Chernin's soldier. Was Sena likely to risk being cast aside in favor of Kim Chernin's newest passion?

A word of caution, before we go too far. The corrections all through these pages were in Kim Chernin's handwriting. (I, of course, have edited them too.) But, were they letters meant to be sent to Sena? Knowing Kim Chernin as we do, did she shred her memories to hide her love for a woman?

I don't believe it. Why would she? Someone who believes love is beyond law would not hesitate to love a woman. Kim Chernin smashed up her memories because she was a coward. Twice, according to her own code. She ran from the soldier before he could forget her; she ran from Sena, who asked her to run, without once trying to persuade Sena to leave with her. Did she think I wouldn't notice this small detail?

I found her passport. She was at Araht from Rosh Hashanah until just before Purim. She arrived in Scotland toward the end of February. In five months, if her story is true, she managed to mess up Simon, change the course of Dov Aviad's life, ruin Sena's marriage, neglect Devora when Devora was in the major crisis of her life. Because of Kim Chernin Boaz turned violent. She almost brought about a love affair between Boaz and his law-and-order man, who left Araht just after Sena got pregnant. No one has heard from him since.

I know what Kim Chernin would say. The crucial moment in the life of each. Why else out of those sixty people did Devora and Simon, Dov and Boaz, Kim Chernin and Sena drift together?

If Kim Chernin is telling the truth, it was Sena who persuaded her to leave. Knowingly, to protect herself, she sent Kim Chernin back to a world in which she had no mooring. Kim Chernin would have prided herself on not complaining.

When Boaz kicked in Kim Chernin's door none were where they had been a few months earlier. None ever returned to that place. Each had gone over a crossing from which there would be no turning back. Kim Chernin did not cause this. Yet one could wonder if (at least explosively, violently like that) it would have taken place without her.

Of them all, Sena forgot her most completely. Kim Chernin was not the only one who did not survive.

I have read Kim Chernin's letters slowly. (How they came into my possession I shall tell in time.) I began to suspect she had written them to me. She would have wanted to cast herself forward, she must have known she was coming to an end, with those letters she hoped to anchor herself in me. If I had read fast, staying up all night, unable to put them down until I had finished, Kim Chernin would have made her way back.

Yes, back. Of course, back. I must have known she would not stay dead forever.

I developed my own strategy. I took notes, allowed myself to work on them only in the morning, searching out contradictions, gaps, inconsistencies in the story. I'm not convinced Sena came to Kim Chernin's room that first night because she had been secretly longing for Kim Chernin. I doubt if she would have used her family, her contacts on the kibbutz, the promise of helping Kim Chernin bring her daughter because she hoped to keep Kim Chernin for herself. Unless, after all, she saw in Kim Chernin the possibility of the crucial encounter. The one, among all others that breaks through the hardening crust of the self to thrust you forward? I'd hate to believe this. It would mean, when Sena got rid of Kim Chernin she got rid of those larger possibilities.

Just what Kim Chernin would want me to think!

The cunning of that fiend, Kim Chernin! Breaking her memories into fragments. Then, to assemble them could only become a portrait of me. The letter that mattered, Kim Chernin's letter to Sena, the letter discovered by Boaz! It went unsuspected by me. I was dazzled by the soldier running, weeping. She knew I would fall for it. I assembled the oldest story in the world. The older woman betrayed by the younger man. She knew I would be only too happy to know her betrayed. If she is telling the truth I am the fool. Unless one cares to remember how many people she picked up, tossed out, going after her Canaanite sexual secrets.

I think she might prefer that version. Therefore, can we believe it?

The apologetic Kim Chernin would contrive for herself, the sum total of her wisdom? Human beings cannot do without love but they also cannot bear it!

Yesterday, I decided to call Devora's mother. After twenty years I wanted to find out where Devora was. Of course I had wondered before. Who wouldn't wonder? I had picked up the phone, once I had even written a letter. I didn't think Devora would have forgotten Kim Chernin. She had been there the whole time, she would have her own version.

Was that what I wanted? Devora's version? Before the letters arrived, before my own story got kicked in the teeth, my task was reconstruction. The noble warfare: what might have happened, what had been set down. My task was memory.

To my relief, Devora's mother is a generous talker. "Now you'll get the whole story," she says. She tells me Devora is still married to Sol, they live in Maine, she has two children. They moved there from Brooklyn, after they moved from Rhode Island after they went to graduate school at USC, after they left Jerusalem. There is Moshe (seventeen), Gigi (nine). Moshe plays the violin in a rock band; Gigi dances.

Devora teaches ten or eleven classes a week to children. She teaches Yemenite music, dance, old children's songs that are no longer taught to children. To the older kids Devora tells folktales. She works during the hours her children are in school. Lately she has been asked to give workshops for schools, churches, libraries.

Devora's father has had a heart attack in the last year, since then he had a twenty-four-hour spell in which he entirely lost his memory.

Miriam, Devora's younger sister (that wonderful girl whom Kim Chernin met on Mount Carmel, when Sena and Kim Chernin spent their last day together in her room) died in 1977 of an allergic reaction to medication. She was twenty-two, at Smith.

Just before I hung up, Devora's mother told me she had visited Araht in 1983. This surprised me. Because Araht has been out of bounds for me, I made it into an inaccessible world. Or was I afraid people who had known Kim Chernin would be disappointed in me?

Devora's mother found Araht depressing. The food

was unappetizing, people were not friendly. They had lunch with a friend of Miriam's from Mount Carmel who had gone to live there. (She might have been the little girl who looked into Miriam's room when Sena kissed Kim Chernin.) There were some new houses, otherwise nothing had changed.

The farm still hadn't acquired a barn, or diversified its agriculture. People seemed depressed, there was no vitality or enthusiasm. She had the impression that many of the founders were still there. And yes, there were children.

"Araht depressing?"

"You can't live by the view alone. I never thought Devora should be there. Too close to the border. No older people to give balance. Devora's father tried to tell them to grow herbs, to diversify their agriculture. They never listened."

Araht depressing? The small farm on the border, depressing? All the vitality burned out of it twelve years later when Devora's mother went to visit? Maybe the law-and-order faction prevailed, hunted down, drove out its free spirits. Simon, other local prophets, Devora, with her admirable devotions. Sena left a few years later, in despair. She had wanted to create a new type of collective, invent a new educational system, develop relations with the Arab villages, train teachers for the impoverished village of Moroccan Jews.

Devora answers the phone after several rings.

"This is Kim Chernin. Do you remember me?"

"Oh, hi, Kim," as if we had run into each other last week at the library. Almost twenty years later, "Oh, hi, Kim."

"You do remember me?"

"We were very close at Araht."

I see her through the long late-afternoon light of memory in a straw hat on New Year's Eve twenty years ago. There is no reason to cry about this, I do not start crying. "I too had the impression we were close. But there were conversations we never had."

"I used not to be aware of some things then, I was vague, I didn't notice things I would notice now."

"There were things I didn't talk about."

"I've always wished I had asked you some questions. I half noticed things, but since you didn't bring them up and they were painful to you, I didn't think I should mention them."

"Not too late."

"And then there was that incident of course."

Twenty years later it is still that incident. "What did you make of it?"

"I didn't think about it too much. I tried not to. Of course, I wondered if it might have had something to do . . . you know. . . ."

"I know."

"With Sena? But you didn't talk about it and I put it out of my mind."

"Why didn't we talk about it?"

"That was then. Things were different. I've known a lot of women since then who get involved with women. I've felt at home with them."

"I never mentioned Sena?"

"You talked about her all the time. She was going to help you with Larissa, you were going to study together at

Oranim. I could have guessed. You and I took to one another the first time we met. I guess that's why you came to
Araht in the first place."

"Then there were all those things we didn't say."

"Well, I was twenty. But there was that incident, and
the thought passed through my mind, maybe you had
something with Sena. Some people said Boaz tried to kill
you."

"I guess he did."

"It didn't seem likely, and it seemed likely. No one
ever got close to Sena, everyone wanted to."

"I wrote to her a few years ago."

"Whatever happened?"

"Boaz started an affair with a volunteer. He and Sena
had a son by then. I guess he might be eighteen now. He
might be in the army. Then after the divorce Sena met up
again with Roni. He was part of the volunteer army unit
holding down the kibbutz before the collective came. He
was up there for a month or two when you first got there.
I think she only married Boaz on the rebound, because
things didn't get going with Roni. They were in the same
children's group at Mishmar Haemek. So they didn't get
together until she divorced Boaz, then Roni started coming
up to visit and they talked about leaving kibbutz life altogether. He wanted to be a sculptor. She wanted to study at
the university in Jerusalem. Then Mishmar Haemek offered
to send him to learn building design for the kibbutz. After
a while they didn't leave kibbutz life, they moved back to
Mishmar Haemek. She's had four more children, three
boys and a girl. She works as the kibbutz librarian."

"You and Sena never had a chance. Araht wasn't for

you. You and I were caged birds there. You would never have stayed. Didn't you just tell me Sena's still living on her parents' kibbutz? Those people are afraid of life. They've never written a check, paid a bill. The city seems lonely to them; they can't imagine neighbors, not comrades. I don't care how much Sena loved you. You couldn't expect Sena to give all that up. That wasn't just twenty years ago. Israel is still like it was twenty years ago. Two women living together? How would you have made a living? Where would you have gone? To Tel Aviv? You wouldn't have had friends. You would have been in hiding. There wasn't even a woman's movement, was there? In Israel then?"

"Sena, in a way, doesn't remember me at all."

"What good would it do her to remember? Is she ever going to spend one hour alone with you again? Where? On her kibbutz? Does she even have a room to herself? Sena'd better not even think about you, or see you again, or even write to you. Does that mean she doesn't love you? If she didn't love you she'd get right on the phone. I don't care if it is twenty years ago. She'd grab the phone, she'd say, 'Shalom, old chum, hey, how're you doing?' Sena always had her aloof beauty. When you were friends, she was lit up, transported. Everyone was happy for Sena. We were always afraid she would go back to Mishmar Haemek. After you came, when you and Sena were first friends, we thought you might be friends for the rest of your lives at Araht."

"Dov came here a few weeks ago."

"Who's Dov?"

"You called him the soldier with the beautiful face."

"What about him?"

"You don't remember Dov Aviad?"

"Maybe I never met him. Maybe he was there when I was sick. Did you know I got pneumonia when I went to Jerusalem?"

If I had called three months ago, before Dov Aviad came to visit, would this conversation have made me doubt the existence of Dov Aviad?

"You and I went to Jerusalem together. Your father picked us up on the kibbutz."

"I remember you spent time with us in Jerusalem. I took you to Sarid but you didn't want to stay. After that, I was sick for two months. After that, I met Sol. A week later we moved in together. My parents were worried, now they see he must be right for me."

"I saw you after you left Jerusalem. You came to stay with us. I've met Sol. Our dog barked at him."

When Devora was at Kibbutz Araht she tried to introduce Israeli folk dancing, she invited a woman from Gedera to hold a workshop. Kim Chernin showed up, Simon went because Kim Chernin was going, the pregnant woman walked through the steps, then stood to one side clapping. Devora was heartbroken. When she held a workshop on Yemenite music after dinner in the dining hall, no one showed up.

Did the kibbutz fail when it failed to take root in those people who fell for Kim Chernin? I am going to write Devora to ask her that. Perhaps they were its wild core, its passionate future, although I doubt it. People that young never seem to do anything but fall in love.

I used to wonder. If Kim Chernin had fallen apart at

Kibbutz Araht, would I have been able to stake out the place for myself? What if Sena and I had become friends? We would have gone to study together at Oranim. Sena would have become a therapist, a more appropriate destiny perhaps than librarian on her parents' kibbutz.

If Sena had left Kibbutz Araht with Kim Chernin the Sena Kim Chernin loved might be alive today.

This is a dangerous thought. I had better keep an eye out for Kim Chernin. It is she, not I, who would have thought it.

I n September 1972 Dov Aviad returned to Israel from his trip to Scotland. His grandmother had died while he was away. He enlisted in the army for two years of active service. War seemed unlikely. He preferred two years at risk to the relative safety of a desk job. Because he did not sign up for four years as an engineer, he was posted as an officer to an artillery battalion.

On October 5, 1973, Yom Kippur weekend, unusual activities were observed among the Syrian and Egyptian armies. The Israeli Defense Forces (IDF) were put on general alert. This was a routine precaution.

On Saturday, October 6th, the Egyptian Army, following a heavy barrage of fire, began to cross the Suez Canal. Secondary units from the IDF began moving toward the canal along desert roads.

On Monday, October 8th, General Ariel Sharon, whose division was located in the center of the Sinai Peninsula, received orders to move south toward the Giddi

Pass. Later that day he received orders to attack the Egyptian Third Army. Still later that afternoon he received orders to attack in the north of Sinai.

Between Monday, October 8th and Monday, October 15th, Ariel Sharon quarreled with the senior commanders of the southern division. According to him, the surprise Egyptian attack had caused confusion and panic among the command forces. According to them, he had refused to come to the aid of his colleagues, determined to be the first general across the canal regardless of the danger to his forces.

On Monday, October 15th, although the delivery of bridging equipment had been delayed, Sharon began the operation to place his paratrooper brigade on the west side of the canal. He would not be able to reinforce his soldiers. They would fight on their own, unsupported, behind enemy lines.

Sharon's division opened a heavy artillery barrage. The crossing operation started. During the first hours the patrol unit reached the eastern bank of the canal. But the paratrooper division was behind schedule. The Egyptians blocked the road that had been cleared for the transportation of bridging equipment. Sharon ordered the commander of the paratroop brigade to transport his men on dinghies. Within the next few hours the brigade had been transferred to the western bank of the canal. At 3:00 A.M. Sharon showed up with ten more tanks; an hour later another ten arrived. Sharon mounted a bulldozer himself and began breaking through the embankment where it was marked with red bricks.

On the morning of October 16th it became evident

that Sharon's plan had not been fully carried out. His forces had been successful at crossing the canal, they were able to move freely between the two Egyptian armies, but they had not been able to establish a reliable bridgehead.

By 11:00 A.M. on the morning of October 16th the Israeli casualties had reached two hundred; the number of damaged tanks, fifty. On the morning of the 17th, when the first Israeli barges reached the canal, the Egyptians opened fire with Katyusha rockets, then with mortars. Panic set in. Cries of "take cover" could be heard from all sides. During the fighting in the following days Sharon repeatedly claimed the Egyptian army had collapsed. It repeatedly fought back.

On the morning of October 22nd, the United Nations Security Council called for a cease-fire along the Suez Canal. The Israeli government accepted this decision. The general staff was forced to admit that its military objectives had failed. The Egyptians held well established positions on the eastern bank of the canal. More than thirty-six hours would pass before the cease-fire went into effect. Meanwhile the Israeli southern command was ordered to complete the encirclement of the Egyptian Third Army. During this period the fighting was fierce.

Dov Aviad had been assigned to Ariel Sharon's division in the southern command (a rebuke, because he had not enlisted for four years as an engineer?). He was among the first Israeli soldiers to cross the canal in the period of heaviest artillery bombardment. Life had delivered Kim Chernin's beautiful soldier into the hands of an ambitious, vainglorious man.

At first, Dov Aviad was not afraid. In this state he

moved mechanically through routine procedures, charted the path of artillery shells, issued commands, was kept busy. Then, in a moment of distraction, he noticed four paratroopers huddled together in an improvised dugout. From where Dov Aviad stood, some yards away, it was clear that they were shaking violently. Now fear broke through for him too. It didn't last long. Within moments the unreality returned. One night, sleeping next to his truck, he awoke to heavy shelling in his immediate neighborhood. He gathered his sleeping bag, moved to the other side of the truck, fell asleep. When he told me this story he said there was, of course, no safety on the far side of the truck. In an artillery bombardment the entire area is in mortal danger. Morale was low, the army was insufficiently prepared, his unit knew it was alone out there, difficult to reinforce, unsupported.

On Wednesday, October 17th, Dov Aviad saw Moshe Dyan and Ariel Sharon strolling together (yes, strolling) through the heaviest Egyptian artillery fire. After that, morale improved noticeably, although Dov Aviad himself never lost his sense of unreality.

In 1974, when his two years of active duty were over, Dov Aviad enlisted again. He was sent to train cadets in the Golan Heights. He had become a senior lieutenant, the commander of an artillery battalion, a respectable rank for a young man of twenty-six. He had also become something of a legend. When the artillery cadets graduated, ninety percent of them requested Dov Aviad's battalion. Several generals tried to talk him into making the army his career. Something hard, precise, authoritative had come out in him. If he had stayed, he might be a general today, the sort of man who could tolerate his role on the West Bank, who could order his men to fire into a crowd of stone throwers. If he had stayed in the army it is possible he and Simon might have met on a dirt road in Gaza, on the opposite ends of a stone's throw.

In 1975 he signed up for another year of service. The following year he was about to reenlist, believing in the purity of arms that most army men admired in those days. Then something happened. Kim Chernin had predicted it.

One day, when he was training cadets in the Golan Heights, a fast-moving black cloud became visible on the horizon. He had never been in a sandstorm before. When he had made all the right decisions, when he had saved his life and the lives of his cadets with his cool thinking, when he had fulfilled everything that could be asked of a young, tough Israeli soldier who had brought them all back safely to camp, a few days later he sat alone in his truck and sobbed.

A man without a soul does not cry. Dov Aviad had not cried since he had walked back from the beach in Boar Hills because Kim Chernin was not there, because he was going home into the army. He does not remember if he cried when his grandmother died. He is sure he had not cried during his years in the army, although the IDF might be the only army in the world in which it is debated by the general staff whether its senior officers may weep at funerals.

A man who does not cry drinks desolation in the sunrise. He thinks about women in a certain way, he believes at all costs in defending his country. If Dov Aviad is going to worry about his soul, he will have to live again the loss of Kim Chernin, the roundness of his grandmother's death, the death of the enemy soldiers who died in the artillery fire from his battalion in the Sinai. If he can face all this, he can have his soul.

He had by then decided to make the army his career. He hadn't seen Kim Chernin for five years. But he was thinking about Kim Chernin, that's what he told me. She had said he would never work as an engineer. She was right about that. She had told him he would never kill anyone. There she was wrong. She became for him the Image of All Longing because she had once casually said he would never be able to give up his soul. That's what he told me three weeks ago when I picked him up in my car.

He had left a message on my telephone answering machine. It said, "This is a voice from the past." I listened to the message again. This man spoke with an English accent. He called himself Dov Aviad.

Here we enter the domain of old women, ancient mariners, other repetitive talkers until the tale that cannot be told finally emerges. Then the tellers grow silent, release you from their gaze, break the intolerable flow, stare down at their hands. This rarely happens. I am coming to that.

It is like one of those dreams in which you are walking down the stairs, suddenly the stairs aren't there. I go to the door to look out into the garden. Why do I expect it to look different than it did five minutes ago? In the rock pool, slightly ruined, which the gardener has promised to fix, where the tough neighborhood cat has taken to watering an hour before sunset, a violent dislocation has taken place.

Sometime during these years I must have persuaded

myself Kim Chernin had made him up. As if he were only a story I'd been writing in her name. While I am standing here watching the garden change he might be waiting by the telephone twenty years later for Kim Chernin to call.

And I? Am I too waiting for Kim Chernin to call? Is the garden changing because (from the moment I heard his name?) it is she, the Kim Chernin of twenty years ago, who has been looking at my garden?

I should have known. I did not want to believe. Kim Chernin was dead, wasn't she? She had done away with herself, on a rocky cove in Scotland, hadn't she?

I lived for a long time with the man who brought me home from Scotland. Sometimes I tried to tell him how Kim Chernin had come to a bad end, leaving me to assemble what I could of her memories. Then, after our marriage ended, I lived for several years with Kim Chernin's daughter. With her I never pretended. She knew the Kim Chernin who had gone to Israel never came back. She was always kind to me, knowing how hard I was trying to be her mother. She never looked into my eyes. That was her way of being tactful. She went off to Harvard in 1981. Since then, there has been little to stop me from my work of remembering. Most days I take notes during the mornings. In the afternoons I have regular sessions with other people trying to make sense of their past, the life they had as children maybe.

W hen Kim Chernin lived in this neighborhood with her daughter the garden behind her house across the street ran straight up into the woods. In the evening deer would come down through the old rosebushes. The other night I walked up behind Kim Chernin's apartment to pick roses for the kitchen. Kim Chernin had liked wild animals. If she were out picking roses, if a deer came out of the woods, when it caught sight of Kim Chernin it would stop, stare back, she could hold the thing transfixed for a quarter of an hour. When wild animals set eyes on me they bolt.

Last night that didn't happen. Is this a sign? Is Kim Chernin returning?

Some wild night I may remember the Afghan dogs walking around and around the chicken house, one behind the other beneath a sharp shiver of moon across which dark clouds are burning. Or I will dream another of those insatiable dreams from which Kim Chernin will wake up in full possession.

Dov Aviad. Would she want him? She could thumb through my Rolodex, pick up the telephone, dial him directly. I took him to the plane three weeks ago. He lives in a stone house in the Cotswolds, in a village near Chichester. That's all twenty years would mean to her.

I go to bed early. If Kim Chernin comes back it will be late at night. I make sure to eat a good breakfast. She liked to starve until noon, eat nonstop until dinner. I avoid bread. Kim Chernin could have survived years on that farm by bread alone. I'm not kidding. If her daughter looks me in the eyes the next time she comes home for vacation, if she demands the mother who went off to Israel, Kim Chernin will be back in a flash.

Would she call Sena? Would she dare to call Sena?

Several years ago, I wrote Sena to tell her I was coming to Israel. She was living on her parents' kibbutz by then; there would have been no question of Araht. I had been invited to a women writer's conference in Jerusalem. More than fifteen years had passed. I trusted Sena to attribute my difference to that.

Sena invited me to her kibbutz. "I always used to be afraid to have you come, because of what I had done with my life. I thought you would be vindictive. Now I am at peace. Roni and I have been very happy."

After that letter I lost my nerve. I didn't go to the writer's conference, I didn't visit Sena. I didn't go anywhere near Israel. The stamps on the envelope, Sena's handwriting, if anything had the power to bring Kim Chernin back from the dead, they would have done it.

I stayed awake all night, I examined every comma for its hidden meaning, telling myself I was trying to find out what Kim Chernin had meant to Sena. Then, as from my own memory, I drew up what must have been the particular grief letters had brought these women. The letter searched out by Boaz, the incomprehensible letter in Hebrew, the letters Kim Chernin wrote before her death.

I, who do not easily cry, went to the quick of how Kim Chernin would have met up with Sena. It would have been the owl again, the days of naked awe, Kim Chernin would have drowned herself in the long dark hair, if she had been called back from her death by drowning.

Of course, it made no sense to me at the time.

By morning I came to my senses. I wrote back to say I had changed my mind, I wouldn't be coming to Israel. I was going to Italy to a house I had rented in Asolo for the summer.

I must have meant to offend Sena, to keep her from writing again. I must have succeeded. During the last five years no letters addressed to Kim Chernin have arrived.

Therefore, a few days ago I called the kibbutz. I didn't use my own name. If I had said it was Kim Chernin they would have thought I meant Kim Chernin. They might have hung up right away. They might have invited me to visit.

I don't know which would have been more disturbing.

I wanted information, hard facts. If I couldn't reach the past I would never be able to hammer myself into the present. The founders were no longer there, all but five or six had left. My informant, who had been living at Araht for a few years, had never heard of Simon, Devora, Sena, Kim Chernin. The farm had grown. There was a new club, a coffeehouse with a television, a library. There was also a factory that made metal goods and pipes. New houses had been built for the members, the old buildings were gone. In the new buildings, everyone had private quarters, their kids lived with them, the collective had broken into families. There was a swimming pool.

I got the impression most people took their meals in their own rooms. Newcomers would no longer have much of a problem finding a place in the dining hall.

If I went back to Araht I would not find the man with the headband, who said *"Lila tov,"* who is no longer a Zionist. He would not be sitting at the end of the table, his eyes fixed mournfully on the speakers, three men who constantly interrupt one another. No woman, who has not yet said anything, will rap the table next to her plate three times with her forefinger. Then, it had been an expression of disagreement.

In the new community, still called by the name of Araht, they all have private telephones; no one up there will be pacing about on cold nights by the public phone near the laundry. I guess that means none of them will ever see the wild Afghans marking off their circle near the chicken house.

Maybe the young soldiers from Safad are no longer the type to fall for an older woman.

In the community that failed before Kim Chernin got to Araht, all the clothes had been held in common. When you got done with work for the day you threw them into a common pile, from which they emerged several shades lighter but neither larger nor smaller (which was usually too large or too small for whoever ended up with them). Back then, in those days, that meant a lot of trading went on, accompanied by a great deal of collective laughter.

When Kim Chernin was at Araht she liked pulling on a collective garment, she hated being limited to her own skin.

In the new Araht there are fifty adults, some sixty kids, there are also workers and their families who live on the kibbutz but are not full members. My informant was hesitant to give me this information. She did not know the name of the first child who had been born at Araht a few days before Kim Chernin left.

Most people up there are in their thirties (Araht may have remained a place where it is impossible to grow old). The kids study off the kibbutz two days a week; they are allowed to study what they like. It doesn't have to be of benefit to the community. They can also work off the kibbutz when they graduate, they are not especially socialist or anything like that, they are finding a way to reconcile privacy with enlightened collectivization.

If they were not on the northern border, I would admire them.

Buses come up to Araht four or five times a day now. Its isolation has ended. The security road, being built when Kim Chernin was there, is now thoroughly established along the border, connecting Araht to neighboring kibbutzim. I guess that means the explosions up there are now shells falling.

Probably you could still get shot if you took your clothes off one day in the orchards and went frisking in a born-again body over the border.

The woman on the telephone did not have precise details of why the second Araht had folded. There seems to have been a stage when certain members wanted more individual freedom, a move resisted by other members. Perhaps the freedom party wanted to have their children sleep in their parents' rooms once a week, a breach of collective etiquette that would have caused fierce debate in the club, similar I suppose to what happened the time Kim Chernin asked for permission to stay through the winter.

In time, new people joined who were in favor of the new freedoms, which in the end they took so far there was virtually none of the old collective structure left. So the original founders left too, both those who had wanted more freedom and those who hadn't.

Many people from those earlier days would have felt

it a violation of kibbutz principle to have hired workers living on the farm, doing work the members declined to do. I didn't ask if they were Arab workers.

I wanted to call back, to find out if the kibbutz had friendlier relations with the Arab villages, if the villages had electricity or running water, now that the kibbutz had a swimming pool. On second thought, I felt the questions would sound aggressive.

The farm has orchards, chickens, and avocados, as well as cotton fields, wheat fields, sunflowers. I don't know where these new lands have come from. If they were part of Araht when Kim Chernin was there she was not aware of them. They never got their barn.

I was curious about the kids who had been born and raised at Araht. I wanted to know if they stayed on after they went into the army. Apparently, a whole bunch of them had gone into the army. That could mean Lebanon, Gaza, the West Bank. Any one of those kids, who was not yet even born when Kim Chernin was at Araht, is old enough to be killing innocent people this very day.

Yes, I am beginning to sound like Kim Chernin's mother.

One thing more. I should have mentioned it sooner. In 1975, when Dov Aviad was still in the army, after Sena had divorced Boaz, before she got married to Roni, Dov Aviad went to Araht for a visit.

That weekend, three years after I imagined Dov Aviad had fallen for Sena, more than three years after Kim Chernin had left, he spent the night with Sena. After that she waited for him to call, she didn't hear from him. I don't think she waited by the telephone next to the laundry. She waited for him to write, he never wrote to her. During our brief correspondence five years ago it was she herself who told me this story. Of course, at the time, I took it as confirmation of the narrative I had assembled, as if the incident were the final chord in what had begun years before. I always believed Dov Aviad loved Sena for her closeness to Kim Chernin.

As it turns out, she told me in the same letter that her sister had left their parents' kibbutz. Since then the sister has been living with her lover, a woman, in London.

D ov Aviad called on a late Saturday afternoon three weeks ago. He invited Kim Chernin to attend a Sufi conference at the Berkeley campus. His lecture was scheduled for Sunday. What would Kim Chernin have done? Would she run around getting her hair cut, buying a new skirt? If Kim Chernin would have put on her old white linen suit, gone down to see him in all the arrogance of knowing he could never stop loving her, why shouldn't I?

If he didn't recognize me, if he didn't want to know me, did it matter?

I told him on the telephone my hair had gone gray. (I said it had turned silver.) I warned him he might not know who I was when I walked into the lecture. He said, "I will always recognize you."

"Even you won't find it easy after twenty years."

I thought Kim Chernin might say something like that.

I must have been right from the way he responded. He said, "I'm married now. I have an eight-year-old son."

He told me, on the telephone, about the Israeli generals who had wanted him to stay in the army. He spoke with pride about finding my name in the phone book, as if he had imagined I would be impossible to discover after twenty years. Kim Chernin never lived in this house; she lived across the street in the garden apartment where she used to hear doors slam day and night.

It is I who drive down the hill, wondering what he will look like. If his voice has become unrecognizable, if he has given up even the slightest Israeli accent, maybe the man I will see for the first time in all these years will not be all that Kim Chernin promised.

I park illegally behind Sproul Hall. Did he tell me the lecture would begin a half hour later? Was that simply how I heard him? It was the sort of thing Kim Chernin would have done, walking in when everyone else was seated, when the man standing at the podium might or might not be Dov Aviad.

He is tall and slender, dark-haired. Dov Aviad never wore a pin-striped suit with a dark tie, he did not have the authority of this man, who is reading from a paper about the Sufi abu Bakr Mohammed Ibn 'Arabi of the Arabic tribe of Hatim al-Ta'i. I gather that in certain circles of Islam Ibn 'Arabi is called "the greatest master."

I sit down at the back of the room. I find it hard to see from here. While the tall man is reading his paper, I move closer. He does not glance at me. If this is Dov Aviad, the man she dreamed up twenty years ago, he has managed to get back out of the past. No matter what each of us privately makes of him, he exists. Hair slightly graying, somewhat hollow beneath the eyes, the sign at the elevator announced a conference on the wisdom of the prophets.

It isn't easy to hold on to him. Perhaps Kim Chernin was not to blame for her inability. He is reciting some kind of devotional poetry in abstract philosophic words. His listeners seem gripped, as I am, by the intensity of the speaker. His hands rise from the lectern with the authority of one who knows, whose dependence on Scripture is a kindness to his listeners. These hands give him away; gestures of admonishment, exhortation, a sensitivity immediately banished by the expansive outward sweep, fingers spread, the munificence drawn back by spiritual discipline into foldedness, obedience, contemplation.

The speaker seems to be talking about the cry to God from a soul in despair. He is saying this love cry is the beginning of longing for self-realization in God. His audience listens with rapt attention, although the language is more abstract than I would have guessed any group of thirty people could easily follow.

I cannot make more of what he is saying. The words are spoken with authority, slowly, with a precise articulation. At times they seem intricate, severe, abstract, icy. These are not qualities one would associate with Dov Aviad. The man up there likes to play with contradictions. Dark, intense, supremely handsome, this face seems to have come from a long way off. He seems more Arab than Jewish, a spiritual teacher more than a young man who might have become a general. This man could not be swept off his feet by passion, unless that is how he feels in his love for God.

At the end of the talk, while the audience is on its feet clapping, while people are coming forward to congratulate him, he walks away from them in a straight, sharp line through the crowd to me. I stand up, I am no longer in doubt. This is the man Kim Chernin loved twenty years ago. He is taller than I would have imagined, he almost has to bend forward when she reaches up to put her hand on the side of his face and then they stand there.

Dov Aviad and Kim Chernin. I see her from a distance. The linen suit looks just fine on her, she has put on a pair of black and white sling-back heels, her hair makes a wave of bright silver around her face. I see the same lines near the mouth I saw this morning in the mirror. Perhaps because he is observing them they have become the expressive transformations of a face he would recognize anywhere. He was right about that.

They say nothing. In that crowded room of people talking excitedly Kim Chernin and Dov Aviad look at each other as if love had not yet happened, he bending forward looking slightly dazed, she triumphant, as if she always knew he would become after twenty years just what she had always predicted. She's impressive, I have to admit. As if he has become whatever he is only for her, for this moment when she will walk in late into a room to hear him lecture. Completely at home in her role, the woman he has not forgotten for twenty years, as if she had been waiting for me to bring her to this.

After a time, with a slight smile, he says, "Hello, beloved."

I would never have believed any two people simply by standing face-to-face could efface twenty years that completely.

That time, Kim Chernin didn't make it down the stairs, into the car parked illegally. I made sure of that. By the time I got to the wheel she was only a memory, perhaps even had made a fool of herself, reaching up to lay her hand along his face. I saw the yellow in the cuffs of my linen suit. When she had been wearing it the whole thing gleamed as if it had been bought yesterday. The heels pinch. The last time she wore them was twenty years ago.

I must have known it would be dangerous to set eyes on him. Kim Chernin, who should have been dead, Kim Chernin who had walked herself out on a cold morning on a beach in Scotland twenty years ago, here, in my own world?

O n Monday night, the day after Dov Aviad's lecture, he is waiting for me at the window of a house near Stern Grove in San Francisco. When I pull up he runs down the steps, opens the door to the car, leans toward me. "Have you noticed I am afraid to look into your eyes?"

No doubt he thinks he can find Kim Chernin in them. When I try to tell him he has nothing to fear, fear overtakes me.

By the time he gets into the car it is almost dark. He has been talking fast, about the Image of All Longing. That is what he says Kim Chernin has become for him.

Then, because she will not permit him to evade love, because she cannot tolerate his distance, because she has returned in this moment to rebuke him for his austerity, she says, "Ever since you called I have been crying on and off, constantly."

She knows her man. She knows him better than I could. She isn't surprised when he puts his face in his hands to weep.

Against this force, which has not allowed itself to diminish in twenty years, I am powerless.

I draw over to the side of the road. I don't know if Kim Chernin is lying. Maybe she has been crying. I am shattered by her reappearance.

He says, without looking at her, "I don't want anyone to be hurt by this." From the distance at which I now have been placed, I imagine he is speaking of his wife and son.

Because he has had tears in his eyes, one suddenly imagines him as he might have been the day she first stared at him from the kitchen, wide mouth holding something back, a cry of joy, terror? Perhaps he had foreseen this particular ending?

"All I had to do was pick up the phone, find your number to have you back. Not as if you were mine to have."

"Why did you wait until now?"

"Ibn'Arabi talks about *al-hayrah;* it means 'perplexity.' It is the correct way to feel about something that passes beyond rational understanding."

Because he means to say his bond with Kim Chernin is a connection higher, more perplexing than reason, the severe words take on a strangely sensual power. Or maybe because, even in his retreat from her, she means so much to him.

She says, "I have tried to remember the last time I saw you."

"There was no last time. There never could be." In the silence that follows, these words assemble themselves as love's declaration. "I could not dismiss my dreams, I received them as a very precious gift from Him, which came to me through you and maybe at the same time pointed out my obligation to you."

He cannot keep it up. The face of the young soldier makes its way back through. Because of this face, so passionately absorbed in her, every word he speaks unfolds a pure line of desire.

"I didn't think you would have forgotten me although some people have wished to believe I was dead."

"Margo gave me your letters to Sena."

Margo gave? Letters? To Sena?

In the months after Kim Chernin left Israel he spoke to Sena daily. His mother was very worried about him. He almost dropped out of school. At night, he woke up his grandmother talking in English. When he says this his hand comes to rest on her hair, as if it had done nothing these twenty years but wait to complete this gesture.

"I never had heard of such things between women. Even when you tried to tell me I had no idea what you meant. You had no idea what an innocent boy that was."

If Kim Chernin wished to protect him, that would have been her moment. The simplicity of this, wanting her to know, not wanting to blame her, would have seized her heart.

But letters to Sena? That desperate writing day and night had been letters to Sena?

She leans toward him, puts her head on his shoulder. It is the sort of thing she would do. It seems to console him. She says, "In America, when I was growing up, there was never innocence."

I don't know if she offers this as an apology. Maybe she feels, where love is concerned, none is needed.

"You happened to me the way you did in order to bring me to Him. That was my grief. That I did not mean the same to you. I think, for you, the initiator would have been Sena."

Even his renunciation before the power of love cannot disguise the ancient longing that has brought him back to her.

"If Sena was to bring me to Him, it would have been a very circuitous path."

"Have you become bitter?"

"I have been dead."

"Your eyes say different. These eyes will haunt me to the end of days." Again, that silence in which his words, played back to him through her response, seems to awaken terror. "Or perhaps you mean, you have died to yourself, to begin in Him?"

She has become sure of her power, used to his retreat, has grown arrogant in her refusal to let it happen. "Have you come here to forgive me? Is that what you think? Will I forgive you for taking those letters?"

"You were my initiator, the one whose task was to water for the first time the seed of yearning, which is the yearning for beauty, not for the sake of self-satisfaction but for the sake of the yearning for yearning. I know you understand what I mean."

Does she? Would she understand yearning for the sake of yearning? To her, it would be blasphemy to shove God into the place of a man or woman she had loved, just because she had lost them. He'd better be careful or she will not forgive him.

She is ruthless, she doesn't care about time, she has no life he can threaten, he is hers, she wants that acknowledged.

As for me, I knew she would be like this if she ever came back. I have a life to preserve, even if she does not. I'm going to warn him.

"Sena showed you those letters. Sena, not Margo. She wanted you to understand what sort of person you loved back then. I don't think you have grasped that."

"Sena forgot Kim Chernin. For her, Kim Chernin was not the initiator. Sena would not be able to survive yearning for yearning, self-perpetuating and insatiable."

The severe, distant words suddenly crack. Every one of them gets charged with feeling. Their emptiness fills with grief and loss, his face throws itself back to the boy still trying to get over her. It lasts only a second or two. He has control of himself again. In the dark, his hands are not shaking.

"You imagine Kim Chernin is no longer a threat to you because you have made her into the Image of All

Longing?" I think my words sound more bitter than I had intended.

"How could one forget a connection that outlasts memory? A connection derived neither from past articulation nor from the possibility of convergence of two paths?"

"If you didn't come here to forgive why did you come?"

"Maybe it sounds presumptous but I am bringing you these books. "The Wisdom of the Prophets." With them, I am giving you back your letters. I understand why you wrote them to Sena. She was your first glimpse into the awesomeness of the Reality of Love. The Beloved reveals Himself in the faces of those whom we love. Through you He was revealed to me. To you, through Sena. That is what I wanted to tell you."

His face is transfigured by an inner light. What does he know? What did Sena tell him? I suppose a man would have to look like this in the moment he can no longer distinguish a living woman from The Beloved.

We pull up in front of a restaurant on Union Street, we don't manage to get out of the car. Sometimes he leans toward me, with that look of a face cracked open. His hands make wings, gestures of prayer, supplication, he twines his fingers together, the abstractions begin again, he is back in control, the severity transforms his features so that it becomes unthinkable this Sufi teacher was a boy who hung his rifle on the chair next to her desk, trembling with desire before he knew she was his initiator into Wisdom.

"I thought you would like to know my father had departed from this world about two years ago. It happened in a very short space of time, and I am glad to say that he did not suffer much."

He has already told me his mother died eight years ago. His grandmother died when he was in Boar Hills looking for Kim Chernin.

He has put into my hands a stack of letters that will make a fool of me. I know this, even before I read them. Their terrible weight, Sena's name written in large Hebrew letters, the address scrawled in Kim Chernin's abominable handwriting, the laughter he cannot hear as Kim Chernin takes off.

This man has made his way out of a memory in which he was falsely charged to face me, his accuser.

Across the street from my house, from which Kim Chernin's daughter used to wave to me from the window, he folds his hands together close to his heart.

The Sufi teacher, the luminous sage, the innocent soldier boy, the man of passion afraid to look into her eyes, the husband keeping guard over his family, the man of truth, simple, heartfelt, in this form so reminiscent of Kim Chernin's father. I cannot get used to how fast he changes.

It is a warm night, more likely in Berkeley in late autumn than in summer; Dov Aviad and I sit on the deck. He leans against the railing, reading the landscape from right to left, the swift flame from the Richmond refinery, the shadow humps of Mount Tamalpais, the lights that piece together the Golden Gate. The mountains remind him of Safad.

"You are being watched over," he says. "You must have done something to deserve this. What is it?"

"What does one have to do?"

"I had this feeling once myself. Maybe in your way, you have been to war?"

"I am at war even now?"

"Yes."

What does he mean, yes?

He is sitting across the table from me, this ghost who has been haunting the dreams of a dead woman. He pulls on his sweater. It messes his hair, he does not bother to straighten it. The hands start up again, demonstrating his control over the expansive, outward movements. I wonder what his eyes were like during the years he reenlisted in the army. Did he look into, at, through then, too, the person to whom he was speaking? Because one cannot imagine him tough, hard, issuing commands, it seems likely he has been at the edge; maybe he is still falling. At moments, his intensity is alarming. It charges the air between us, demanding the presence of Kim Chernin.

And what then?

He shared a room with his grandmother. He is a storyteller. I had almost forgotten that. The night air inspires him, he does not touch the champagne. He speaks of the flight of wild quails over the Mediterranean, of Phineas the prophet, blinded by Zeus because he could foresee the future. There is the cave in Safad where the Jewish sage is buried. When he was training cadets in the

Golan Heights, Ibn'Arabi was buried forty miles away from where he was standing. This time, when he tells the story of the sandstorm, he doesn't mention Kim Chernin.

It has taken time and diaspora to bring out the Mideast in him, this man from the Levant whose family line on both sides had never before him touched the shores of Europe. This dark-skinned Jew, intensely feeling, somber, hard to grasp, harder to hold on to, so fully present you suddenly think if you touched him your hand would come away burning. I imagine God would be happy indeed to have him for a lover.

During the last twenty years, while I have been putting together Kim Chernin's memories, this man has been stripped of all identifying marks. If he is at times remote, too much the wandering sage, that must be because so little has been left him. He has lost his grandmother, his mother, his father, his home, his homeland, his national identity. He has quarreled with his sister. Sometimes, when he lets me look into his eyes, I see knowledge, terror.

Do they always go together?

He is one of those souls that wear down pure under the world's stresses. When he stands up to take one last look at the view, there is a momentary break. In that moment he is not soldier, Sufi teacher, storyteller, misbegotten lover. He has the hurt, hard look of a boy the first time he does not wish to be hugged by his mother.

He takes Kim Chernin by the hand. He holds her hand against his chest. He is not kneeling, he gives the impression of the young lover, walking across the room when he thinks she is sleeping. He says, "I have wanted you to be happy. In my prayers I have often wished for your happiness. You were so lost. I was the rock. But I couldn't save you. I didn't know from what to save you. From me? From yourself? From Sena? Seeing you here, with all of this, I think you may have been running from God."

When I drop him off in San Francisco he places his hands on my shoulders, leans forward to look into my eyes. His gaze never arrives. I throw my arms around his neck, wishing I had not thrown my arms around his neck. He needs Kim Chernin at a distance, the organizing image for a string of unbearable losses. Up too close, he is in danger of falling prey to her.

As he gets out of the car he gives me the impression he could cast himself off with a shrug, unthinkingly in a moment of distraction.

When I look back he is standing on the bottom step rolling a cigarette. He does not look up, he does not go inside. Kim Chernin turns over with an icy jab. She takes hold of the steering wheel, pulls over to the curb, springs out, runs back down the twenty years that mean nothing to her. "Don't you say good-bye? Are you going to write? Will I ever see you again?"

"You were always like that," he responds with an exhausted smile. "Maybe you will see me when you take me to the airport?"

A few days later I take him to the plane. During all that time I have fought every hour to keep him from Kim Chernin. I sit at my desk, gathering statistics, clipping stories. He calls her to say he has been on the ferry, looking up at the Berkeley Hills, it has reminded him of Safad, when he used to walk there looking up at Araht.

He lives in a stone cottage in the Cotswolds. Every

morning he drives twenty miles to work. Two years ago he was a printer. Last year he computerized the publishing house, inventing the software. His wife picks out his clothes (he is always beautifully dressed), drives their son to school, puts dinner on the table. After dinner he goes upstairs to his devotional odes. His wife is the art director of the Sufi magazine in which he publishes his abstract musings. The first time he saw her he was pierced by the arrow of love. Kim Chernin is not the only woman he has loved. No matter what she has in mind, I say he will return to his wife and son. I will not allow her to disrupt this life, its order, it reclusion. She has no idea how frail he is, this man who is falling forever unless God flicks out a hand to save him.

At the airport, he has to have the toy guns he has bought for his son approved by a man in a lower office. When we go down the stairs he takes my hand. Kim Chernin says, "I wonder if I will see you again during the next twenty years," as if she were planning to stick around for a while. But he too knows this may be the last time. And so he says, in a desperate rush, taking her face between his hands, as if he will never forgive himself if he doesn't finally speak, "I don't want you to cry. Please don't cry. I thought you shouldn't come today but I wanted to see you. It is like those times you used to walk with me to my car and I could see you standing alone on the road when I drove off down the mountain. And then the time came when, without knowing, it was the last time. And then I never saw you again."

The package of toy guns is opened, inspected. The inspector rewraps them, stamps his approval, they can be

taken on the plane. Kim Chernin does not ask him why
he is bringing guns to his son. Maybe she doesn't wonder.
She is used to contradiction, perhaps she doesn't find it
strange that a servant of love was once a senior lieutenant.
Neither of them says a word about the West Bank, although I have been wondering whether he would have
refused to serve there if he were still in the Israeli
army.

A few weeks later a hand-sewn pouch arrives in the
mail, a small amulet in black leather. Inside, in Arabic, are
the words of a protective prayer. Kim Chernin is requested
to wear the amulet on her person (a chain is enclosed). Although severe, it is the love gift to his Beloved from a soldier of god. Because of this I have thought it only right to
keep the amulet around my neck. I must have known Kim
Chernin would show up to claim it.

K im Chernin liked wind. If she tries to get back it will
be on a windy night. When she was a child she
thought of the wind as a messenger. From whom? For what
purpose? She never figured it out. I have been studying
weather reports. If there are winds of twenty miles an hour
I put up the storm doors, meticulously.

There was supposed to be a security zone, a no-man's-
land, some small margin of safety. Kim Chernin crosses
borders as if for twenty years she had been hiding in caves.
What choice do I have? Become Theirs or collapse back
into Kim Chernin? She will fight me over an acre of rock.
And if I don't fight back she gets possession? And if I fight

back, who am I then? Theirs? Like it or not, that's what she's made me?

Kim Chernin better not believe I will go down without a struggle, as she did. I avoid the sea, my fortifications are well tended. The only threat could arise from a fifth-column of the interior. If Kim Chernin got back she'd be all on fire with notions of union. I will not give up without a fight. But am I set up to fight Kim Chernin's yearning for Kim Chernin?

K im Chernin interested in politics? She never had a sense of history, before. Reality, I thought, was the one impenetrable fortress, outside her range, over her head, beneath her. Here, I was certain, I could live out my days, gathering statistics, clipping stories. She would have no interest I thought in these studies of a land she boarded exclusively from the romantic side, never having bothered to mark the historic traces. The Arab trellis in what is now a Jewish town, to take up the most obvious example.

Perhaps, during the years I thought her dead, she has gained some knowledge? Perhaps secretly, over the years, she has been keeping an eye on me? Why else would she have staged last night as a reappearance?

I had looked up from my work (a report by B'Tselem, the Israeli Information Center for Human Rights in the Occupied Territories). It had gone dark meanwhile. I saw the reflection of the desk lamp in the rock pool. I saw Kim Chernin (the unruly, irresponsible Kim Chernin of my youth) beneath the lamp, cupping her eyes to observe me more closely. I did not like the expression in her eyes, measuring the distance for a calculated spring.

At first, I imagined Kim Chernin was weeping for her own exile. For her impotence. Her inability to get at me. Mine the desk, the room, the heavy Spanish door, the house with its three stories across the street from the garden apartment where Kim Chernin lived with the child Larissa.

I went out to slip the chain lock into the door. I should have known better. When I returned Kim Chernin was at my desk, savaging through my papers.

I had been sure, if Kim Chernin were confronted with the burning tires, the bombings, the massacres, the rocks, she would see it as the ritual struggle for a land promised to two brothers. When a Palestinian is tortured, when an Arab boy throws a rock, when an Israeli woman is knifed to death, when Palestinians are driven out of their village just beyond the security zone, when an Israeli truck is exploded by a hand grenade, when children are trapped in a school by terrorists, Kim Chernin would perceive a ceremonial violence of sure mythic proportions, the inevitable violence before the two brothers reconcile, divide the land between them, close the agon with a conversion to the lying down of lion and lamb.

Kim Chernin always liked the story of Rachel, the way Jeremiah pictured her, rising from her grave to weep over the Hebrew children exiled to Babylon. No doubt, in her reappearance, Kim Chernin fancies herself another Rachel. Just now, she has adopted the blind Palestinian girl in flight from Kfar Rumman, ten miles north of the border where in her day the security road was being built. She lords it over me because I do not weep. Soon, she will cob-

ble together a resemblance between our domestic strife
and the blood struggle for the homeland. I can just see her
with her map of the interior, erasing the security zones.

I sit sternly, clipping, posting, assembling, recording.

Much has been lost; the memory of the land in its
blood struggles has fragmented. The claims are driven back
to a sharp cut of antiquity, exclusive, absolute, irresolvable
on either side. I would say neither can have the land without the other, if both cannot possess it, it cannot be home
to either. Always, the other, across the border.

I do not weep. I search the papers, comb through old
bookstores, I visit Palestinian groceries south of Market
trying to pick up a trace here, something there. Now that
my work on Kim Chernin has come to an end, I have been
sent on to other restorations. If she thinks there is a way
to live out the passionate destiny of the romantic dreamer,
now, in this place, if she imagines I am terrified by her outrage, her weeping, her clenched fists because she is pounding the work table where my papers have been spread out,
so be it.

If Kim Chernin thinks I am afraid she will set these
notes on fire because she cannot find the way to say *shin
bet* and mean Jewish men interrogating Palestinians with in-
sults and verbal abuse, fists and rubber truncheons, broken
ribs, and death, she'd better think twice.

Now she is making notes next to my notes in the
margins of my clippings. In Ramallah hundreds have
marched through the streets, some six miles north of Jerusalem in the West Bank, to celebrate peace negotiations. A
young woman and a young man are said to have climbed
Israeli army jeeps to lay olive branches on them.

If Kim Chernin wants to regain possession she will have to acknowledge: the first-born boy on the farm near the border could have been one of those young soldiers, who lied about his age, who enlisted early, who was seen sprawled on his tank just outside the walls of the camp listening to Simon and Garfunkel on the radio while some eight hundred, some say one thousand civilians, were shot and quartered in Sabra and Shatilla. It was he, or one of his pals from another kibbutz, who set off the flares at night by which Phylangist soldiers murdered. The killing went on for three days and three nights. Is this night different from any other?

If Kim Chernin cannot believe her Palestinian neighbors from the village were shut up in closetlike cells, in closets, in refrigerators to make them talk to their Israeli interrogators, if she does not want to make this knowledge part of herself, if she prefers to rend her garments, cover herself in the biblical manner in ash, Kim Chernin at my desk, savaging through my notes, had better weep for her own loss of innocence. If Kim Chernin wants to cry let it be for the lost family romance with her own people. If Kim Chernin cannot make memory of this, why should I any longer fear Kim Chernin?

Do you hear?

Why should I any longer fear Kim Chernin?

W elcome her back? Forever thirty-one years old in her straw hat? My youth self still coming of age with her uproar and disorder? In her old sandals worn down at the heels from twenty years of constant traffic, the low-cut yellow blouse no less exuberantly displayed for all its tatters. Welcome her back, not quite laughing in her face, a quick nod of the head, so there you are, what do you know, and I thought you were dead!

I could give her Larissa's room down the hall from me, knowing full well (and accepting this) that when she looks out the window she will not see the Richmond refinery with its sulfurous fumes. She will have a view of the immortal valley, birds winging through the dusk that brings on homelessness no matter where in the world you are when twilight falls. If she drags a chair across the floor to nail in the poster of the eight-year-old daughter, if she uses Scotch tape on the Victorian wallpaper, pastes a tattoo on the hand-painted desk, these things should not matter.

I cannot shut her away in the garden apartment across the street where doors would be slamming. I cannot keep her from Larissa, who will wish to set eyes on the mother who never made it back from Israel. I came back in her place.

I have seen Larissa stride out on a recent visit, a black leather bag over her shoulder. She is not the woman to wear a straw hat. Muscular legs carry her boldly in those big shoes women wear these days with their short skirts. A handwoven scarf around her neck, gold ring in her left nostril, head back, shoulders easy, there is no trace of the waif in this woman who lets you know with every step she is not going to let life escape her. I wonder what sort of impression she would make getting off the bus at Kibbutz Araht. She is the age Kim Chernin was. I mean, when she set out on the wanderings that led to her death.

May life prove kinder to her daughter!

She has a sense of humor, that makes a difference. She knows where reality begins and ends, sits up late nights talking to me at the foot of my bed, braiding her hair into small tight braids. That night she announced she was moving back to California.

Why suddenly now, after ten years?

Kim Chernin never stayed up chatting with her mother. She never sat at the foot of her bed. For twenty years Larissa has had my protection. Every morning she lets down her hair into a mass of waves, honey colored, medieval, thicker than Kim Chernin's.

These hands that move so deftly dividing and braiding, useful hands that can knit, weave, embroider, fold intricate paper forms. To these hands, against all dangers of heredity, I entrust her. From them over the years have come scarves, sweaters, opera bags in purple velvet, hand-painted shoes, paste-and-paper scrolls in which I have recognized the mature forms of her childhood art.

Her mother's hands were good for almost nothing. For typing, for (yes), all-night improvising at the piano. She couldn't do much that was useful (I know this is not fair) until she learned to prune trees.

Larissa does not tell lies, not even the kind that might be called exaggerations. Perhaps in her the worst of Kim Chernin has been burned off, leaving a bolder, sounder, more capable woman. Yet strangely, year after year, that well-groomed girl who went off to Harvard, studied philosophy, has given way, (what shall I say?) grown into, been taken over by something reminiscent of Kim Chernin. You can see it in the way she paints. There have been canvases so large it is difficult to get them out of her studio. She has the same laugh, maybe for the same reasons. You could pick it out from a hundred others, contagious, raucous, rising above the early sorrow. Suddenly, standing next to me at the breakfast table, she is in tears because she has remembered something until that moment meticulously forgotten.

I must have always known it was useless to protect her from Kim Chernin. I always knew I had to try.

On the last night of Larissa's visit her father showed up to take us out to dinner. He brought Larissa her schoolwork from that time, the drawings she had made, a book of poems she had put together. He also brought Kim Chernin's letters. Oh yes, the entire stack of them, with their Israeli stamps, the name Kibbutz Araht written sometimes in Hebrew in the left corner.

I could have wished them shredded forever, dispersed into the past, tossed out during a housecleaning. No doubt they contain small details that once again would set the story at odds with itself. Fortunately, Larissa showed no interest in them, gave them a deliberate, respectful push across the table.

"Don't you want to read them?" I asked, relieved that she did not.

She gazed at them thoughtfully. "They were so sad."

Therefore, Kim Chernin's letters have gone unread into the box with other memorabilia, the notes from Simon slipped under Kim Chernin's door, the recent letters from Dov and Devora, the passports, other "letters" from that time. The collection is now complete. The details have been assembled to do what they can against memory. If Larissa doesn't care to read them, why should I? Still, they have had their effect on her. She who never expressed even the least desire to read my story about her mother.

I don't say she sat up all night reading. For all I know she may have slept now and again. She didn't look particularly tired at breakfast, didn't eat much, gave me for the first time in all our years together the first look of that kind that stops at nothing.

"I always knew you did not come back from Israel."

"Well, Kim Chernin did not come back. But what does that mean?"

"Before you left for Israel I used to worry about you a lot."

"You think that mother of yours is on her way back? That's why you're moving back to California?"

"I never said she was dead."

"You expect to set eyes on her again!"

"That was the worst year of my life." She says this calmly. Then, with an intensity reminiscent of her mother, "I didn't know it was the worst year of your life too."

Does that mean the daughter Kim Chernin abandoned feels sympathy for the mother who has abandoned her? Has forgiven her? Loves her more than she loves me who has tried so hard all these years?

"I'm not sure Kim Chernin would have called it the worst year of her life. There was something unrepentant about her, right to the end. She might have said she lived herself out at the extreme edge where life takes on meaning. Maybe she wasn't even thinking about you then."

That wonderful laughter Kim Chernin's daughter has in common with Kim Chernin.

"She must have been thinking. How else could she have sent you to take her place?"

Okay, welcome her back. My perpetual waif, still coming of age at every age with her uproar and disorder. Welcome her back. Throw out my arms to embrace her. Leave a saucer of milk on the doorstep for her. Scatter birdseed all over the garden. Sit up nights waiting for her, letting her bring back the sleeplessness, the banging doors, the trouble she's sure to cause the neighbors playing Wagner through open windows in her room all night.

Share my house with her. Spend my days gathering in her wet sweater thrown across the living room couch, her sandals left out in the rain, her notebooks with their paper napkins stuffed here and there in any corner. It will take me hours to flake off the yogurt she drips on the oriental rugs. She will eat the crust off my bread, she'll leave cheese rinds and cherry pits in the terra-cotta pots I took the trouble to bring home from Italy.

She will not have changed. She will drag her sleeping bag into the garden, curl up with the tough neighborhood cat, plant herbs by moonlight, eat the wild blackberries from the neighbor's side of the fence, snap off the finest Joseph's Coat in the public rose garden, prowl through the order twenty years have meticulously laid out. Have I really missed her these twenty years, my wandering spirit who should have been trampled out in the name of maturity? She will leave muddy paw prints all over the new green and white chaise pads on the deck where last year I grew cactus.

Welcome her back. A me not entirely me, a self violently outgrown on a cold morning in Scotland, an incorrigible me newly back from the dead, staking its claim to the living. There are fresh springs in Berkeley. They flow underground to surface unexpectedly in a neighborhood hill street. She will find them. She will take up with the one-eyed duck in the park up the hill from my house, boasting she has saved his life by feeding him daily. She will want to confess her dreams over a breakfast of cigarettes and black coffee. She will develop a passion for the study of some arcane subject. Sufi mysticism will be high on her list.

Of course, she will have a story to tell. If she hasn't been dead these twenty years, what has she been doing? She will sit up by the fire late into the night to tell me about the lost years of Kim Chernin. She will come running into my room before it is light to disclose some impossible love affair just remembered. I suspect there will be more than one broken heart.

Would I have to admit I too have missed her all these years? Will I have to confess my life cannot go on without her?

When she lived in Berkeley she knew where edible mushrooms grow, in the fastidious shadow cast by the hill of purple thistles.

Acknowledgments

Books are created in part by their readers.

My first, most consistent, critical and inspiring reader has been, once again, Renate Stendhal, who also edited the first and all subsequent drafts.

To her, and to Cathy Galligher and Michael Rogin I spoke about the meaning of every detail, large and small, which preoccupied me during the book's composition.

Cathy also helped me understand why I was writing, what I was writing about, and whose story I was telling.

Michael, who has known this story for some twenty years, knew where things were going and when they were going wrong.

To all three of them, for their friendship and love, I am deeply grateful.

Jerilyn Fisher read a late draft of the manuscript. Her detailed response led me to changes I am very happy to have made.

My first readers for the finished manuscript took very seriously their responsibility as my "little public." For their perceptive readings and responses, I am grateful to: Michael Bader, Larissa Chernin, Peter Elkind, Sue Elkind, Margot Duxler, Tobey Hiller, Louise Kollenbaum, Amy Rennert, Lillian Rubin, Frances Tobriner, Phillip Ziegler.

Diane Cleaver, my agent, has consistently, from first idea to final draft, represented this book with her usual combination of vision, intelligence, wit and toughness.

Joanne Wyckoff has been an insightful, hard-working and scrupulously honest editor.

Andrea Schulz has made the endless process of changes and galleys far more enjoyable than anyone has a right to expect them to be.

To them, and to the National Endowment for the Arts, I give thanks for their support of this project.

ABOUT THE AUTHOR

KIM CHERNIN has written about women's lives for more than a decade. Her books include a trilogy of works on hunger. (*The Obsession, The Hungry Self, Reinventing Eve*), *In My Mother's House*, a memoir, and *The Flame Bearers*, a novel. She is the coauthor, with Renate Stendhal, of *Sex and Other Sacred Games*. She is a writing consultant and psychoanalytic consultant in Berkeley, California.